'Abdu'l-Bahá in Philadelphia, Pennsylvania, USA, June 1912

A Love Which Does Not Wait

ISBN 1-890101-17-6

Palabra Publications
3735 B Shares Place
Riviera Beach, FL 33404
407-845-1919
407-845-0126 (Fax)

A Love Which Does Not Wait

by
Janet Ruhe-Schoen

**The Stories of
Lua Getsinger ▪ May Maxwell
Martha Root ▪ Keith Ransom-Kehler
Hyde Dunn ▪ Susan Moody
Dorothy Baker ▪ Ella Bailey
and Marion Jack**

Palabra Publications
Riviera Beach, Florida, 33404

Dedicated to Chris, Anna, Joshua, Jaleh, and Colin

MOURN LOSS IMMORTAL HEROINE MARION JACK . . .
TRIUMPHANT SOUL NOW GATHERED DISTINGUISHED
BAND CO-WORKERS ABHÁ KINGDOM MARTHA ROOT, LUA
GETSINGER, MAY MAXWELL, HYDE DUNN, SUSAN MOODY,
KEITH RANSOM-KEHLER, ELLA BAILEY, DOROTHY BAKER
WHOSE REMAINS LYING IN SUCH WIDELY-SCATTERED
AREAS GLOBE AS HONOLULU, CAIRO, BUENOS AIRES,
SYDNEY, TEHERAN, ISFAHAN, TRIPOLI, DEPTHS
MEDITERRANEAN ATTEST MAGNIFICENCE PIONEER SER-
VICES RENDERED NORTH AMERICAN BAHÁ'Í COMMUNITY
APOSTOLIC FORMATIVE AGES BAHÁ'Í DISPENSATION.

—Shoghi Effendi, March 19, 1954

Table of Contents

List of Illustrations

Acknowledgments

Extracts from *Martha Root: Lioness at the Threshold,* by Mabel Garis, Copyright © 1983 by the National Spiritual Assembly of the United States, are reprinted by permission of the Bahá'í Publishing Trust of the U.S.

The first stanza of "The Hardy Garden" by Edna St. Vincent Millay, from *Collected Poems*, HarperCollins, Copyright © 1928, 1955 by Edna St. Vincent Millay and Norma Millay Ellis, is reprinted by permission of Elizabeth Barnett, literary executor.

I thank both George Ronald, Publisher, and Kalimát Press for permission to quote from any books published by them.

I also thank Roger Dahl and Louis Walker at the U.S. National Bahá'í Archives for prompt and thorough replies to my requests for information and prompt supplying of the information, even though that involved copying and mailing hundreds of pages, and most of the time I was researching this book I lived in Chile.

And thank you to the many people who shared their own research, reminiscences, and impressions. I especially thank Rúḥíyyih Khánum for her reminiscences of her mother, May Maxwell, shared at the 1990 convention in Buenos Aires; for the photo of herself with her mother; and for the ways that both her presence and her writing have illumined Bahá'í history for me.

Beginnings

Lua Getsinger, an actress; May Maxwell, an invalid; Martha Root, a high powered journalist; Hyde Dunn, a traveling salesman; Keith Ransom-Kehler, a socialite with a background as a Christian minister; Susan Moody, an artist and vocalist who became a medical doctor; Dorothy Baker, a wife and mother; Ella Bailey, a schoolteacher; and Marion Jack, a landscape and portrait painter. What do these nine people have in common?

Eight of them were women, but one was a man. Not all of them were from the United States. They had varying degrees of education, different levels of intellectual attainment. But when Marion Jack died in Sofia, Bulgaria, in 1954, they were all mentioned in the eulogizing telegram sent by the Guardian of the Bahá'í Faith because, like Marion, they had died far from home while working with one common purpose: to establish the Bahá'í reality of peace through unity among all people. Within this purpose, they shared a rare attribute which enabled them to do their work under the most adverse conditions with incomparable grace: they were transformed and animated by a love which does not wait but rushes forth to serve, unburdened by expectation of reward, unfreighted with selfish concerns. They were truly Bahá'ís—followers of Bahá'u'lláh, Light-bearers. The source of their light may have seemed obscure to much of the world, but to them it was as apparent as the sun.

* * * * * * * * *

If asked the dawning place of the sun which illumined their lives, they would have answered: S<u>h</u>íráz, Iran, in May of 1844, when 'Alí Muḥammad, a 25-yearold merchant, announced the beginning of a new epoch in the global history of religion. Speaking to His first follower, a young Islamic theologian named Mullá Ḥusayn, He referred to Himself as the Báb, meaning "the Gate," and said He was a Messenger of God but, more importantly, the portal through which the Promised One of All Ages would come.

His teachings caused tumultuous religious revival. He was imprisoned almost immediately as a heretic; thousands of His followers were killed because they refused to recant their belief in Him; and just six years after He announced His mission He was shot by a firing squad on a July noon in a barracks square in the town of Tabríz. Then the political and religious leaders who opposed Him assumed they had forever quelled the revival, for all His greatest defenders were dead—except One.

And that One they enchained in a dungeon called the Black Pit. His name was Ḥusayn 'Alí of Núr, and His death seemed certain. If He didn't die of the privations of imprisonment, He would certainly be killed, as every day one of His fellow believers was taken out of the prison, paraded through the streets of Ṭihrán, and slaughtered by brutal mobs using means so savage they defy description.

He had a young family, a wife and three small children. They had lost their regal ancestral home to rioters and they lived in a small house near the dungeon. Daily, they listened in terror to the killings, and at night the eldest child, a boy of nine, ventured out to learn who had died. Was it His Father?

But the Prisoner was the Son of a distinguished man, descendent of two noble families, and by His own spotless bearing and wisdom since youth He had won great respect. Through the intervention of a Russian diplomat—and Russia was a force to be reckoned with in the Iran of the 1850s—He was released and sentenced to exile in Baghdád. When that failed to stifle His influence, He was exiled again, and then again, until He was finally imprisoned in the prison-city of 'Akká, a penal colony belonging to the Ottoman Empire.

His suffering at the hands of His enemies was constant; His triumph over His enemies was measured by that which He deemed wealth: joy, patience, simplicity, love, and the steadfastness of his disciples. He said, "My calamity is My providence, outwardly it is fire and vengeance, inwardly it is light and mercy."[1]

It is by the name of Bahá'u'lláh, the Glory of God, that He is known today. The Báb Himself had bestowed that name upon Him, and, during the decade following the Báb's death Bahá'u'lláh slowly educated the confused and oppressed remnant of the Báb's followers so that they came to see of their own volition how He fulfilled it. By the time He died in 1892, He had perpetuated the revival begun by the Báb, and He promised that religious renewal would be global. His followers were called Bahá'ís, and they lived in Iran, Iraq, Syria, Palestine, Egypt, and India.

His death did not bring fragmentation to His creed, for its centerpiece was unity, and to maintain unity He named His Son—the One Who, at nine, had ventured into the streets of Ṭihrán to learn if His Father lived or died, and who had been the companion of all His Father's sufferings—to be His successor.

This Son, 'Abbás, called the Master by His Father, preferred to be known as 'Abdu'l-Bahá, the Servant of Glory. He was a prisoner under house arrest when His Father died. While mourning the Person who had been the Lode-Star of His life, He also had to bear and grieve for the jealousy and intrigues of petty egotists who imagined they could usurp His spiritual power, though it could never be understood by them because it was born of humility.

Therefore, when the first Bahá'í pilgrims from America and Europe arrived at 'Abdu'l-Bahá's house in the prison city, climbed the stone stairs to His room, and saw in Him the reflection of His father and the answer to their prayers, He rejoiced poignantly in their pure-hearted love.

****

The occidental pilgrims who came to 'Abdu'l-Bahá were people whose childhoods had been touched by the Advent Movement, the expectation of Christ's return as preached by William Miller and others. When Christ failed to appear in the sky in 1844 as Miller prophesied, disillusionment was deep and bitter. Yet hopes, visions, and dreams persisted, especially in the hearts of people who allowed that God was subtle, mysterious: the Christ spirit may have come and gone and it may not have been apparent to everyone. So, they sought Him. Unlike most of their contemporaries, they opened their minds to other religions besides Protestant Christianity. They read books with strange names, joined oddly assorted groups, and were branded kindly as eccentrics and unkindly as cranks; yet they persevered. And when they met 'Abdu'l-Bahá they embraced His precepts and example so whole-heartedly that they became His disciples and took the Bahá'í message everywhere, endeavoring to transform the world as they themselves had been transformed. They believed they had found the new heaven; all that remained was to make a new earth. They were pioneers of a truly virgin frontier.

This book tells the stories of nine star disciples of 'Abdu'l-Bahá. It is an elaboration of an article, "A Love Which Does Not Wait," written by the author for the U.S. based publication, *Bahá'í News*, in 1975, briefly presenting the lives of Marion Jack and her co-workers. Because the article was well-received and well-remembered over the years, the author began this book in 1991, hoping to pay tribute to people whose greatness transcends our usual understanding of the word, for their grandeur is not so much structure as radiance, an outpouring of the selfless love that was born in them when they met 'Abdu'l-Bahá.

So, in relating their stories, the author starts by touching on the pivotal moments they spent with Him when they knew within themselves the courage and passion to follow His maxim: "Behold the candle, how it gives its light. It weeps its life away drop by drop, in order to give forth its flame of light."[2]

They became candles. And winds blew against them mercilessly, violent winds toothed and clawed with war, yet their fragile flames, lit by vision and love, still burn. Radiance.

Chapter 1

Lua Getsinger

Lua Aurora Getsinger, circa 1910

We reached the door and stopped—before us, in the center of the room stood a man clad in long raiment with a white turban upon His head, stretching out one hand to us, while His face, which I cannot describe, was lighted by a rare sweet smile of joy and welcome! We stood thus for a moment unable to move—then my heart gave a great throb and scarcely knowing what I was doing I held out my arms, crying, 'My Lord, my Lord!!!' and rushed to Him, kneeling at His Blessed Feet, sobbing like a child; in an instant my husband was beside me, crying as only men can cry! He put His dear hands upon our bowed heads and said, in a voice like a strain of sweet music, 'Welcome, welcome, my dear children, you are welcome, arise and be of good cheer.'[1]

Thus Lua Getsinger—among the first group of western pilgrims to visit the Holy Land—described her initial meeting with 'Abdu'l-Bahá, which took place in His home in 'Akká early in the morning of December 10, 1898.

At the time Lua was a twenty-seven year old* actress and singer with thick, wavy auburn hair and blue eyes. She was considered a great beauty, and her wardrobe, dramatically ruffled and plumed, was something of a legend among her friends. Edward was a thirty-two year old scientist with a highly independent spirit and an inquiring mind; he had been an atheist for much of his life. He had light brown hair and aquiline features, a pointed beard and handlebar mustache, and a shrewd gaze.

---

* There may be some discrepancy as to Lua's actual date of birth. She notes in her own journal on her birthday in 1898 that she had turned 26, thus making her year of birth possibly 1872 and not 1871 as official records appear to indicate. See Velda Piff Metelmann, *Lua Getsinger: Herald of the Covenant*, p. 8. (Oxford: George Ronald, 1997.)

'Abdu'l-Bahá immediately trusted the Getsingers and saw qualities in Lua which, for others, were hidden by her glamour. She had fierce purity and strength, and great tenderness of heart. He named her "Livá," meaning "the Banner," and told her to give the Bahá'í message in His name. Through constant travel punctuated by much-needed, frequent visits with 'Abdu'l-Bahá, she rose to meet the challenge, bringing honor to her own name as well.

Fortunately, Lua's entire description of her first pilgrimage is preserved in a letter she wrote to friends in Chicago.

She and Edward first arrived in Haifa at 10:30 P.M. on December 8. Haifa, then a small, straggling Arab town on an ancient shore, seemed familiar to Lua because her childhood had been steeped in Biblical lore and the expectation of Christ's return; as for Edward, he had seen the place in a vision a few years before. A warm welcome from Iranian Bahá'ís who met them when their boat docked heightened the feeling of familiarity. Among the welcomers was 'Abdu'l-Bahá's elderly uncle, sent by Him to extend special greetings. Lua said the old man "saluted us and his countenance beamed."[2] At the home of one of the Bahá'ís, Lua and Edward had tea, and then some accompanied them through the dark, narrow streets to their hotel while the hotel keeper walked ahead with a lantern. They conversed with the Bahá'ís till after midnight and then could hardly sleep; they were consumed with eagerness to meet 'Abdu'l-Bahá.

But, all day on December 9, no word came. However, that evening they arrived at a Bahá'í home and the host happily informed them that 'Abdu'l-Bahá had sent a note saying He'd be awaiting them the next morning and His heart "longed to see the first American pilgrims."[3]

Lua wrote,

As you may imagine, sleep was out of the question that night. My husband and I were talking all the time and congratulating ourselves upon our great blessings and good fortune and counting the hours, which passed much too slowly, until the dawn of the morrow. . . . We arose early, dressing ourselves with much care, feeling the best we had was not half good enough to wear upon this our first visit to the Holy City, and shortly after eight o-clock the carriage drove up and . . . my husband and myself started for the place of all places.[4]

The way from Haifa to 'Akká was a short jog, just about five miles, and charmingly picturesque, for the road was, as Lua described it, "... close to the sea—indeed, in the sea, for the horses were walking in the water and at times the waves dashed nearly to the top of the wheels. After riding for about a quarter of an hour we could see the City in the distance."[5]

Soon the horses were trotting by the ancient double walls of 'Akká. The carriage passed through the massive Land Gate, proceeded down the narrow streets which swarmed with people even at that early hour, and continued on to the home of 'Abdu'l-Bahá. Lua and Edward alighted within His flowering courtyard, then climbed the stone steps to His door and entered His room.

He was fifty-four years old. His long hair and full beard were black streaked with steel gray, and he radiated both physical and spiritual strength. He had a scent of attar of roses and His voice held resonant authority; there was a certain ring to it. Many who heard it remarked that it rang in their ears for the rest of their lives. When Lua rose from her knees after her effusive first greeting, she stood in what was for her a bright new world, and 'Abdu'l-Bahá was, and would remain, the light of it.

Her initial steps in that new world were taken along the corridors of 'Abdu'l-Bahá's house as He led her to meet His sister, and His wife and daughters. The teachings of Bahá'u'lláh clearly state the equality of women with men, so the women of 'Abdu'l-Bahá's household were educated, but because of the suspicions and enmity surrounding them they had to follow Islamic custom by wearing veils and leading secluded lives. 'Abdu'l-Bahá's sister, Bahíyyih <u>Kh</u>ánum, the great one among them, witnessed the sufferings of her brother as she had witnessed those of her Father—in silence. She endured everything without complaint, transmuting pain into resignation—and more, into love. When she saw Lua, she simply took her in her arms and kissed her, Lua wrote, "very tenderly on both cheeks."[6] Bahíyyih <u>Kh</u>ánum's joy at welcoming Lua and Edward was like 'Abdu'l-Bahá's. The Getsingers were overwhelmed at the joyful reception they received.

Yet, in the midst of such joyful welcomes, the pain and suffering of life for 'Abdu'l-Bahá and His Family were apparent to the Getsingers. 'Abdu'l-Bahá, designated the Center of the Covenant by His Father, was the target of constant attacks against that very Covenant that were so vicious their perpetrators had to be named Covenant-breakers. With infinite love and patience, 'Abdu'l-Bahá tolerated the most unthinkable insults and arrogance from disloyal Bahá'ís before declaring them Covenant-breakers and instructing the other Bahá'ís to cut off communication with them.

Besides these internal enemies, external enemies continued their persecutions. No wonder that 'Abdu'l-Bahá had been eagerly awaiting the fulfillment of His Father's prophecy, "In

Edward Christian Getsinger,
around the time of his marriage to Lua

the East the light of His Revelation hath broken; in the West the signs of His dominion have appeared."[7] When news had reached Him of the first Bahá'ís in America, He had written jubilantly to the oppressed Iranian Bahá'ís, saying a holy choir was now raising its voice from America. He would write to them of Lua and Edward, and of the stream of western pilgrims that followed.

As Lua sat at His table on that first day, He told her, "The love of God burning in your heart is manifest upon your face and it gives us joy to look upon you."[8] Though she could not understand the extent of that joy, when night came she found herself unable to sleep; she said she was "too infinitely happy."[9]

The next day, 'Abdu'l-Bahá took Lua and Edward to the Garden of Riḍván (Paradise). The Garden, blossoming under a crown of old mulberry trees, was on a small island in the midst of a slender river. It had been used by Bahá'u'lláh as a refuge and also as a picnic spot. He had named it after the garden of nightingales and roses in the midst of the Tigris River in Baghdád where, in 1863, He first publically stated His mission and purpose. Beneath the large trees which, Lua said, formed a "green tent," she and Edward and the party of accompanying Bahá'ís sat down before the bench where Bahá'u'lláh used to sit, and they were served tea while the gardener brought fruit and flowers. Then the Getsingers were taken into the small cottage where Bahá'u'lláh had sometimes stayed. They wept, and the Bahá'ís with them wept also. On Bahá'u'lláh's chair were "a wreath of flowers and some beautiful cut roses."[10] 'Abdu'l-Bahá gave the flowers to Lua and Edward, along with four large oranges which were on a table in the room.

From the garden, 'Abdu'l-Bahá took Lua and Edward to the Shrine of Bahá'u'lláh. This Shrine was (and is) His tomb at Bahjí, the country house where, though nominally a prisoner, Bahá'u'lláh lived the final years of His life in comfort and dignity. Because He had died just six years before the Getsingers' visit, grief was still very fresh in the hearts of His companions, most especially in the heart of His Son. Yet the tomb had none of the coldness or bathos often associated with death. There was no chill of abandonment, no hysteria of attachment to the departed One, but instead a warmth, a presence.

Writing of the place, Lua said, "you must excuse me if I do not go into detail about this—I cannot find words to express myself."[11] 'Abdu'l-Bahá had taken her by the hand and led her inside, where she knelt and begged God to make her pure, to "kindle" within her heart "the fire of His love."[12] Then the Getsingers walked with 'Abdu'l-Bahá through the garden of Bahjí, and He picked flowers and leaves to make fragrant souvenirs for "the faithful believers in America."[13]

That night, Lua said, she had "a long delicious sleep." In the morning, she and Edward took tea with 'Abdu'l-Bahá and He presented her with a beautiful sheaf of white narcissus. Then He had other business to attend to, so the Getsingers returned to Haifa. "As we were quitting the city," Lua wrote, "we saw Him standing by the gate and He smiled at us as we passed."[14]

Lua left the prison city feeling that there was "no other place in the world worth seeing."[15] Thus the squalid penal colony, infamous as one of the foulest spots on earth, was transformed, for her, into heaven. Of 'Abdu'l-Bahá she said, "It seems to me that no one could doubt should He smile upon them."[16]

'Abdu'l-Bahá perceived her loyalty and sent her a tablet in Haifa: "Oh thou shining and spiritual Gem! Glad tidings to thee from the Generosity of Thy Lord. Be happy on account of the Gifts of Thy God which shall soon surround thee; and thou art confirmed in the Covenant."[17]

Lua had found what she'd been seeking all her life. From the moment of birth, in fact, from the time of her mother's pregnancy with her, destiny had aimed her like an arrow towards 'Abdu'l-Bahá in 'Akká.

* * * * * * * * * * * * *

Lua's mother, Ellen McBride Moore, was born in 1843 when the great Adventist, William Miller, was at the peak of his career in the northeastern United States. Since the 1830's he had preached over 3,000 sermons predicting the return of Christ. He fixed various dates, and each time his followers prepared to ascend with Christ to heaven while the world came to an end. They stayed up all night, watching the skies where the Lord would appear in the clouds with great glory, only to find themselves, when morning came, still on earth, with onlookers laughing at them. Despite this apparent ignominious failure, when Miller died in 1849 he was murmuring of victory. What bright vision hovered at his deathbed to inspire that final fulfillment? Lua's mother grew up wondering.

She was also intrigued by the feminist movement. She was just five when the first Women's Rights Convention was held at Seneca Falls, New York, in 1848. That gathering was followed by others, well-publicized, and Ellen read about them. As an adult, she was haunted by the question of why Christ had not returned during the mid-1800s, and she had no qualms about speaking out in church, asking questions. She was finally silenced by a visit from her pastor to her husband. Ellen was a disturbing element, said the minister, and must learn to keep her thoughts to herself. At that time, Ellen was pregnant. She bowed her head and kept her mouth closed in church, but she prayed, "If this child in my womb is a girl, may she be given the chance to speak out and know the truth that has been so long denied me."[18]

Lua Aurora Moore was born on November 1, 1871, on the Moore farm in Hume, New York. As a child she was, her sister said, "straight and slender as a white birch."[19] She was unusually articulate, had a beautiful voice, and was so brilliant that she often stayed after school because the teacher couldn't satisfy her hunger for knowledge during regular classroom hours. When she was about twenty, she went to Chicago to study theater. It would have seemed more logical to go to New York, but Lua said some sort of guidance drew her to Chicago. She was soon distracted from the stage by the pageantry of all sorts of churches, mystical societies, cults, and philosophies. Looking for a faith that would satisfy her, Lua was constantly disappointed but never discouraged. She was twenty-two when she ran across the name Bahá'u'lláh while reading a newspaper report on the 1893 World Parliament of Religions, which was one of many special gatherings convened at the Columbian Exposition in Chicago.

It isn't surprising that, with her searching spirit, Lua read the report of the parliament, but it is surprising that the ecumenical event even took place, for Christianity was on the defensive. Darwin's theories of evolution and new findings by Biblical scholars had upset age-old beliefs, while missionaries had found various so-called "pagans" to be more intractable than expected. So, of the 170 speakers at the parliament, most were Protestant ministers, although Jews, Jains, Zoroastrians, Confucians, Buddhists, and Hindus were represented, and, in fact, the Hindu speaker, Vivikananda, went on to establish quite a career for himself in America as a swami.

Yet the man who spoke Bahá'u'lláh's name for the first time in the occident, on September 23, 1893, was a Protestant missionary from Syria named George A. Ford. He delivered a paper written by Henry Harris Jessup, his mission director. Reverend Jessup, like other missionaries in Islamic countries, felt warmly disposed towards Bahá'u'lláh because he thought the Bahá'í teachings, with their embrace of Christ, would help christianize the Muslims. He wrote, and Reverend Ford read, of Bahá'u'lláh as "a Persian sage"[20] who had "died a few months since,"[21] and who had said, shortly before His death, to the British orientalist E.G. Browne: "That all nations should become one in faith and all men as brothers; that bonds of affection and unity between the sons of men should be strengthened; that diversity of religion should cease, and differences of race be annulled—what harm is there in this? Yet so it shall be; this fruitless strife, these ruinous wars shall pass away, and the 'Most Great Peace' shall come."[22]

It is not known precisely how Lua, soon after reading this, met Ibráhím Khayru'lláh,* the Syrian who had come to America to teach the Bahá'í Faith, but it is known that she attended classes organized by Khayru'lláh and in 1897 she was listed among the approximately 1,000 Bahá'ís of the United States. Bahá'í groups existed in Philadelphia; New York City; Kenosha, Wisconsin; Ithaca, New York; and Chicago.

Khayru'lláh had been in the United States for several years, talking religion with many people, before Thornton Chase became the first American Bahá'í in 1894. Like Lua, Chase came across reference to Bahá'u'lláh for the first time in reports of the World Parliament of Religions. He was a Theosophist, seeking the Avatar, and he met Khayru'lláh while look-

---

* Ibráhím Khayru'lláh's name is also commonly transliterated as "Ibrahim Kheiralla."

ing for someone to teach him Sanskrit. He was also a Civil War veteran, an insurance salesman, a poet, a fine baritone, a connoisseur of ice cream, and the one who taught Edward Getsinger about the Bahá'í Faith.

Back in 1893, at the Columbian Exposition, Edward had attended a scientific gathering. He was an atheist at the time, so he had no interest in the religious parliament or in newspaper reports of it. But, to his surprise, he had a vision while sitting in the lobby of his Chicago hotel. He saw a blue bay, a mountain, and a welcoming oriental Sage. This aroused his interest in mysticism. When he met Thornton Chase, he found someone who could answer his questions, and he became a Bahá'í in Ithaca in 1897. He and Lua married shortly afterwards.

Edward Getsinger probably wouldn't have become a Bahá'í through <u>Kh</u>ayru'lláh, who was, sad to say, a charlatan yearning to establish a cult of personality. This was not immediately apparent, but Edward felt it and it was anethema to him. <u>Kh</u>ayru'lláh presented the Bahá'í teachings in a series of lessons wrapped in mystery, climaxing in one during which the students learned the Greatest Name, Yá-Bahá'u'l-Abhá, an invocation which means "O Thou Glory of the Most Glorious."

Lua didn't wait to take all the lessons before insisting that she be told the Greatest Name. Then she wrote home of "great news."[23] Soon she was on her way back to the farm to tell her family that the Advent, the day prophesied by William Miller, had dawned. Ellen McBride's prayer that her daughter find the answers to her long-standing questions had been fulfilled. Lua's sister reported that Lua came home looking "ethereal and radiant."[24]

And, she went on, "One moonlit night, Lua, Mother, another of my sisters and myself went into the parlor. Whenever any momentous decisions were to be made in the Moore family, they were all made in the parlor."[25] Lua chanted a prayer, then told how Bahá'u'lláh had come to usher in the promised millennium. Her sister recalled, "It is impossible to describe the feeling of wonder . . . the excitement Lua's words generated in our hearts."[26] But the family also felt sorrow, for they could see that the passionate Lua was wholly given to her new-found Faith, and, in a sense, lost to them.

Then Lua accompanied Edward to California, where there were as yet no Bahá'ís, and established the first Bahá'í group there. Edward's medical theories had been written up in newspaper articles that caught the eye of Phoebe Hearst, widow of the mining magnate, Senator George Hearst, and she invited Edward to California so she could consult him. Edward espoused homeopathy, and Mrs. Hearst was so enthused about homeopathic medicine that she had helped found the Hahnemann Hospital in San Francisco. She was also interested in peace, so Edward wanted her to know about the Bahá'í Faith. He felt Lua should be the one to teach her.

As Lua sat sipping tea with Mrs. Hearst in the elegant drawing room of the mansion called the Hacienda, she noticed that the butler was very attentive to what she was saying, so she directed herself to him, too. His name was Robert Turner, and he was a man of integrity and dignity, greatly trusted by Mrs. Hearst. He embraced Lua's message and became the first African American Bahá'í.

Mrs. Hearst was so enthused that she arranged for Lua to give classes in her apartment atop the Examiner Building— named for the newspaper owned by her son, William Randolph Hearst—in San Francisco. Ella Goodall Cooper recalled meeting Lua there in 1898. Lua was still using <u>Kh</u>ayru'lláh's system of lessons, and since Ella had missed the first lessons she couldn't be included in the group but had to wait in a bedroom of the apartment to talk to Lua. She waited for a long time and finally, Lua burst into the room, very radiant, and very hungry. They sent out to a nearby saloon for an oyster loaf and some white wine—in those days, the American Bahá'ís didn't know that Bahá'u'lláh had prohibited alcohol except for medicinal purposes—and they ate, shared a little wine from one glass, and talked. Ella soon became a Bahá'í and, like the other new believers, wrote a declaration of Faith to 'Abdu'l-Bahá. She subsequently received a Tablet from Him and longed to go and meet Him.

Phoebe Hearst decided to include 'Akká in an Egyptian tour she was planning, and with her usual largesse she financed the trip for Lua and Edward. Robert Turner traveled with her as her valet, so he was able to enter 'Abdu'l-Bahá's presence as a pilgrim. The travelers stopped in England, where Mrs. Hearst invited an old friend, Mary Virginia Cropper, to come with them, and Mrs. Cropper's mother decided to accompany her daughter. Later, Ella Goodall and Nell Hillyer joined the party, and so did May Maxwell (Bolles at the time) in Paris.

The travelers separated into three groups when they neared the Holy Land and went to meet 'Abdu'l-Bahá that way, so as not to arouse suspicion by arriving in a large party. Seemingly by chance, Edward and Lua were in the first group to meet Him; <u>Kh</u>ayru'lláh and his family made up the rest of their group.

The Getsingers stayed much longer in the Haifa-'Akká area than any of the other pilgrims, for Lua, from the beginning, found the thought of leaving 'Abdu'l-Bahá impossible to contemplate. Edward, always scientific, recorded 'Abdu'l-Bahá's voice, using the brand-new technology developed by Thomas Edison, and took photographs which he later had tinted and published as an album, one of the first Bahá'í works published in America. In 1899, when the Getsingers reluctantly left the place they considered heaven to return to the United States, they were both sobbing even though 'Abdu'l-Bahá had told them great tasks awaited them. Edward later related that, one day, 'Abdu'l-Bahá told Lua He was giving her the gift of eloquence: when she had to speak of the Faith, she was to think of Him and He would be with her. Even with this promise, she wept copiously upon departure.

* * * * * * * * *

She and Edward might have wept even more had they suspected the hellishness of some of the great tasks ahead of them. They had to help protect the Bahá'í community from the machinations of Khayru'lláh. Pilgrimage had not done him any good. He had for some time secretly harbored the notion that 'Abdu'l-Bahá could captain the Bahá'ís of the orient, while he would take charge of the Bahá'ís in the occident. Upon meeting 'Abdu'l-Bahá, he realized no one could possibly share His authority. But Khayru'lláh couldn't bow his ego to that reality and joined forces with the Covenant-breakers, who encouraged his delusions. When he returned to the United States he started making false claims, causing discord and distress among the Bahá'ís.

Edward had disliked Khayru'lláh from the first and the feeling was mutual, so there was little Edward could do to try and placate him; he could only try to protect the Bahá'ís from his lies by championing the true, unifying teachings of Bahá'u'lláh. However, Lua was sent on missions by the worried Bahá'ís to try to "conciliate" Khayru'lláh. But he wouldn't be conciliated. Although he didn't succeed in causing lasting division among the American Bahá'ís, he did cause a lot of pain, especially to 'Abdu'l-Bahá, who wrote to Lua telling her to exemplify servitude to God, for that alone pleased His aching heart. Following 'Abdu'l-Bahá's advice, she and Edward treated Khayru'lláh as kindly as possible until the time came when 'Abdu'l-Bahá had no other recourse but to instruct the Bahá'ís to shun him.

'Abdu'l-Bahá's constant personal guidance through His letters was a rallying point of unity for the Bahá'ís, and so was their desire to build a House of Worship, or Mashriqu'l-Adhkar ("The Dawning Place of the Mention of God"). In Russia the first Bahá'í House of Worship in the world was under construction in Ashkhabad, in what is now Turkmenistan, near the northern Iranian border. This inspired the American Bahá'ís with a dream of building their own House of Worship, and 'Abdu'l-Bahá gave to the Getsingers and other energetic souls the mission of rousing people to donate to the Temple Fund. Since money could only be accepted from Bahá'ís who gave voluntarily, and most Bahá'ís had limited means, the donations represented personal sacrifice and, more than that, faith in a project which seemed phantasmagoric, for when the first Temple Unity Committee came into being there was no site, no architectural design—nothing but a dream.

The Bahá'ís were also educated in unity through teachers 'Abdu'l-Bahá sent to try to save Khayru'lláh, chief among them Mírzá Abu'l-Faḍl, a renowned scholar who arrived in America in 1901 accompanied by an interpreter, the young poet and diplomat Ali-Kuli Khan, who later said that if he had never met 'Abdu'l-Bahá he would have thought Faḍl the most wonderful being on earth.

Mírzá Abu'l-Faḍl was a tall, spare figure, garbed in robes and a turban, subsisting on Persian tea, delicate biscuits, and, until he stopped smoking, thin Egyptian cigarettes. To expound the Bahá'í truths convincingly, he relied on a prayer revealed especially for him by Bahá'u'lláh, and it was said that 'Abdu'l-Bahá found his wit refreshing.

Lua was with Faḍl in America and in Paris, but it would have surprised both of them if they could have known that one day they would share the same burial ground in Cairo, Egypt, with a monument over it supporting a globe symbolizing the unity of East and West. Odd as this may seem, it is suitable for many reasons, one being that Lua, in France, made one of the great early gestures that opened the way for solidarity between the Bahá'ís of the East and the West at the same time that Faḍl was helping the Bahá'í group of Paris to consolidate itself. This occurred when Lua delivered a petition from 'Abdu'l-Bahá to Muẓaffari'd-Dín-S͟háh, the ruler of Iran at the time.

The S͟háh was in Paris being educated by his Prime Minister in the wonders of the West. During the course of this education, he narrowly escaped assassination by an anarchist's bomb as he viewed the splendors of art and science at the Exposition Universalle. However, though he was a timid-souled despot, the allure of the West was apparently greater than the threat of dynamite, for he remained in France, ensconced at the Elysèe Palace Hotel. Lua was to go to him there and personally present 'Abdu'l-Bahá's petition requesting that he extend protection to the persecuted Bahá'ís in Persia.

Following the assassination of the S͟háh's father by a socialist in 1896, the Bahá'ís had been scapegoated. A poet named Varqá (the Dove) had been killed along with his twelve-year-old son, Rúḥu'lláh. Six other Bahá'ís were also martyred, and the oppression was increasing. The Bahá'ís of France added their own petition to 'Abdu'l-Bahá's, and Lua went to the hotel accompanied by a French Bahá'í, Hippolyte Dreyfus, to request an audience with the Sháh.

Lua was pale and elegant in a black dress she'd had made especially for the occasion. But the Prime Minister refused to see her. He was not receiving anyone, because his son was dying. Lua asked if he would consent to see her tomorrow should his son be healed? The Prime Minister's secretary didn't want to ask that question, but Lua, with transcendent calm, wouldn't leave the room, so he finally had to communicate it and the Prime Minister agreed to Lua's conditions. That night the Bahá'ís of Paris held a prayer vigil till dawn. Lua learned in the morning that the boy was recovering. When she and Monsieur Dreyfus returned to the hotel the Prime Minister promised that measures would be taken to grant the petitions. But Lua wanted to hear that from the Sháh himself and she managed to get past the Prime Minister, put the petitions into the Sháh's hand, and hear him say he would do all that was within his power.

Her success as a messenger was clear, but the success of the message was less clear. In 1903, a savage rash of persecution broke out in Iran against the Bahá'ís and the Sháh did nothing because his Prime Minister, his chief advisor, thought it politic to let a restless populace vent rage on the Bahá'ís rather than on the rich and powerful foreigners who might otherwise have been victimized. However, the Prime Minister resigned or was dismissed in mid-1903, persecutions eased, and there were a few isolated cases near the end of the Sháh's reign in 1907 in which he did intervene in favor of the Bahá'ís. Meanwhile, the Bahá'ís of Iran accomplished a great deal, even managing to open their own schools and hospitals. Occidental Bahá'ís were able to collaborate with them in these efforts. (See chapter 6.) So Lua, at the request of 'Abdu'l-Bahá, had taken a first historic, giant step towards unifying the Bahá'í world.

* * * * * * * *

In 1902, Lua was again in Haifa with 'Abdu'l-Bahá. She spent over a year in His household, teaching English to His grandchildren. She learned that if she wanted to achieve her dearest wish, to follow in His footsteps, the way would be stony. An anecdote she related was of the time He told her He was too busy to visit a friend of His who was ill and asked her to go in His place. She felt honored to be sent to visit His special friend. But she found the man in rags, lying in a reeking hovel. She nearly fainted because of the stench, the filth, and the fear that she herself might contract some horrible disease. Feeling there must have been some mistake, she rushed back to 'Abdu'l-Bahá. Regarding her sadly and sternly, He told her that if the man was dirty, she must bathe him; if his house was filthy, she must clean it; if he was hungry, she must feed him; and if he were ailing, she must make sure he had whatever remedies he needed. 'Abdu'l-Bahá said that He had served the man in just that fashion, many times. He asked Lua if she couldn't do it, just once?

Lua learned the lesson well: she often volunteered to nurse the poor and wounded. She also began to dress in clothing that resembled a nursing sister, and that, too, was because of 'Abdu'l-Bahá. He designed an outfit for her, a simple dress and coat, and a hat with a long, cloak-like veil. He told her she should wear the outfit at all times, and He even chose the color, royal blue. She had the garments made in lightweight cloth for summer and in heavy cloth edged with blue velvet for winter. The days when she wore delicate ruffles, pastels, and lace were over.

A friend of Lua's, Ramona Brown, recalled how beautiful Lua looked in the royal blue, and how the color complimented her eyes. A few years after Lua's stint as an English teacher in 'Abdu'l-Bahá's household was over, she gave Ramona a poignant gift. They were in a hotel room in San Francisco when Lua suddenly rose, opened a drawer, took out a long, flat white box and handed it to Ramona. The box contained a pair of white kid gloves, the last remnant, Lua explained, of all her finery.

Lua told Ramona she was grateful to 'Abdu'l-Bahá for the blue outfit, for its modesty protected her from thieves and other pests during her ceaseless travels. And, as the gift of the fine gloves showed, she didn't impose her own austerity on others. But it was her deepest desire to attain the humility and simplicity exemplified by 'Abdu'l-Bahá.

Because of her pure-heartedness, she was a comfort to Him. During 1902, because of the machinations of His maliciously jealous enemies, He was strictly confined to 'Akká and couldn't visit Bahá'u'lláh's tomb, where He loved to go and pray daily and water the flowers. He used to ask Lua to sing His favorite hymn, "Nearer My God to Thee," while He stood in a room He'd had built on the roof of His house that looked across the plain to Bahjí. Shoghi Effendi later told some Bahá'ís in England that Lua's voice rose and fell like a nightingale's as she sang, and that its sound would make 'Abdu'l-Bahá weep. Then 'Abdu'l-Bahá would chant the "Tablet of Visitation," a prayer revealed by Bahá'u'lláh and chanted in His Shrine, and Lua would weep. She said her heart broke when He reached

the stanza, "Waft then, unto me, O my God and my Beloved
. . . the holy breaths of Thy favors, that they may draw me
away from myself and from the world . . ."[27]

'Abdu'l-Bahá later kept a small framed portrait of just one
Bahá'í on the little table in an airy blue and white room where
He took pilgrims to rest while visiting Bahjí: a portrait of Lua.

He knew nothing was easy for her. Not only was she
empathetic and sensitive in the extreme, but she was fragile
due to a heart condition. At one time 'Abdu'l-Bahá report-
edly said to Edward Getsinger, "I told the Angel of Death to
stay away" from Lua.[28] Yet He required great things of her,
and she spared herself nothing.

She didn't even have a home. She and Edward were based
in Washington, D.C., but they traveled constantly all over the
United States, giving Bahá'í classes. 'Abdu'l-Bahá had told
them to visit small towns where most teachers didn't go, never
stay too long in one place, and teach people of all types, not
just the upper crust and intellectuals. No one, then, was unimportant. Ramona Brown observed Lua as she gave talks in
Ramona's family home in Berkeley, California. Lua always sat
in a certain corner of the room from which she could look
into every face and read all eyes as she spoke.

Lua's teaching method was a compound of common sense,
certitude, and inspiration.

In 1905, a young man named Harlan Ober attended her
classes in Boston.[29] He was dubious, and she told him, "You
must discover the reality of this Faith and, if it is true, you
must accept it, but if it is false, you must denounce it."[30] He
was interested in Hinduism, but she told him his path to understanding Bahá'u'lláh would be through Christ because he
had been raised in the Christian tradition. She told him to
pray. He distrusted prayer as a form of self-hypnosis, but he

said he would pray if she could supply him with a supplication that was "sufficiently universal."[31]

However, it wasn't until the spring of 1906 that Harlan retired to a hotel room in Boston with the prayer she'd given him, along with other literature. There he found his search fulfilled through, he later said, turning in prayer to God through Christ. Then he went out and walked around Boston Common, gazing ecstatically at the magnolias which symbolized for him the spiritual springtime. When he next saw Lua he excitedly described his awakening, and he wrote to 'Abdu'l-Bahá.

Shortly afterwards, Lua's brother, Dr. William Moore, suddenly died. William had been preparing to go to India and Burma at 'Abdu'l-Bahá's request to visit the Bahá'í groups that had been there since the time of Bahá'u'lláh, for 'Abdu'l-Bahá felt they would be cheered by meeting an American Bahá'í. Lua suggested that Harlan go in place of her brother, and he did. So Lua, despite personal grief, placed 'Abdu'l-Bahá's wishes first and, with her usual generosity and resourcefulness, served Him and also Harlan Ober—the young man with an interest in Hinduism.

But the quality which most distinguished her teaching was the way she communicated a feeling of 'Abdu'l-Bahá's presence. Louis Gregory, the African American lawyer who was posthumously named a Hand of the Cause of God due to his distinguished services to the Bahá'í Faith, wrote in his memoirs that he first met 'Abdu'l-Bahá when he heard Lua speak. It was the winter of 1907 in Washington, D.C., and because the night was frigid and stormy not many people attended the gathering. It was, Louis recalled, small and intimate. Lua presented the Faith by telling its history. Obviously, Khayru'lláh's mystically muddling classes were a thing of the past, and Lua had found her own eloquence based on knowledge and emotion.

'Abdu'l-Bahá told Lua's friend, Juliet Thompson, that she should teach like Lua, and He added, "You will never find Lua speaking with dry eyes."[32]

* * * * * * * * *

In 1909, Lua received a letter from 'Abdu'l-Bahá containing great news to share with her fellow Bahá'ís. His long imprisonment was over because the Turkish Sultán had been overthrown, and all political and religious prisoners were released. Also, He had finally succeeded in interring the remains of the Báb in a Shrine built especially for the purpose on Mount Carmel. He'd begun that project eleven years before, in 1898, while Lua and Edward were on their first pilgrimage.

However, the project to preserve the remains of the Báb was even older than that. When the Báb was martyred in 1850, His body was thrown into a field for wild animals to devour. His followers, however, came in the night, sealed the remains into a coffin, then secretly hid the coffin in various places over many years, moving it ever nearer to the Holy Land, until at last it was hidden in the home of 'Abdu'l-Bahá where it stayed while 'Abdu'l-Bahá built a place to contain it: a simple, small, square building of sand-colored stone. Covenant-breakers aroused the authorities against Him, saying He was building a fort and fomenting revolution. As a result of their lies, His life was endangered, yet He persevered.

When at last He was free and the Shrine was finished, He said, "Every stone of that building, every stone of the road leading to it, I have with infinite tears and at tremendous cost, raised and placed in position."[33] His grandson, Shoghi Effendi, later recalled how 'Abdu'l-Bahá "His silver hair waving about His head and His face transfigured and luminous," finally interred the remains of the Báb. He "rested His forehead on the border of the wooden casket, and, sobbing aloud, wept with such a weeping that all those who were present wept with Him."[34]

In His letter to Lua, 'Abdu'l-Bahá included the coincidental news that, on the very day of the interment, He received a cablegram from Chicago saying that the site for the first Bahá'í House of Worship in the western world had been selected.

Immediately, now that He was free, He began receiving pleas from the Bahá'ís in the United States urging Him to come and visit them. In a letter written to Lua, He told them, "Abiding places in the hearts are needed."[35] In other words, they must be united; their love must draw Him to them.

* * * * * * * * *

To make abiding places in the hearts, Lua traveled and taught with more enthusiasm than ever. In 1911, while 'Abdu'l-Bahá visited the Bahá'ís in England and France and the American Bahá'ís hoped His arrival on their shores was imminent, Lua went, at His request, to California. In just a few months she spoke to a tremendous number of people, including the captain and crew of a naval flagship, prisoners at San Quentin Penitentiary, and 900 women at a Jewish Ladies Council. Then she went to Tijuana, Mexico, where civil war was in progress, and volunteered as a nurse.

She was still in California when 'Abdu'l-Bahá arrived in New York on April 11, 1912, but Edward Getsinger was one of the Bahá'ís who greeted Him. Edward served Him assiduously, giving Him massages in an effort to help Him relax, and making travel arrangements. But Edward found that although 'Abdu'l-Bahá's hair and beard had turned white and the deep lines on His face bespoke His well-taxed sixty-nine years, He had matchless energy; and He also responded with unnerving spontaneity to train schedules. After a few weeks, it was Edward who had to relax.

Meanwhile, Lua had made her way to Chicago and was eagerly awaiting 'Abdu'l-Bahá's arrival there. Because of 'Abdu'l-Bahá's improvisational attitude about schedules, that arrival became particularly exciting.

Lua was in Chicago to attend a Temple Unity Conference, and 'Abdu'l-Bahá was en route to join them and help them dedicate the land for the Temple. She was one of the many Bahá'ís who went to the station to greet 'Abdu'l-Bahá on April 29. All morning and afternoon they met incoming trains and He did not appear. That evening the *Chicago Daily News* reported, "Baha'ist Chief Missing."[36] The article said that 'Abdu'l-Bahá seemed to have mysteriously disappeared on His way to Chicago.

Yet the Bahá'ís remained faithfully on the platform. Sure enough, 'Abdu'l-Bahá finally arrived on a night train, and in their joy the Bahá'ís cried out His name in chorus so the whole station rang with their voices.

On a chilly and cloudy May 1, 'Abdu'l-Bahá joined some 300 Bahá'ís in a tent on the Temple land in the suburb of Wilmette. The site overlooked Lake Michigan, and Chicago's famously cold winds blew in from the water. 'Abdu'l-Bahá addressed the crowd briefly, then left the tent, followed by all 300, and asked for the dedication stone.

What stone? The plan had been merely to have 'Abdu'l-Bahá bless the property. As far as most of the guests knew, there was no stone.

But a dressmaker named Nettie Tobin, thinking there should be a stone, had acquired one from a construction site on her way to the dedication. With help from passers-by, she had lugged it to Wilmette in a little wagon and she'd gotten it to a place near the tent. So, when 'Abdu'l-Bahá asked for it, some men found it and brought it to Him.

Then he was handed a little golden trowel. With this, He was to symbolically turn over some earth. But now there was real stone. A real hole would have to be dug, and the little trowel couldn't cut through the spring grasses. A young man ran to a nearby house to borrow an ax, while another loped down Linden Avenue looking for a shovel. The young man with the ax returned first, and when 'Abdu'l-Bahá took it and swung it vigorously up over His shoulder and then down to cut into the turf, the Bahá'ís were so thrilled that they burst into song. Then the other young man dashed to 'Abdu'l-Bahá's side with a shovel he'd borrowed from a crew at the Isabella Street Elevated Railway.

'Abdu'l-Bahá turned to Lua and called her to come forward and turn over the first shovelful of earth. She demurred, but He insisted. So Lua took the shovel and dug into some of the ground He'd broken. He then asked Corinne True, the indefatigable worker for the building of the Temple, to turn over a shovelful, and she did, after which He invited people representing various races, religions and nations to help enlarge the hole. Then He placed Nettie Tobin's stone in the hole they'd dug, announcing that there it stood, on behalf of all the people of the world.

From Chicago, 'Abdu'l-Bahá went to Cleveland, Pittsburgh, and then Boston, returning to New York in late spring for His second visit. It was during that visit that He named Lua a "Herald of the Covenant." It happened while Juliet Thompson was painting His portrait. He could only give her a few scattered hours. During an early morning sitting on June 19, Lua was in the room. He told Lua that He was getting sleepy, and asked what he should do. Lua translated for Him and Juliet said He should, of course, rest. But when He closed His eyes and slept, sitting upright in His chair, Juliet found she couldn't continue working. She and Lua just looked at Him, for He was so majestically peaceful. Then He suddenly opened His eyes, rested an electrifying gaze on Lua and, in Farsi, said to her, "Herald of the Covenant."

"I?" exclaimed Lua in amazement.

'Abdu'l-Bahá told her to summon one of the Persians to translate, to make sure she understood perfectly. Then He said, "I appoint you, Lua, the Herald of the Covenant. And I am the Covenant, appointed by Bahá'u'lláh . . . Go forth and proclaim, 'This is the Covenant of God in your midst.'"

Juliet wrote that Lua's eyes were alight, her face bright with joy. She begged 'Abdu'l-Bahá, "Oh, recreate me."

Juliet, overwhelmed, was reduced to tears, and the tenderhearted Lua, who wouldn't forget a friend even at such a moment, said to 'Abdu'l-Bahá, "Julie, too, wants to be recreated."[37]

Soon after this Lua descended from the heights, for 'Abdu'l-Bahá instructed her to go and teach in California. Lua didn't want to leave Him, but He was adamant. So, while attending a picnic hosted by Him in New Jersey, Lua slipped into the woods, took off her shoes and stockings, and traipsed through poison ivy. The next day her feet and legs were so swollen she couldn't walk, and she happily told Juliet to inform 'Abdu'l-Bahá that she couldn't possibly leave for California. 'Abdu'l-Bahá, amused, gave Juliet an apple and a pomegranate to take to Lua and said, "Tell her to eat them, and she will be cured. Spend the day with her, Juliet."[38]

Lua, obedient to His wishes even after she'd tried to disobey them so thoroughly, ate the fruit down to and including the seeds. Later in the day, 'Abdu'l-Bahá came to see her. He looked at her feet which were, Juliet said, beautifully slim again. He laughed heartily: "See? I've cured Lua with an apple and a pomegranate."[39]

Lua actually tried a few more schemes to avoid California, but she had to go at last—so, she was there to greet 'Abdu'l-Bahá in October. The Bahá'ís hadn't expected that He'd make the long train trip across the continent, but He was moved to do so by the concerted prayers of the California Bahá'ís, and Lua had the privilege of making the arrangements for His stay, after which He boarded the train again for New York. He left America on December 5, 1912.

* * * * * * * * *

Photos of 'Abdu'l-Bahá and copies of His talks had been printed in countless newspapers, often with banner headlines across front pages. His talks had been attended by large audiences, His days crowded with personal interviews. People holding high, influential positions were reverent towards Him, in need of Him, grateful to Him—yet, for the most part, their inmost hearts were unmoved. There is a story of Him in California, walking by a pond: the ducks swam to the shore, and He gazed at them while they gazed at Him, and then He remarked that the ducks came to Him but the people did not.

Such incidents made His disciples more eager than ever to serve Him. Lua and Edward were fortunate to be with Him in Egypt in 1913, and then to visit India at His request. He told Lua before that journey, "Thou must be firm and unshakable in thy purpose, and never, never let any outward circumstances worry thee . . . Look at me! Thou dost not know a thousandth part of the difficulties and seemingly insurmountable passes that rise daily before my eyes. I do not heed them; I am walking in my chosen highway; I know the destination."[40]

Longing to live up to His expectations, Lua, though severely ill, kept up a hectic schedule of public talks and private visits. Edward recalled, "She never spared herself. Time and again I have seen her in a state of utter exhaustion yet she would pull herself together by sheer willpower in order to keep her appointments . . . She was generous to a fault, depriving herself often that others might have."[41]

From the fullness of her heart, Lua begged 'Abdu'l-Bahá to allow her to take upon herself the burden of atonement for wrongs done by any of the Bahá'ís. 'Abdu'l-Bahá knew her sincerity. Someone criticized Lua to Him, and He only remarked that she loved her Lord.

From India, she returned to Him in 'Akká. Soon afterwards, the Great War (World War I) began. For safety, 'Abdu'l-Bahá sent the Bahá'ís of 'Akká and Haifa to live in a Druse village. Although still suffering from the after-effects of her illness, Lua worked as a nurse with a Bahá'í surgeon in a dispensary in the village. So long as the U.S. remained neutral in the war, 'Abdu'l-Bahá let her stay. However, one day a United States gunboat appeared at the port of Haifa. Sooner or later the United States would enter the war against Germany; and Turkey, which still ruled Syria, was allied with Germany. Lua couldn't stay in enemy territory. She left Haifa on August 30, 1915, with 290 refugees on the U.S. cruiser *Des Moines*.

The ship touched on Crete, then docked at Port Said, where Lua disembarked. She was so ill that she couldn't get back on the ship. Despite wrenching exhaustion, she sent letters during September from Port Said to America, England, and India, assuring the Bahá'ís that 'Abdu'l-Bahá, though surrounded by difficulty and danger, had been in good health when she left. She imparted His message: "Tell everyone that now is the time to teach and spread the Cause!"[42] She planned to go France, and then home, but she was hemmed in by illness and trapped by war.

As soon as she could stand she volunteered as a nurse to wounded soldiers, but she soon got pneumonia. She lodged with a Persian Bahá'í couple in Cairo, who cared for her devotedly. When she was well enough, she gave talks in their home. A Bahá'í from Egypt reported that some people were transformed by her eloquence. When spring came, she accepted an invitation to stay at the home of another Bahá'í, and his family regarded her as a sister.

But she was very weary. In April she remarked to some friends: "Little by little I am seeing all the reasons why many things are as they are, and the lessons I have to learn thereby. I am sure until the last day of our lives we will be learning lessons, for this world is a school, from which we graduate only when we leave it. I shall be so glad when the last day comes, and the school is forever (so far as I am concerned) dismissed. His will, not mine, be done!"[43]

Her prayer was answered. On May 2, 1916, she woke in the middle of the night with a severe pain in her heart. The family phoned for a doctor but she died before he arrived.

She had managed to repeat three times the Greatest Name. She was forty-five, and her childlike simplicity and yearning heart made her seem much younger.

'Abdu'l-Bahá received the news of her death in silence. After remaining silent for a long time, He finally sighed, "What a loss."[44] And, many times over the ensuing days, He was heard to repeat, in grieving tones, "What a loss."

Lua, the delicate, simple child walking through poison ivy in a silly scheme to stay by 'Abdu'l-Bahá's side, the lonely woman in the dark blue dress wishing to take upon herself atonement for wrongs done by her fellow believers, the pioneer teacher searching every soul for an answering spark to the great flame that burned within her—Lua was gone. At last, out of the deep well of His own sorrow, 'Abdu'l-Bahá revealed a prayer for Lua, praising her humility, telling how she had "traveled to distant countries and remote regions . . . throughout vast and spacious continents," and had "healed every sick one with the antidote" of the knowledge of God, until "her frail body failed her." He asked that she be established "in the midst of the Paradise of Immortality."[45] Thus, her homelessness was ended, her place assured.

Chapter 2

May Maxwell

May Bolles, with Thomas Breakwell, in Paris, 1902

I stood on the threshold and dimly saw a room full of people sitting quietly about the walls, and then I beheld my Beloved. I found myself at His feet, and He gently raised me and seated me beside Him, all the while saying some loving words in Persian in a voice that shook my heart.[1]

So May Maxwell began her description of her first encounter with 'Abdu'l-Bahá, which occurred early in the morning on February 17, 1899, in a house in Haifa that He had rented for the American pilgrims. In that voice which shook her heart, He told her, "Now your troubles are ended, and you must wipe away your tears."[2] He said that the soil of her heart, plowed and furrowed by her life's experience, was ready for "the seed of life."[3]

May had certainly had troubles. She was at the point of death when the mere fact of 'Abdu'l-Bahá's existence, related by Lua Getsinger, rejuvenated her. She was twenty-nine, petite and ethereally lovely, and an invalid since the age of twenty-one. At one time, she had been able to play tennis all day and dance all night but, when she met Lua, after suffering for years from an ailment that doctors could not diagnose, she lay weakly among her pillows, her face peaked, her eyes huge.

It was November, 1898. Lua and Edward Getsinger, en route to 'Akká with Phoebe Hearst, were in Paris so that Mrs. Hearst could visit her nieces, Anne Apperson and Agnes Lane. Mrs. Hearst and May's grandmother were old friends, and May's mother was chaperoning Anne and Agnes. When Mrs. Hearst learned May was ill in bed, she sent Edward to examine her. His diagnosis was that his wife had just the remedy, and Lua arrived at the apartment on the *rue du Bac* to tell the invalid, "There is a prisoner in 'Akká who holds the key to peace."[4] In those days, that was the typical way of introducing the Bahá'í Faith. May cried, "I believe! I believe!" and fainted.[5]

When she revived, she told Lua that, two years before, she had seen in a vision a kingly figure in oriental robes, beckoning to her from across the sea. She thought He was Jesus, but Lua said He was 'Abdu'l-Bahá. After learning that Lua was going to visit Him, May decided that she, too, must go.

Although she was almost thirty, she was so transparently beautiful and so dependent on her mother after her years of illness that all who knew her then, and for years afterwards, thought of her as a young girl. However, she was independent within herself. She asked no one for assistance to pay for her journey but immediately started trying to sell her gold watch and other jewelry. Mrs. Hearst heard about it and invited May to travel with her as her guest. The Hearst nieces were going, too, along with their governess, Julia Pearson, and Mrs. Hearst took May and the other young women out and bought them Paris gowns so they could be presented to 'Abdu'l-Bahá in style.

Then May journeyed to Marseilles to set sail for Haifa. She and her companion, the elderly Mrs. H. Thornbourgh, left Marseilles on February 9, 1899, on the *S.S. Carthage*, and reached Port Said on February 13. For passengers going on to Bombay, Port Said, at the entrance to the Suez Canal, was the rowdy place where the picturesque and risky East began, but, for May, Port Said was the joyous place where she first experienced the loving hospitality of the oriental Bahá'ís. The pilgrims were welcomed in the home of a Bahá'í family, where they each received a photograph of 'Abdu'l-Bahá and a lock of Bahá'u'lláh's hair; then they were served abundant tea and pastries. The pilgrims and their hosts couldn't speak each other's languages, yet, May said, "We felt that no language could have been more eloquent than that silence in which our hearts alone had spoken."[6]

On February 15, the pilgrims boarded the boat for the short sail to Haifa. As they sat on deck, twilight fell, shadows deepened, and in the gathering darkness the stars shone "large and effulgent in that clear atmosphere."[7] Soon May saw "looming up through the darkness, dimly at first, but growing ever more distinct and grand, the noble outline of Mount Carmel, then the twinkling lights along the shore," and she caught "the breath of the Holy land . . . laden with the perfume of roses and orange blossoms."[8] Two Russian Jewish pilgrims stood motionless, praying, at the ship's rail, and May and her companions joined them as the ship entered the bay and cast anchor.

May spent her first night in Haifa "between waking and sleeping, waiting for the sunrise."[9] Just after sunrise, she learned that 'Abdu'l-Bahá would arrive momentarily. "We had barely time to dress," she wrote, "when a sudden stir without set all our beings in commotion. We went out into a large central hall from which opened all the rooms of the house and opposite the door of one of these we saw the shoes of the believers."[10]

After May knelt at 'Abdu'l-Bahá's feet and He spoke to her, the two Russian pilgrims arrived. May said their faces were radiant with happiness, but, for her, all radiance dimmed in the luminosity of 'Abdu'l-Bahá's face. "We drank tea with Him at His bidding," she said, "but existence seemed suspended, and when He arose and suddenly left us we came back with a start to life: but never again, thank God, to the same life on this earth!"[11]

The meeting had certainly sown a new seed of life in May's heart. 'Abdu'l-Bahá wrote to her mother that May had been dead, but now she was alive; she had been mute, but now she was gifted with wonderful eloquence.

It was His love that revived her. She tells in *An Early Pilgrimage* of the special attention He gave to each person, and she was deeply touched by His consideration for her in her illness. One evening, she wrote,

He invited all the pilgrims to meet Him on Sunday morning under the cedar trees on Mount Carmel where He had been in the habit of sitting with Bahá'u'lláh. We were all most happy in this hope, and great was my disappointment next morning when I found myself quite ill. As soon as the Master arrived for breakfast He came directly to my room and walking over to my bedside took both my hands in His, passed His hand over my brow, and gazed upon me with such gentleness and mercy that I forgot everything but the love and goodness of God, and my whole soul was healed and comforted. I looked up into His face and said: 'I am well now. . . .' But He smiled and shook His head and bade me remain there quietly, until He should return at noon. Although I had been suffering during the night, all pain and distress were gone. . . . On Sunday morning we awakened with the joy and hope of the meeting on Mount Carmel. The Master arrived quite early and after looking at me, touching my head and counting my pulse, still holding my hand He said to the believers present: 'There will be no meeting on Mount Carmel to-day. We shall meet elsewhere . . . in a few days, Inshá'alláh (God willing), but we could not go and leave one of the beloved of God alone and sick. We could none of us be happy unless all the beloved were happy.[12]

May and her companions were astonished. How amazing that such an important meeting, in such a significant spot, should be canceled just because one person couldn't go! "It was so contrary," she said, "to all ordinary habits of thought and action, so different from the life of the world, where daily events and material circumstances are supreme in importance, that it gave us a genuine shock of surprise."[13] She felt that 'Abdu'l-Bahá's decision gave the pilgrims "a vision of that infinite world whose only law is love."[14]

He also taught His disciples sterner lessons. One afternoon, in her room with two friends, May criticized a fellow Bahá'í. When 'Abdu'l-Bahá came to the house, He called for Lua and said He knew one of the pilgrims had spoken unkindly of a fellow believer and it "grieved His heart that the believers should not love one another."[15] He told Lua to pray about it. At suppertime, May, totally unconscious of her wrong-doing, raised her eager eyes to His face and saw, she said, something in His eyes which showed her, as in a "pure and perfect mirror" her "wretched self."[16] She realized that, in finding fault, she'd acted without love to vent her own malice. She began to weep. 'Abdu'l-Bahá kindly ignored her and everyone followed His example, going on with the meal while she sobbed. But 'Abdu'l-Bahá only let her suffer for a few moments. Smiling, He spoke her name several times, as if, she felt, He were calling her to Him; her heart was comforted with "sweet happiness" and "infinite hope."[17]

She also learned from Him the power of prayer. One day, He instructed the pilgrims to prepare to leave Haifa for 'Akká at six o'clock the next morning. That evening, May told Lua that He evidently didn't realize how ill and weak she was, or He would never have expected her to be able to go. Lua smiled and said, "You will soon realize something of the power of 'Abdu'l-Bahá." May recorded, "It was about dawn when I woke, feeling myself stirred by a breeze. I cannot describe what followed, but through my soul was flowing an essence; a mighty, unseen force was penetrating all my being, expanding it with boundless life and love and happiness, lifting and enfolding me in its mighty strength and peace." She realized that 'Abdu'l-Bahá was "praying for His servants," and she left her bed feeling refreshed and well.[18]

May was able to join the others for the pilgrimage to Bahjí, preceeded by a visit to the lovely little Garden of Riḍván. May wrote that "the sky was blue and clear, the sun shone with eastern warmth and splendour, a light breeze stirred and the air was perfumed with roses."[19] At Bahjí, they found "a group of more than one hundred oriental believers. . . . Knowing that we were among the first American pilgrims to that Holy Spot they had come from all directions to behold our faces, and their own shone with a love and joy which amazed us, and which we can never forget."[20]

Before the pilgrims entered the Shrine, 'Abdu'l-Bahá said, "We are now going to visit the Holy Tomb. When you are praying . . . remember the promise of Bahá'u'lláh, that those who attain this pilgrimage shall receive an answer to their prayers, and their wishes shall be granted."[21] Then they followed Him into the Shrine, first removing their shoes, and found themselves "in a square court with a glass roof, and in the centre a plot of earth where flowering bushes and mandarin trees were growing." There was a door to one side of the courtyard, leading into the tomb. Before the door, "in the mellow light of a stained glass window," they stood silently until 'Abdu'l-Bahá asked one of the group to sing "The Holy City." May said, "No pen could describe the solemn beauty of that moment, as, in a broken voice, this young girl sang."[22]

Nowadays, pilgrims remain in the courtyard, but in those days 'Abdu'l-Bahá led them into the tomb. May did not describe that experience, saying that thought could not encompass the feeling of the place. Afterwards, standing again in the court, they sang "Nearer my God to Thee" at 'Abdu'l-Bahá's request. And then they were outside in the cool evening air, following 'Abdu'l-Bahá across green fields, under a full moon rising, to the waiting carriages. It was their final evening with Him.

In the morning, May awoke feeling that she faced utter darkness because she had to leave 'Abdu'l-Bahá. Sitting before Him, waiting to hear His parting words, some of the pilgrims sobbed and He asked them "for His sake not to weep."[23] In fact, He wouldn't speak until tears ceased and all were calm. Then He said, "Pray that your hearts may be cut from yourselves and from the world, that you may be confirmed by the Holy Spirit and filled with the fire of the love of God. The nearer you are to the light, the further you are from the darkness; the nearer you are to heaven, the further you are from the earth; the nearer you are to God, the further you are from the world." He assured them, "Nothing shall be impossible to you if you have faith."[24]

Then He led them into an adjoining room so they could view portraits of Bahá'u'lláh and the Báb which were placed on a divan against the wall. The portrait of the Báb was a Persian miniature, while the one of Bahá'u'lláh was a photograph, a passport picture taken when He was exiled from Edirne, Turkey, to 'Akká. May said the Báb's face was young and beautiful, but she couldn't keep her eyes from the eyes of Bahá'u'lláh. She was kneeling, gazing into His eyes when, suddenly, "in a tone so poignant," wrote May, "that it pierced every heart," 'Abdu'l-Bahá said,

> Now the time is come when we must part, but the separation is only of our bodies, in spirit we are united. . . .

Great mercy and blessings are promised to the people of your land, but on one condition: that their hearts are filled with the fire of love, that they live in perfect kindness and harmony like one soul in different bodies. If they fail in this, the great blessings will be deferred. Never forget this: look at one another with the eye of perfection; look at Me, follow Me, be as I am; take no thought for yourselves or your lives, whether ye eat or whether ye sleep, whether ye are comfortable, whether ye are well or ill, whether ye are with friends or foes, whether ye receive praise or blame; for all of these things ye must care not at all. Look at Me and be as I am; ye must die to yourselves and to the world, so shall ye be born again and enter the Kingdom of Heaven. Behold a candle how it gives its light. It weeps its life away drop by drop in order to give forth its flame of light."[25]

Then the pilgrims had to leave Him. They wouldn't turn their backs on Him, because they couldn't stand to lose sight of His face a moment too soon. May said, "For a moment it seemed that we were dying, but our Master never removed His compassionate gaze from our faces, until we could see Him no longer, for our tears."[26] As they said final farewells to His family, with warm embraces, May recalled that "it seemed as if all the cords of life were breaking." Then, "suddenly His spirit came to us, a great strength and tranquillity filled our souls. . . . We had left our Beloved in His glorious prison that we might go forth and serve Him."[27]

It would be ten years before May saw 'Abdu'l-Bahá again. During that time, and throughout her life, she served him with complete, selfless devotion. She was one of His disciples, and from His pen received over sixty Tablets. In the last one, written shortly before His passing and translated on October

24, 1922, He addressed her, "O thou dear daughter!"[28] He described her in a letter to one of the early believers: "Mrs. Maxwell is really a Bahá'í. This is why whomsoever she becomes acquainted with, she imbues with the Spirit of Life."[29] Later, Shoghi Effendi would refer to her as "'Abdu'l-Bahá's beloved handmaid" who attained the crown of martyrdom. She indeed went forth and served her beloved Master well.[30]

* * * * * * * * *

Mary Ellis Bolles, usually called May throughout her life, did not come from a family that had spiritual tendencies, and she wasn't raised to be a handmaid to anyone. She was born on January 14, 1870, in Englewood, New Jersey. Her grandfather owned the Ocean City Bank in New York, and her mother, Mary Martin Bolles, was accustomed to luxury. May's father was John Bolles, an engineer, but her mother took May and her brother, Randolph, to live in the grandfather's well-appointed house.

When May was still quite young, however, her grandfather suffered a reverse. The bank was robbed, and May's grandfather made up all the losses out of his own pocket. Then the family retired from New York, in reduced circumstances, to their home in New Jersey. Sometimes, May even wore hand-me-down clothes from her wealthy New York cousins. But this probably did not bother her as much as it bothered her mother, for May was an unworldly person.

Though her family was not religious, May used to go out into the woods alone to pray. She was convinced that she was living at the time of the return of Christ, and she had remarkable dreams. At the age of eleven, she dreamed of a light so dazzling that she woke up blind and remained blind until the following day. When she was fourteen, she refused to continue her formal schooling because, she later said, "I felt very distinctly there was another way of acquiring knowledge."[31] She lived with her mother, grandmother, and brother in Paris, where she became fluent in French; she often thought in French, and loved the language, referring to it as a "lyric, plastic tongue."[32] She read the Qur'án, a very unusual proceeding for a young American woman during the late Nineteenth Century, and studied cults such as Rosicrucianism. Her vocation was religion, but she wasn't able to discover which religion until she met Lua Getsinger.

After her pilgrimage, the purpose of her life was clear. To fulfill it, she relied on courage and faith, for she was always physically frail. Her daughter recalled, "I never walked two blocks with my mother in my whole life. She just couldn't do it. And this increased after she grew older."[33] May transcended her weakness with her philosophy: "The mortal cage is nothing; the soul's motion in relation to the Beloved is the unfolding of all the meaning of life."[34] 'Abdu'l-Bahá said May had been born with an unusual nervous ailment for which there was, as yet, no cure. He also noticed and highly praised her beneficent influence on others. Her daughter said: "Many people inspire more or less love in others, but I don't think I ever knew anyone who inspired the love Mother did—so that it was like an event when one was going to see her. And this I felt all my life, day in and day out, and it never became commonplace."[35] On another occasion she remarked, "I can truly say of her that I never knew anyone to cross her path whom she did not in some way benefit — and that is saying a lot."[36]

May was a powerful presence. Her friend Juliet Thompson praised her "personal fascination . . . so fragile, so luminous . . . and the most delicate, perfect beauty, flower-like and star-like."[37] A number of Americans, like Juliet, came into the Faith in Paris through her, and so May, the first Bahá'í on the European continent, established the first Bahá'í group there.

Edith McKay, a member of that group, was in Paris studying to be an opera singer. She later recalled, "It was in 1900 that I became a Bahá'í. I was twenty-one years old. One evening (it was Christmas) I was invited to my godfather's home and on entering the salon I saw an angelic creature. It was May . . . A mysterious force drew me to her and I said: 'I believe you have something to tell me.' 'Yes,' she said, 'I have a message for you.' She then disclosed to me this secret, which was the Bahá'í Faith . . . Later, my mother, Madame Marie-Louise McKay, also became a Bahá'í, as did my friends H. Dreyfus (Hippolyte Dreyfus, the first French Bahá'í) and his wife, Madame L. Dreyfus-Barney, Edith Sanderson, and others."[38]

Berthalin Allen, one of the Bahá'ís of Paris, remembered:

> I first heard of the Bahá'í Cause a little before 1900, while I was in school in Paris. There I met . . . a few American students . . . who seemed to be involved in a new religion stemming from Persia. I can't say that I was especially impressed by what they said. Rather I was attracted by these people as unusual people—one in particular, a very beautiful girl who seemed to radiate a special magnetic charm. I was completely captivated by her and, not understanding what she was saying, I just silently sat in wonder. . . . Her name was May Bolles. . . . The Guardian many years later wrote me how blessed I was to have been a member of that group. A small group but there was radiance . . . the spirit of Bahá'u'lláh so strong, a tightly united group; it made me speechless; all I wanted was to be with them; my whole life was changed. . . . There were no books, just a few words

brought back to us from pilgrims who had gone to 'Akká to see the prisoner, 'Abdu'l-Bahá."[39]

Agnes Alexander, who would establish the Bahá'í Faith in Hawaii, Japan and Korea, first learned of it in Rome, where she was given May's address in Paris. She wrote to May asking for more information, and May's reply was, she said, "so permeated with divine love" that it captivated her heart and she immediately made her way to Paris, found May's apartment, and knocked on the door. A woman opened it, and Agnes threw herself into her arms. There was an awkward silence. Then the woman said, "I think you want to see my daughter." May received Agnes so sensitively that, although Agnes was just a few years younger than May, she felt, she said, from that day on, "May's tender mother love," and through the years to follow that love was her "guiding star."[40]

Another person taught by May was Thomas Breakwell, the first Englishman to become a Bahá'í. He benefited from May's steadfast adherence to 'Abdu'l-Bahá's will and her resistance to her mother's. During the spring of 1901, Mrs. Bolles was preparing to go to Brittany, as she always did during hot weather. She assumed May and Randolph would accompany her. But May announced, "I can't leave Paris because 'Abdu'l-Bahá said I had to stay here and teach."[41] Mrs. Bolles wrote to 'Abdu'l-Bahá asking permission for May to leave, but He responded that she must stay. Then Mírzá Abu'l-Faḍl wrote to Him on behalf of Mrs. Bolles, and no reply came. When departure time arrived, Mrs. Bolles was very angry. She said to May, "I don't know what you're going to do, but I'm closing the apartment and I'm going away for the summer."[42]

Although May was thirty-one years old, she had no money of her own and had always lived with her mother. Undaunted, she went to stay with one of the Bahá'ís, Edith Jackson. Then one day, a Mrs. Milner, who knew the Paris Bahá'ís but was not one of them, brought Thomas Breakwell to meet May. She'd met Thomas aboard ship, crossing from New York to France.

May wrote, "I shall never forget opening the door and seeing him standing there. It was like looking at a veiled light."[43] Thomas and May chatted, but she didn't mention the Bahá'í Faith. As he was leaving, he told her he would only be in Paris for a few days but he wanted to call on her again and hear about the teachings Mrs. Milner had mentioned. May invited him to visit the next day. When he arrived, his face and eyes were shining. His voice trembled with emotion as he looked at her intently and said, "Yesterday after I left you, I walked alone down the boulevard and suddenly some great force nearly swept me off my feet. I stood still as though awaiting something and a voice announced to me distinctly, 'Christ has come!'"[44] He asked May if she thought he was crazy. She thought he had just become sane, and she told him about the Báb and Bahá'u'lláh, and of her meeting with 'Abdu'l-Bahá. He then yearned, she later said, for just one thing: to go to 'Akká and meet 'Abdu'l-Bahá.

Immediately after that, May went to get her mail and found a little blue cablegram. It was from 'Abdu'l-Bahá: "You may leave Paris at any time."[45] She made her way to Brittany, joined her mother and Randolph by the sea, and told them what had happened. Mrs. Bolles burst into tears and said, "You have, indeed, a wonderful Master."[46]

Thomas Breakwell was soon in 'Akká. He could only stay for two days because of restrictions imposed by the authorities, but his life changed entirely. He returned to Paris and stayed there at 'Abdu'l-Bahá's request. He took cheap lodgings far from where the other Bahá'ís lived and walked to all the meetings; he only wanted to use his money to further the Bahá'í Cause and not for his own comforts. He became, May said, "the guiding star of our group."[47] His charitable acts were many, and he also perceived nonmaterial needs and filled them. May's mother had not yet become a Bahá'í, so, when he went to the Bolles' home, he paid special attention to Mrs. Bolles, almost ignoring May. Yet, when he took May's hand to say good-bye, he always slipped a cheering note on folded paper into her palm. "He knew well," May said, "the secret of imparting happiness. . . . His kindness and love to my mother . . . produced a great effect on her and . . . he was . . . a joy and a consolation to her."[48]

But Thomas became ill with consumption and, after great pain, died in 1902, just a few months after his pilgrimage. 'Abdu'l-Bahá wrote a long prayer for him, a eulogy that was heart-rending. A year later, 'Abdu'l-Bahá, sifting through His mail one day, picked out an envelope which He said had an especially pleasing fragrance. It contained a pressed violet and a beautiful card with a message from Thomas' father, saying he had picked the flower at Thomas' grave. 'Abdu'l-Bahá stood up, pressed the card to His brow, and wept.

****

May's years with the rapturous new Bahá'ís of Paris came to an end in 1902 when she married William Sutherland Maxwell and moved to Canada. She had given no indication of wanting to be married before she met Sutherland. In fact, she said that in 1902 she reminded herself of a certain French heroine who had all her handkerchiefs embroidered with the words, *"A quoi bon!"* (Loosely translated: "Whatever for?")[49]

And a friend of hers, Louise Bosch, said, "As often as I looked upon her, and contemplated her attitude to life and her disposition of it, I would distinctly feel that she was only visiting here."[50]

She really was detached from everything except the Bahá'í Faith in its most mystical aspects. And then she fell in love with Sutherland Maxwell, a young architect who wasn't a Bahá'í and had no intention of becoming one. (May was the only person who ever called him Sutherland; everyone else called him William.)

They met when he came home for lunch one day with Randolph; he and Randolph were fellow students at l'École des Beaux Arts. He was a very tall, broad, Scots Canadian with rosy cheeks, bright blue eyes and curly chestnut hair. After he left the Bolles' apartment, May ordered her brother, "Don't you ever bring that big Canadian here again." Randolph considered Sutherland his best friend, so he was naturally alarmed by this ultimatum. "Why not?" he asked. "Because," May said, "he stared at me all the time."[51]

She later learned that he had stared at her because he had immediately made up his mind to marry her. And Randolph was not one to be bullied. He continued to bring Sutherland home, and May fell in love with him. But Sutherland, naturally reticent, had trouble when it came time to make the marriage proposal. He could not quite get the words out. Finally, May said, "Sutherland, are you proposing to me?" He said, "Yes," and she said, "I accept."[52]

'Abdu'l-Bahá consented to May's leaving Paris to live in Montreal. In fact, He instructed her, "With the strength of thy heart promote the word of God . . . in that remote region."[53] She was the only Bahá'í on Canadian soil when she arrived, but she wasn't alone for long because Sutherland's cousin, Martha McBean, became a Bahá'í in around 1903 and others followed.

Sutherland himself became a Bahá'í at around that time, but his conviction grew slowly and was not really confirmed for some years. Meanwhile, his architectural firm became the biggest in Canada and built landmarks such as the Parliament Buildings in Regina, the Chateau Frontenac Hotel in Quebec, and the Church of the Messiah in Montreal.

Sutherland was an artist who would watch the carving of ornamentation he had designed and take the chisel or gouge from the craftsman into his own hand to "sweeten the lines," as he put it.[54] Artisans admired and loved him, as did other colleagues. He became a Fellow of the Royal Institute of British Architects, was at one time President of the Royal Architectural Institute of Canada, and helped found the Pen and Pencil Club and the Arts Club in Montreal; his watercolors were often exhibited. The home he built at 716 Pine Avenue in Montreal in 1907–1908 was beautifully adorned. He would often come home bearing a new acquisition, an antique vase or such, and then experiment for hours, rearranging the parlor, putting various brocades under the vase, until it finally looked perfect.

May was a lovely asset to the house, wearing Fortuni gowns—custom tailored tunics from Italy embellished with a stamped design and lacing at the sleeves, and tied with wide belts. It was easy to look elegant in those gowns without wasting thought on them, and that was what May wanted, because all she really wanted to think about was the Bahá'í Faith. This caused a crisis in her marriage.

Her daughter remembered: "My mother, you see, just existed for the Faith. . . . One day, my father said to her, 'You know, May, I will never love any woman but you. But I have my profession. I'm interested in it, and you're only interested in the Bahá'í teachings. And we're getting farther apart in our marriage.' And Mother said she was terrified, absolutely terrified of losing him, because she loved him. Nevertheless, she said, 'I told you, Sutherland, when I married you that this Cause would have to come first in my life always. And I will just have to go on alone. I'll have to go on alone.' And she said that, then, he took her hand and held it, and said, 'I'll go all the way with you.'"[55]

Her daughter commented, "If she had been weak at that point . . . her service to the Cause would have been greatly reduced. So . . . you see . . . people don't become great people by accident."[56]

But May was not insensitive to Sutherland's needs. She did not do a lot of traveling for the Faith until he was strong in his belief. They both had to contend with opposition to the Bahá'í Faith in Montreal, which was a stronghold of Catholic conservatism. Even Sutherland's Protestant friends tended to be flippant about the strange oriental cult Mrs. Maxwell belonged to, and the Bahá'ís of Montreal were variously labeled Muhammadans, Sun-Worshippers, and Heretics. May's teaching style, maternal and tolerant, overcame this, and her undeviating devotion to her Faith was rewarded in 1909 when Sutherland, while on pilgrimage with her, received a lesson from 'Abdu'l-Bahá.

One mealtime, as the Maxwells, with other pilgrims, sat at 'Abdu'l-Bahá's table, Sutherland remarked to Him, "The Christians worship God through Christ; my wife worships God through You; but I worship Him direct."

'Abdu'l-Bahá smiled and asked, "Where is He?"

"Why," Sutherland replied, "God is everywhere."

"Everywhere is nowhere," 'Abdu'l-Bahá said.[57] And He

proceeded to demonstrate that humanity can only attempt to know God, the unknowable, through the Manifestations of His Reality in Beings like Christ and Bahá'u'lláh. Sutherland said nothing, but bowed his head in acceptance, and his own great devotion to the Bahá'í Faith was born.

During that pilgrimage, one day in 'Abdu'l-Bahá's home, May was chatting with a woman who was holding a baby, making a fuss over the baby, when 'Abdu'l-Bahá saw her and said, "Would you like to have a child?" May answered, "Oh, yes, I would love to have a child." 'Abdu'l-Bahá said, "I will pray that God will give you a child if it will never interfere with your service to the Cause of God." May told Him, "Nothing could ever come before my service to the Faith."[58]

Her daughter, Mary Sutherland Maxwell, was born in 1910. May was forty. She had been a semi-invalid for years, and, also, at that time it was very dangerous, even for a robust woman, to give birth to her first child at the age of forty.

'Abdu'l-Bahá wrote to May, "In the garden of existence a rose has blossomed with the utmost freshness, fragrance and beauty."[59] And He counseled her not to neglect her husband now that she had a baby.

****

After the birth of their daughter,* the crowning glory for May and Sutherland's home was the visit of 'Abdu'l-Bahá in 1912. Montreal was the only city He visited in Canada and His plan to go there had been discouraged by people who told Him

---

* In 1937, their daughter, Mary Maxwell—later known as Amatu'l-Bahá Rúḥíyyih Khánum—became the wife of 'Abdu'l-Bahá's beloved grandson and successor, Shoghi Effendi, appointed Guardian of the Bahá'í Faith, and in 1952 was appointed by him a Hand of the Cause of God.

how conservative the city was; however, He said their "stories" did not affect his "resolution" and He found that, "through the effort of the maid-servant of God, Mrs. Maxwell," there was a Bahá'í group in Montreal full of "joyous exhilaration."[60] He enjoyed His stay there, and felt it was fruitful.

He arrived on a bright moonlit evening, August 30, and lodged at the Maxwells' house on Pine Avenue. In the morning He visited a neighbor who had a sick child and had asked that 'Abdu'l-Bahá come and see her. He held the little girl in His arms and said she would soon be well; a few months later, she was running and playing, completely recovered. Then He went to a shop owned by the child's family and bought watches, rings, and other items to present to people as He traveled. He always kept a supply of gifts on hand, and was also always generous with tips to porters, waiters, chambermaids, and others.

In the afternoon, He was taken for a drive and, passing the majestic Notre Dame Cathedral, He decided to stop and go in. After touring the sanctuary, He stood outside and remarked to His companions how the church was there in Canada, so far in time and place from Galilee and Calvary, because of the self-sacrifice of the early Christians, who had left their loved ones and all they possessed to propagate their new Faith. They had never returned home, but had died in distant lands as martyrs.

This was a challenge to the Bahá'ís to follow the example of the early Christians. May, perhaps the most delicate of the group, was the one who heard the challenge most clearly and responded most ardently. 'Abdu'l-Bahá knew her heart and wrote of her: "May Maxwell is really a Bahá'í. . . . Her company uplifts and develops the soul."[61]

The next day, He spoke to Unitarians at the Church of the Messiah and, afterwards, the Maxwells' phone rang continually as large numbers of people made their way to Pine Avenue.

A few days later, in order to be more accessible to the general public, 'Abdu'l-Bahá moved to the Windsor Hotel, still as the guest of Mr. and Mrs. Maxwell. He addressed Socialists at Coronation Hall and a crowd of 1,200 at St. James Methodist Church. Montreal received Him with interest and respect, and the city's newspapers gave Him some of the most intelligent coverage He received during His North American journey. He left Montreal on September 8 and continued west.

* * * * * * * *

Several years later, some of the most important letters 'Abdu'l-Bahá ever wrote arrived at the Maxwell home. They were addressed to the Bahá'ís of Canada, and they were part of what is known as the "Tablets of the Divine Plan," 'Abdu'l-Bahá's mandate to the North American Bahá'ís to establish the Bahá'í Faith all over their continent and the world, to try to heal the terrible ills of humanity.

'Abdu'l-Bahá had foreseen the coming of World War I and had even instructed the Bahá'í farmers living in the vicinity of 'Akká and Haifa to grow and store extra grain, which He then used to relieve famine—but foresight and planning did not dull His emotions. Shoghi Effendi, who observed Him during the war years, wrote, "Agony filled His soul at the spectacle of human slaughter precipitated through humanity's failure to respond to the summons He had issued, or to heed the warnings He had given."[62] He longed to travel throughout the world and give the peace-creating Bahá'í message until He dropped in His tracks, but that was not His fate, so He called upon the North American Bahá'ís to do it.

He wrote the first Tablet to Canada as He paced the garden outside the Shrine of Bahá'u'lláh at Bahjí in April, 1916, and the second in the room which had been Bahá'u'lláh's in a house in 'Akká. He called upon the Canadian Bahá'ís to travel and teach in every Province and in other northern regions; He emphasized the importance of teaching the Eskimos in the Arctic. In response, May went to northeastern Canada with Grace Ober in 1916, and also toured with Marian Jack and Elizabeth Greenleaf. She helped form Bahá'í groups in St. John's, Brockville, Ottawa, Toronto, Calgary, and Vancouver. Her home became a stop-off point for Bahá'í teachers passing through Montreal. Still, she felt she was not doing enough.

She constantly tried to inspire her fellow-believers to follow the mandate of the "Tablets of the Divine Plan" and gladden 'Abdu'l-Bahá's heart. At a Bahá'í Congress in Montreal in April, 1919, she spoke of the blessing of being alive during His life-time, saying that the years while He was on earth were like no others, so that a word spoken for Him was worth volumes and teaching in His name was a matchless privilege, an incomparable expression of love.

'Abdu'l-Bahá was seventy-five in 1919. The war was over; the British crown had knighted Him for His famine-relief work; His guidance to the Bahá'ís remained illumined, His insight all-encompassing. He sadly remarked that the word "peace" flourished on the lips of the rulers and peoples of the earth, while unchecked hatred still devoured their hearts.

It seemed His energy was unflagging, but He was weary. It would remain for Shoghi Effendi to guide the Bahá'ís through the coming world chaos. 'Abdu'l-Bahá warned the Bahá'ís in various ways that He would soon die, yet, when it happened, it was a profound shock to them—one from which May Maxwell just barely recovered.

* * * * * * * * *

"The Night Has Come," was the bleak headline in the 12 December, 1921, issue of the Bahá'í magazine, *Star of the West.* Above it was a facsimile of the cablegram from Bahíyyih <u>Kh</u>ánum, dated November 28, 1921, which read, "His Holiness 'Abdu'l-Bahá ascended to Abhá Kingdom. Inform friends."[63]

Soon, comforting news of His peaceful, painless, and very conscious last days and moments reached the Bahá'ís, along with His final messages to them and descriptions of His massive funeral procession and bright burial place within the Shrine of the Báb. There was also His touching plea regarding the Guardian named in His Will and Testament, his twenty-four year old grandson: "O ye the faithful loved ones of 'Abdu'l-Bahá! It is incumbent upon you to take the greatest care of Shoghi Effendi. . . . That no dust of despondency may stain his radiant nature."[64] And there was Shoghi Effendi's first message to the American Bahá'ís, expressing gratitude for their staunch and noble resolution and assuring them that, though the night of separation from 'Abdu'l-Bahá had fallen, this was the day of steadfastness.

But nothing comforted May. She had a breakdown because she had somehow conceived the notion that she was not worthy of seeing 'Abdu'l-Bahá in the next world. Her husband decided that the only remedy for her was to go and meet the Guardian.

Shoghi Effendi, of course, was not a bearded patriarch like his grandfather. He wore a black felt fez but otherwise preferred western suits, and he was clean-shaven except for a small mustache. He had been studying at Oxford when news came of 'Abdu'l-Bahá's death, and he rushed home, in accordance with the provision's of 'Abdu'l-Bahá's Will and Testament, and took upon himself, in the midst of his own grief, the complicated affairs of the Bahá'í world. Nevertheless, it was to this youth that Sutherland Maxwell sent his mourning, invalid wife in April, 1923. With May travelled her personal maid, and Mary, the Maxwell's twelve-year old daughter. May was in a wheelchair, too weak to walk. Shoghi Effendi, at once poignantly young in years but mature in experience and capacity, understood her sad state of mind. Referring to her feeling that she would not be worthy of 'Abdu'l-Bahá's presence in the next world, he more than once said to her, "The thoughts you are thinking, Mrs. Maxwell, are not true."[65]

One day, he invited her to visit the Shrine of the Báb on Mount Carmel. He and another pilgrim helped her out of her wheelchair; she walked a short distance, then fainted. In a room of the Pilgrim House near the Shrine, she remained unconscious for a number of hours. These events proved a turning point in May's life; when she regained consciousness, she slowly began recuperating.

At this period, the Guardian confronted dark crises of Covenant-breaking within 'Abdu'l-Bahá's own family. During May's pilgrimage, one of these crises occurred. Shoghi Effendi, a singularly confiding soul with people he trusted, called May and her daughter to his bedroom, where he lay prostrated by nerves and grief, and told them he could not stand it, he was going away. He went to his beloved Switzerland where he hiked and bicycled over the Alps from dawn till nightfall, day after day for weeks at a time, trying to heal himself of the pain of 'Abdu'l-Bahá's death, seeking strength for his strenuous tasks as the shield and defender of his Faith.

May and Mary Maxwell went to Egypt, and when the Guardian returned to Haifa they were again given permission to visit him.

May was much better, yet she only wanted to talk about spiritual mysteries and life after death. The Guardian, however, talked mainly about Bahá'í Administration. May listened whole-heartedly, and Shoghi Effendi's poignant sensitivity, his urgent need of loyal helpers, his loving-kindness, and the simple grandeur of his vision of the Bahá'í Administration as a seed-bed of peace and a pattern for world unity, all combined to heal her and imbue her with a vision of the Administrative Order, while her devotion to the Guardian grew. She said, "Nothing is too great to suffer for him, no daily discipline, no effort or sacrifice, no surrender of all that is upon this earth."[66]

Soon after she returned home to Montreal—without her wheelchair—she was elected to the National Spiritual Assembly of the Bahá'ís of the United States and Canada. She served on the National Teaching Committee, and was a member of the Local Spiritual Assembly of Montreal for over fifteen years. She was often ill, but she would leave her bed, even in the midst of blizzards, to attend Bahá'í meetings; she said, "This is what strengthens me. This is what gives me life."[67]

She was particularly interested in inter-racial activities and in teaching youth. She did not wait for people to come to her; she reached out to them. Her touch was liberating. Her daughter said, "She often used the example of the butterfly. You know, when a butterfly is going to come out of the chrysalis, it has to struggle, it has to break the chrysalis. If you help it, it won't have the strength to move. It has to come out in its

May Bolles Maxwell and her daughter, Mary,
in Ramleh, Egypt, October, 1923

own way, and stretch its wings and then live as a butterfly. She often compared this to the new Bahá'ís . . . (And) she literally always, every second of her life had the thought of the Master before her as the Servant of the Cause."[68] Because of this, many people saw a reflection of 'Abdu'l-Bahá in May's eyes, in her face. And, despite her fragility, she had a fierce strength which she was not afraid to assert: her daughter once came out of the hotel where they were staying in New York City to find May red-faced after defending a baby whose mother was abusive. The mother had said she was shaking her baby because the baby was in a temper, and May had said, "Maybe she inherited it from you."[69]

****

May kept all the fervor and passion of youth, even as she neared seventy. From 1935 through 1937, moved by the Guardian's appeal to the North American Bahá'ís to teach in Europe, she traveled, sometimes with a relative and sometimes alone, in Germany, Belgium, and France. She felt the approach of World War II. She said, "The dark forces completely envelop the world."[70]

Hitler had taken power in Germany in 1933, had marched his country out of the League of Nations and the Disarmament Conference, had denied Jews the rights of citizenship, restored the draft, and was rebuilding the German militia in defiance of the Versailles Treaty. Simultaneously, fascism was ascendant in Japan, Italy, and Spain, while the totalitarian Stalin ruled Russia.

May was a total contrast to such dark forces. She breathed freedom and light. Lucienne Migette, of Lyon, France, praised her "limpid beauty, her purity, her love . . . her childlike spontaneity."[71] She said May forever imprinted her memory on the hearts of those she taught, and also awoke in them a lasting urge towards action.

In 1937, the Maxwells went on pilgrimage, and the Guardian told Mary Maxwell he had chosen her to be his wife. They were married in a simple, very private ceremony; even Sutherland and May were not present at the wedding. Afterwards, their Mary came to them and sat with them for a time in the Pilgrim House. Then the Guardian joined them for dinner, and he showered love upon them. With the smile his wife described as inimitable, he gave May his handkerchief laden with petals and flowers, saying he had brought them for her from the inner Shrine of Bahá'u'lláh, where he and Mary—henceforth known as Rúḥíyyih Khánum—had gone to pay their respects and pray. One evening, he told May that if Mary had not been her daughter, he would not have married her. And, before she left Haifa, he added one more tender mercy to May's store of them.

Despite his marriage, the Guardian remained immersed in work and, though he ate dinner almost every night in the Western Pilgrim House with Mr. and Mrs. Maxwell, his wife, Rúḥíyyih Khánum, and some of his secretaries, "there was no opportunity," Rúḥíyyih Khánum said, "for any deep personal intimacy to develop." Shoghi Effendi was a very reserved person. However, after lunch on the day the Maxwells were to say farewell to their daughter and leave Haifa, he went alone to May's room. Afterwards, May, her eyes shining, told her daughter, "He kissed me!"[72]

Though honored, May was concerned about her daughter in her new life. She saw her daughter, still quite young, taken far from her and from the western culture in which she had always been a very free spirit, immersed in an oriental world, plunged into depths of service, devotion and self-sacrifice which May could visualize but never plumb. It seemed to May's friend, Marion Hofman, that, although May did not see her daughter after leaving her in 1937, "her home was Haifa . . . in a deeper sense she lived there, hour by hour to her last day."[73]

But May was able to write:

There was a time that I agonized with a mother's weakness and instinctive protection over the terrific deprivation in all her outer human ways, and the austere discipline in the life of my child. It is she herself (combined with a ray of common sense of my own), who taught me the Spartan spirit of that Persian mother who threw back the head of her martyred son to his executioner . . . As I have witnessed . . . the profound and mystic change in Rúḥíyyih Khánum . . . I have marveled at the grace of God and His delicate and perfect handiwork.[74]

That pivotal year for May's family was also pivotal for the North American Bahá'ís, for it was the first time the Guardian called upon them, in his Seven Year Plan, to make a concerted drive to send pioneers overseas to establish and consolidate Bahá'í communities. The goals of the Seven Year Plan were based on 'Abdu'l-Bahá's mandate, the "Tablets of the Divine Plan." May had been mentioned in those Tablets because of her pioneering work in France and Canada, and she longed to pioneer again. In 1921, she had been a strong influence on Leonora Holsapple Armstrong, who became the first pioneer in Latin America. When Leonora, a young social worker, hesitated to make the radical move to Brazil, May, in such a tone of command that Leonora never forgot it, exclaimed, "Go!"[75]

In subsequent years, May, charmed with the thought of Latin America, had always been a good audience for Leonora's stories of Brazil. A few years into the Seven Year Plan, as the guns and bombs of World War II unleashed their fire, she decided to go to Argentina. She was seventy, she had a heart ailment, yet her husband, her daughter, and the Guardian all consented. In fact, the Guardian cabled that he approved heartily of her itinerary. At the same time, he cabled Sutherland, "Profoundly appreciate noble sacrifice dearest love."[76]

She sailed on the S.S. *Brazil* out of Manhattan on January 24, 1940. Her niece, Jeanne Bolles, who traveled with her, wrote that May was thrilled with the voyage and her stops in Brazil and Uruguay, but "she seemed to press forward every minute of the way" to Buenos Aires.[77] At the end of February, late summer in the Southern Cone, they arrived. Jeanne said that May, leaning out of the taxi to admire the city, was "like a girl of sixteen in her joyous enthusiasm."[78]

May and Jeanne dined together in their rooms at the City Hotel. The phone rang, and May was welcomed to Argentina by the small group of Bahá'ís residing there. She and Jeanne discussed Haifa, the Guardian, and the growth of the Bahá'í World Center as it had recently been brilliantly discussed in a letter from Rúḥíyyih Khánum. Joyous in her faith, joyous in her daughter, joyous in prospects for pioneer teaching in Buenos Aires, May went to sleep.

But she woke the next morning, March 1, with a sharp and violent pain in her chest. A doctor was called in, and he assured May and Jeanne that all would be well; nevertheless, May cabled her husband and the Guardian, requesting prayers. Shortly afterwards, she died.

The Guardian, when he broke the news to his wife, took her in his arms and comforted her, saying, "Now I am your mother."[79] He cabled the North American Bahá'ís that May had won the "priceless honor of a martyr's death."[80] He told the Bahá'ís of Iran, "The heavenly souls seek blessings from her in the midmost paradise."[81] And he cheered Rúḥíyyih Khánum by humorously picturing May wandering about heaven making a nuisance of herself because all she wanted to talk about was her adored daughter. He extended his loving hand to Sutherland Maxwell, instructing him to design a tomb for May which he himself would erect, and inviting him to live in Haifa.

In Quilmes, Buenos Aires, eleven people gathered with Jeanne Bolles at May's grave in the British Cemetery. Countries represented were Argentina, Brazil, Uruguay and Colombia. They played the recording of 'Abdu'l-Bahá chanting, which Edward Getsinger had made during that long-ago, early pilgrimage.

At the same time, friends gathered with Sutherland in Montreal and held a memorial service. They knew what 'Abdu'l-Bahá had said of May, and were comforted by it: "The love of God is as a glorious Crown upon thy head, the brilliant jewels of which are glittering forth unto all horizons. Its brilliancy, transparency and effulgence shall appear in future centuries when the signs of God will be spread and the Word of God will encompass the hearts of all the peoples of the earth."[82]

Shortly afterwards, Philip Sprague traveled to Argentina, inspired by May's example, and he brought a small box sent from Haifa. In it was a large Persian silk handkerchief enfolding blossoms which were still fragrant. A note from Shoghi Effendi instructed Philip to lay the bouquet on May's grave, along with the contents of an envelope inscribed to May from her Mary. Within the envelope was a tiny, delicate wreath of pressed flowers—roses and jasmine.

Chapter 3

Martha Root

Martha Louise Root

On the morning of April 11, 1912, several hundred Bahá'ís stood on a Manhattan pier watching the S.S. *Cedric,* with 'Abdu'l-Bahá aboard, glide towards them from its overnight anchorage outside the harbor. They'd been waiting since dawn, and now, when they saw Him at the ship's rail, they waved hats and handkerchiefs high. Among them was Martha Root, the person who would, as the century rolled on, come closest, the Guardian said, to "the example set by 'Abdu'l-Bahá Himself in the course of His journeys throughout the West."[1]

Martha, a successful journalist, was in her forties, tiny, with large, candid, blue-green eyes, a singularly sympathetic smile and a very determined jaw. Her devotion to 'Abdu'l-Bahá impelled her to travel around the world four times in such a selfless spirit that she became, as Doris McKay wrote, "the embodiment of a love which does not passively wait, but which goes forth, with a wholehearted reckless spending of personality, of time, of strength."[2] For Martha, the joy of following in 'Abdu'l-Bahá's way was so great that she called her journeys, despite their physical rigor, "spiritual skylarking."[3]

She was generally reticent about personal matters, so, while myriad papers of hers survive, no description of her private interview with 'Abdu'l-Bahá has come to light. It occurred in Pittsburgh, Pennsylvania, where she lived and worked; she had arranged for 'Abdu'l-Bahá to address some 400 people at the Hotel Schenley on May 7. A friend recalled Martha saying that when she met 'Abdu'l-Bahá, He anointed her with attar of roses and embraced her, drawing her head gently to rest on His shoulder. He also presented her with white roses. Later, she often wore a white rose on her dress.

She took time from newspaper work to attend 'Abdu'l-Bahá's talks in New York City, Washington, D.C., and Chicago.

She was particularly moved by His Unity Feast, a picnic of Persian food that He hosted for over 250 people of varied classes and races at Teaneck, New Jersey—the same event where Lua Getsinger went off into the poison ivy in her effort to avoid going to California. Since 1912, Bahá'ís have commemorated the picnic annually with a gathering called 'Abdu'l-Bahá's Souvenir; and Martha, wherever she was in the world in later years, made a point of doing something special on that day.

She was also profoundly touched on a July night in New York City when 'Abdu'l-Bahá spoke of the martyrdoms of the poet Varqá and his twelve-year old son, the two whose deaths had been motivating factors in Lua's mission to the Sháh in Paris. Almost twenty years later, in Iran, Martha researched and wrote about the two martyrs in detail, titling the story "White Roses of Persia." She said that when 'Abdu'l-Bahá finished telling the tale, He went upstairs and the silent guests could hear Him weeping. She felt the two heroic lives couldn't fail to urge every soul who heard about them to action. They certainly had that effect on her as she went forth through revolutions, riots, epidemics, and more, in places of which the folks back in her hometown had never dreamed.

****

Martha Louise Root was born August 10, 1872, in Richmond, Ohio, to Timothy T. (T.T.) and Nancy Hart Root. The Roots were a large family of British ancestry. Their most famous member, Elihu, was a statesman who won the Nobel Prize for Peace in 1912. He was much older than Martha, and a distant cousin; their shared name served her well in her career as a journalist and then as a publicist for her Faith, but she doesn't seem to have traded very hard on the connection.

Martha grew up in Cambridge Springs, Pennsylvania, a resort town built around hot springs. Her father was a deacon in the Baptist Church, a champion fisherman, and a businessman with his finger in many pies, known for fair dealing and the astute settling of disputes. Martha adored him and was also devoted to her gentle, good-natured mother. A sunny child who loved parties and was a born diplomat, she grew up happily, but she wasn't content to stay at home.

She began writing and selling her work at an early age. At fourteen, she saved enough money to take a trip to Niagara Falls. After graduating from high school in 1889, she went to Europe. Her brothers, Clarence and Claude, started businesses in Cambridge Springs, but Martha went to Oberlin College in Ohio, then took her senior year at the University of Chicago and graduated with a degree in literature. She became principal of a high school in Union City, Pennsylvania, but after a few years she resigned and reinvented herself as a lecturer on Shakespeare. She had a clear, mellow, resonant voice, and her dramatic readings from *Othello* and *The Merchant of Venice* were well-received, even by the most critical audiences. However, in 1900 she moved to Pittsburgh and started working as a journalist.

One day, she followed a new invention, a car, up the street as it bucked and snorted its way to its "stable" (cars wouldn't be "garaged" for some years), and her fascination with the vehicle led her to be a pioneer reporter on automobiles: she wrote about how they worked and what the well-dressed motorist wore, and gave inside stories on marathons and races. She remarked that there was nothing like an automobile race for stirring up the liver.

She also wrote features on Pittsburgh society and culture. The city was home to booming industry led by magnates with names like Carnegie, Mellon, and Frick. The new millionaires' wives gave teas and gala dinners for touring matinee idols and opera stars, while their husbands built palatial homes, invested in art, and established schools and hospitals. Martha knew all the Pittsburgh plutocrats. By the time she was thirty, her stories were earning four-inch bylines.

She was thirty-six when she first met a Bahá'í. She had to write about a religious convention and was dining with missionaries in a crowded Child's Restaurant. Roy Wilhelm, the Bahá'í, happened to be in Pittsburgh doing business (he was a coffee broker), and he was seated near them. Roy couldn't help overhearing one of the missionaries remark about how pitiful it was that all the non-Christian heathens were lost souls. Martha commented that she doubted if any souls were lost. Roy then thought a certain coolness descended upon the table. When Martha and the missionaries rose to leave and he had to stand to let them pass, he overcame his shyness and told them he hadn't been able to help overhearing their conversation. He asked if he might express an opinion. They consented, and he said he'd just been in the East to meet 'Abdu'l-Bahá, and he'd observed how followers of various religions said their prayers and led good lives; he felt humanity was progressing towards the recognition of the oneness of God.

Martha gave him her card and, from New York, he sent her a Bahá'í book. But Martha didn't read it. She later recalled that she left it on a counter in a pharmacy, and the pharmacist's wife read it and became a Bahá'í. Roy sent her Bahá'í literature for over a year and she never looked at it, but she did give it to people she thought might be interested. Roy always visited Martha when he came through Pittsburgh, and Martha looked up Bahá'ís when she was in other cities. Finally, a conversation with Thornton Chase in Chicago led her to identify herself as a Bahá'í in 1909.

Shortly afterwards, Martha's newspaper, the *Pittsburgh Post,* published her article, "The Báb and the New Persian Religious Movement," and Martha, the indefatigable communicator, began her tasks: she mailed several hundred copies of the article to friends and acquaintances, sent some to Bahá'í groups and one to 'Abdu'l-Bahá. A Bahá'í Assembly was formed in Pittsburgh and she was a member, but she longed to travel and meet Bahá'ís in other countries.

* * * * * * * * *

In 1914, as World War I began, Martha decided to make a tour. The high point would be a pilgrimage, a visit to 'Abdu'l-Bahá, and she would be a courier as well as a pilgrim, for Roy Wilhelm had amassed $2,000 in gold for 'Abdu'l-Bahá's famine relief work. Her desire was less to teach than to observe Bahá'ís in places where the Bahá'í Faith was older than in America.

She sailed from New York on January 30, 1915, taking along a camera with which she made lantern slides that she used a lot during later trips, for people were wild about photography and pictures of exotic places. She waited weeks in Port Said for word that she could visit 'Abdu'l-Bahá; Syria, occupied by German and Turkish troops, was dangerous for an American Bahá'í. With the help of the American Consul General, Martha got the gold through, but finally left on April 24 for India. She didn't know that two letters from 'Abdu'l-Bahá, encouraging her to come to Haifa and outlining safety precautions, were en route to her. She proceeded down the Suez Canal, over the Arabian Sea, to Bombay.

Almost all of her travels through India were by rail. Railroads were the lifeline of India and everyone rode them, from the poorest beggar to the most *pukka sahib* British General.

Europeans generally traveled ultra first class in cars fitted with bar-catches and latched windows with Venetian blinds and, since schedules were fluid, railroad officials often requested the Sahibs' permission to leave stations.

Missionaries often did try to mingle with all kinds of people but, even by their standards, Martha's attitudes were unusual. One of her Indian companions always remembered her, on a train with himself and his father, taking a comb out of her purse and arranging his father's tangled white hair. He said the astonished Indian train attendant stood and stared. But Martha was simply doing for the old Indian what she would have done for her own father.

From India she went to Mandalay, Burma, where she was able to visit the Bahá'í Center, which had an orphanage, a school, a home for elderly women and a fund for the sick and unemployed.

In Japan, Martha met Agnes Alexander, May Maxwell's adoring friend from turn-of-the-century Paris. Martha was financing her travels with free-lance reporting, and she got a major scoop when she reported the plans for the coronation of Emperor Yoshihito and Empress Sadako. Meanwhile, she was introduced to the new Japanese Bahá'ís, taught Agnes the rudiments of public relations, and received lectures from Agnes on the importance of Esperanto as an international language.

By August, Martha was bound for San Francisco. Some of the California Bahá'ís met her ship, along with her father, T.T. Root. He was seventy-five years old and his wife was ailing, yet he'd traveled 4,000 miles across the continent from Pennsylvania in his eagerness to greet his daughter after their first long separation.

Shortly after that, Nancy Root passed away. In 1916, Martha moved from Pittsburgh to Cambridge Springs to care for T.T.

He was nearly eighty by then, an impressive-looking man with thick white hair and beard, but weakened by asthma. Martha used to wrap him in his beloved wife's old handknit shawl and take him fishing or to baseball games, the theater or the circus. She kept his apartment neat, made him pancakes for breakfast, and took him to restaurants for lunch and dinner.

During her travels she'd recorded names and addresses of everyone she met, and at home her little portable typewriter was constantly busy as she tapped out letters, connecting people with each other the world over. But while she was generally well-received in the wide world, in Cambridge Springs the reception was often negative, and Martha shed tears over it. When she addressed the congregation of the Baptist Church about the Bahá'í Faith, one pewholder stamped out in a rage, denouncing her as a blasphemer, and many people agreed with him; yet Martha's care for T.T., and for anyone in need, defused the hostility. Keeping her dream of travel in mind, she began learning Esperanto and, during 1918, she wrote to 'Abdu'l-Bahá proposing a world tour.

In reply, He said her letter had given Him great joy, and encouraged her: "My hope is that thou mayest forget rest and composure and like unto a swift-flying bird . . . cover long distances . . . (that) in whatever land thou tarriest thou mayest reproduce the melody of the Kingdom."[4] She was also to "roar like a lion" and proclaim "the call of the Kingdom."[5] She had asked about pilgrimage, but He told her teaching came first and remarked that people were waiting for the summons to Universal Peace.

World War I was just dragging to an end, leaving in its wake refugees and ruins. But Martha's concern for T.T. kept her at home till 1919, when all fourteen of the "Tablets of the Divine Plan" were dramatically presented at a convention in New York. Martha was especially moved by the call to teach in

South America; unable to resist it, yet trembling and tearful over her father, she booked her passage to Brazil for June 21, on the *Albah*.

* * * * * * * * *

After a seamen's strike kept her in New York for over a month, Martha was bound out on July 22. Her father was being looked after by a neighbor's family, her many suitcases (she never had less than a dozen on any of her journeys) were crammed with Bahá'í literature, and she was ill with fatigue and doubt.

Having met many of her fellow passengers, she feared she wasn't apt for her task, for they were mostly a hard-drinking, partying crowd. Her cabin was across from the bar, and her cabinmate, an enthusiastic poker-player traveling with two pet monkeys, was in and out of the bar day and night. Martha said she now understood why 'Abdu'l-Bahá had told her, "Thou mayest forget rest and composure."[6]

Wondering how she could communicate with everyone, Martha turned to the Bahá'í Writings and found advice that became her byword for the rest of her life: "Let not conventionality cause you to seem cold and unsympathetic when you meet strange people from other countries."[7] Her tactful thoughtfulness and sympathetic humor were so attractive that, after she gave a Bahá'í talk aboard the *Albah*, a Christian remarked, "Your talk made a great impression. Even the 'beer bums' say it is a good kind of religion."[8]

After two weeks, the *Albah* docked in Belem (then called Pará), Brazil. Martha disdained injunctions that a woman mustn't go out in Latin America alone, and headed for a newspaper office which, since she spoke no Portuguese, she found by going to newsboys and pointing to papers they were carrying. She arrived at the office of Belem's largest paper where, she recorded, fifteen men sat working and not one of them spoke English. She managed to communicate in French and then sat down to write an article in English; as she was finishing, a man came in who could speak English, so he translated the article into Portuguese and took her back to the *Albah* in his car. Martha thought that was the first time anyone in Belem had ever heard of the Bahá'í Faith. It might have been the first time a Bahá'í set foot on South American soil.

On August 11, the day after her forty-seventh birthday, Martha arrived in Recife (then Pernambuco). She was determined to get to Bahia because 'Abdu'l-Bahá had specially mentioned it in "The Tablets of the Divine Plan." But there was a yellow fever epidemic in Bahia, so the *Albah* had canceled its stop there and was going on to Rio de Janeiro.

In Recife, there was also yellow fever—and a revolution. Passengers on the *Albah* who had planned to visit Bahia were now going to by-pass it, and they also canceled their stopovers in Recife. Martha, though she made reservations on two Brazilian lines for Bahia, was confused as to what she should do. At last, as night fell, she threw herself down on her bunk and, she said, "looked through the porthole into the darkness where all alone Jupiter shone brightly, steadily unmoved in his course."[9]

She got up, ordered her bags ashore, and left the ship. The streets of Recife were dark, empty of civilians, patrolled by soldiers; now and then there was an explosion of dynamite. She'd heard that an American businesswoman, Lilian Vegas, was at the Hotel do Parque, so she went there and looked her up. Almost the first words Martha said to her were, "I am a Bahá'í."[10]

This total directness was characteristic of Martha. It generally served her well, and it certainly did with Mrs. Vegas, who responded, "Did you ever know my cousin, Lua Getsinger?"[11]

Recife hotels were full, so Martha slept on a cot in Mrs. Vegas' room that night, and in the morning the two women embarked for Bahia. However, when the ship docked at Bahia, stories of yellow fever were so horrifying that Mrs. Vegas decided to go right on to Rio. Martha, however, left the ship in the midst of a torrential rain and clambered down into a little boat on the raging sea. She was seasick and running a high fever. A young American missionary accompanied her to her hotel and, once she was settled, ill and alone, she thought of 'Abdu'l-Bahá's words, "Let one not call himself a captain until he stands before the opposing army, nor a Bahá'í until he meets the tests."[12] She later said those words were her healing.

So, there was no sickbed for Martha in Bahia. And her teaching there, in São Paolo, Rio, Santos, Montevideo, Buenos Aires—with press coverage won by herself, numerous contacts with community leaders, and the formation of Bahá'í study groups—set the triumphant pattern she would follow all her life and illustrated the phenomenon that was one of the most fascinating things about her: almost everyone she met seemed to happily and unhesitatingly leap to her assistance.

Marzieh Gail wrote,

> I used ask myself why people would do what Martha wished. 'When a person says no,' was Martha's view, 'that's the time to begin persuading him.' It took you back to that well-known dialogue in *Henry IV:*
> "'Glendower: I can call spirits from the vasty deep.
> "'Hotspur: Why, so can I . . . but will they come when you call for them?'

"In Martha's case, yes, they would. They seemed to . . . recognize and respect what she was."[13]

Just as balky people didn't discourage Martha, balky weather also had no effect. Thus, despite advice from concerned friends, she decided the cross the Andes on muleback in the dead of winter, for she was determined to sail home up the Pacific Coast of South America so she could visit Panama, another place emphasized by 'Abdu'l-Bahá in the "Tablets of the Divine Plan."

"The trip by mule back over the 'top of the world,' for the Andes are among the highest ranges, the Aconcagua rising to a height of 23,000 feet, was thrilling enough for the most sensational," wrote Martha. "The ancient trail led 10,400 feet above sea level. The people on mule back were infinitesimal specks clinging to mighty terraces. . . . They huddled on the edges of jagged peaks, frozen chasms, and stiffened mountain torrents. Everybody felt very small and a wonderful feeling of 'camaraderie' sprang up. Fortunately the sun shone brightly, and the acute cold was not so terrible as all had expected."[14]

The most dangerous part of the passage was came on the Chilean side, on the "precipitous downward slope."[15] The frightened mules slipped a yard at a time, and finally Martha and the others dismounted and walked, or, in some particularly precipitous spots, ran, down the vertical trail. The air was cold and thin; some people fainted from altitude sickness, some bled from their nose and ears. Martha gave away all her useful supplies, for she apparently was fine. Naturally, her mule-driver came away with a Bahá'í booklet and the customs inspector on the Chilean-Argentinean border received one, too.

* * * * * * * *

In all, Martha's Latin American journey took five months. It was November, 1919, when she came home to her father, who was sitting by the window of his apartment, watching her approach down the quiet streets of Cambridge Springs. Along with his welcome, she received a missive from 'Abdu'l-Bahá saying, "Praise be to God the Call of the Kingdom has been received in South America and the seeds of Guidance have been sown in those cities and regions. Certainly the heat of the Sun of Reality, the Rain of the Eternal Bounty and breeze of the love of God will make them germinate; have confidence."[16]

The morning after her return, Martha marched herself to the high school and enrolled in Spanish classes, and soon she could read the letters that piled up on her desk. She wrote full reports on each city she'd visited—population, ambiance, industries—for she wanted the Bahá'ís to pioneer. She said, "If anyone feels timid about asking opportunities to speak, let him remember that no day comes twice."[17] She mailed 1,000 Spanish Bahá'í booklets, wrote 400 letters, spoke on her travels to Cambridge Springs businessmen, and mimeographed a travel journal for the Bahá'ís.

But her father's condition kept her from making more long jaunts. She spent the summer of 1920 taking brief trips through the United States and Canada, helping with events such as the first "Convention for Amity Between the Colored and White Races," held in Washington, D.C., where she worked with Agnes Parsons, who went on to become a treasured friend.

Around the time of the conference, Martha fell ill with such wretched pain that she thought she was about to die. She rarely consulted doctors, partly because she distrusted them after a traumatic operation she'd had as a young woman, and partly because she knew they'd confine her to bed and stop her work, but mostly because she feared a diagnosis of cancer.

In 1912, she'd been sure she had cancer, and she attributed the cure to 'Abdu'l-Bahá.

In 1920, Agnes Parsons wrote to 'Abdu'l-Bahá about Martha's illness and received the reply: "Through the grace of God I implore confirmation for . . . Miss Martha Root. It is my hope that through the Power of the Holy Spirit Miss Martha Root will be cured."[18] This message, relayed to Martha through Mrs. Parsons, started her on the road to recovery and whenever illness returned, she remembered it. Many years later, from Prague, she wrote to Mrs. Parsons repeating 'Abdu'l-Bahá's statement, and remarking, "How many times that has saved my life!"[19]

But she hadn't been passively waiting for rescue. Despite her suffering, she'd arranged a benefit for a sick man in Cambridge Springs. She wrote to Mrs. Parsons that when she first started the effort she could hardly propel herself about to take care of details; but, to her mind, the man was the needy one, and the more she worked for him the stronger she became.

During the autumn of 1921 Martha was in Mexico. Despite civil strife that blocked railroad lines, she went on to Guatemala and arrived as revolution was brewing. She presented Bahá'í literature to the leaders of all factions so that, after machine guns took over and the President and cabinet were imprisoned, she could report that the Bahá'í Message had also been given to the Liberals, some of whom became officials the next day under the new government.

She returned to Cambridge Springs to learn that 'Abdu'l-Bahá had died on November 28. She wrote to the National Teaching Committee expressing her faith that 'Abdu'l-Bahá still spoke tenderly to His flock, and the Bahá'ís could answer Him, and tell the whole world how much they loved Him, by trying to follow His example of love, service, sacrifice, and joy; so they would continually delight Him.

A year later, T.T. Root died. Martha was with him till his last breath and, in the cold November air, she lingered at his graveside after everyone else was gone, to leave a last rose with him. Then she went home, entered his empty room, and was overcome with such reverence that she couldn't remove her hat. But now she could make her longed-for journeys, and she knew she would never be alone. She said she felt as if her father, smiling with his eyes twinkling, was with her, assuring her that she would do all he and she had talked over, and he would help her every step of the way.

****

Four months later, on March 22, 1923, Martha set sail for China from Seattle, Washington, on a Japanese ship, the *Kaga Mara*. She would have left sooner, but family matters, chiefly her brother Clarence's shenanigans about money, delayed her. With a tiny income from her father's estate assured, she was free, and basically possessionless, for she'd given away the household furnishings T.T. had left to her, and she had been deprived of the one thing of his she wanted, a camel hair sweater he'd often worn. It was taken by someone else, causing her to weep. No wonder that, during all her travels, she cherished the white wool shawl which had been her mother's.

However, she wasted no time brooding. She was thrilled to be answering 'Abdu'l-Bahá's call: "China, China, China, China-ward the Cause of Bahá'u'lláh must march! Where is the holy, sanctified Bahá'í to become the teacher of China? . . . Had I been feeling well, I would have taken a journey to China myself!"[20] She was jubilant as she leaned over the rail of the *Kaga Mara*, waving the yellow jonquils the Bahá'ís had presented to her, while the Bahá'ís stood on the pier, waving yellow jonquils back at her, and the ship's whistles blew while it steamed out to sea.

She was taking her spring flowers onto a perilous, wintry Pacific. Cold storms raged almost nonstop. One letter to friends and relations came from Martha during that voyage—it was written on a rare occasion, she said, when her typewriter would stay on the table. As she wrote, her heart was with 'Abdu'l-Bahá: "Everyone who ever met Him loved Him so! He sent back such messages of love: 'Though I go away, I shall always be present with you.' What a wonderful Friend to come! If He was ill, He did not speak of it . . . I am just wishing that on the *Kaga Mara* and in China I could live even a little as 'Abdu'l-Bahá did. He said: 'Take courage! God never forsakes His children who strive and work and pray!'"[21]

When Martha arrived in Japan, it was April, cherry-blossom time. She rejoiced in the multitudinous blossoms as, with Agnes Alexander and Ida Finch, she spent two weeks constantly addressing large groups in various towns and cities, until she departed for China from Osaka.

Martha fell in love with China. She saw and felt the brutality and tumult, for the country was torn by political conflict and war, but she also sensed an ancient peace. She wrote home: "There is so much that is radiant, so much that is beautiful, I wish I could send you the charm, the old-time magic, the lovely art and picturesqueness of Peking. It is glorious here, no one need ask for any greater favor than to live and die in China."[22]

She developed her art of presenting the Message of Bahá'u'lláh. 'Abdu'l-Bahá said the Bahá'ís should always teach as if offering a gift to a king, and this Martha did. She once told the poet Angela Morgan that the words of Bahá'u'lláh "have a spontaneity that proclaims them as the upwelling and outpouring from the vernal springs of creative beauty . . . His utterances . . . are prismatic with primal color. His language is the language of the poet, and this is the secret of His appeal to me."[23] Martha's art was to present that prismatic, primal color, not in fine words, but in unpretentious love.

Chief among her Chinese converts was Dr. Y.S. Tsao, President of Tsing Hua College in Peking. Agnes Alexander was traveling with Martha, and she said, "Martha bravely went out to the college without any previous introduction, but was received most kindly by Dr. Tsao and his wife, who is Swedish."[24] Another new Bahá'í was Deng Chieh-Ming, a scholar who started a Bahá'í university before Martha left China.

But Martha couldn't spend all her time skylarking. She had to earn some money. She worked as an English tutor, as a hostess in a guest home, and as a reporter. She went by boat, by mule, by third-class rail carriage through China, avoiding a few particularly war-torn areas, staying in the most economical, and therefore the chilliest, hotel rooms, sleeping on the hardest beds, eating sparsely. She was bedeviled by her old enemy, pain. By the time she reached Shanghai, she had to stay in bed, but she was buoyed up by a note from Shoghi Effendi saying that her letters (she was his good-news wire service) revived and invigorated his soul.

In March, 1924, Martha was in Canton, where the streets rang with sniper fire all night and bloody fighting went on all day. Foreigners were not welcome. Martha, however, always looking for enduring loveliness, wrote that she was moved by a recital in which a young flautist, following Chinese custom, "went and stood in one dark corner of the platform, with his face to the wall, that the beautiful melody might float out without sight of the human agent."[25]

In the spirit of the flautist, Martha went on, making a brief visit to Saigon, traveling into Cambodia, until she had to leave the tropical heat of Indochina, which she enjoyed, and head for Australia. Now she entered fully into the rhythm and pattern of her almost ceaseless world voyage.

****

Australia, June, 1924: Martha speaks to everyone from New Thought philosophers in quiet salons to men at labor rallies— for which purpose she speaks from the back of a truck. She and Clara Dunn, who pioneered to Australia in 1920, have their hair bobbed in the latest style, and with her new look Martha goes to a radio station and makes her first broadcast in the new medium; she is pleased to learn her voice is perfect for the air waves. During July and August, the coldest months of the Austral winter, Martha perseveres despite a flu that makes her head and neck ache and convinces her she must have a heart condition; and she tours New Zealand, too.

December, 1924: Martha arrives in South Africa on the *Balnarald* after a three-week voyage from Australia during which she bestows on fellow passengers all the chocolate Hyde and Clara Dunn gave her. She works with Fanny Knobloch, the pioneer who, at 74, left a sick bed to take to the seas and settle in Cape Town, and whose wry, gentle humor soothes Martha. So does the sunshine.

March 13, 1925: Martha arrives in Haifa for a pilgrimage and rests her head on what she calls "that threshold of promise" in the Shrine of the Báb, where she says a prayer "of deepest gratitude." At the special invitation of the Guardian, she prays with him in the Shrines and confers with him about her work.

He urges her to publicize the persecution of the Bahá'ís in Iran, and assigns her to help establish the International Bahá'í Bureau in Geneva. She says of the Guardian: "He is the essence of radiance, he imparts happiness to all who meet him. He is also the essence of justice."[26] And he writes to her, when she's en route to Switzerland: "My dearest and most precious Martha . . . the fragrance of your visit has overpowered us all and as the days go by we feel more and more the penetrating power of your sublime love for and devotion to this mighty Cause."[27]

Switzerland, 1925: Martha arrives in Geneva in mid-May. Jane Stannard is already there. She is a British Bahá'í who shared lecture platforms in India with Lua and Edward Getsinger. She has lived much of her life in the orient, speaks fluent French and Farsi and, guided by letters from the Guardian, she's able to demonstrate the international scope of the Bahá'í Faith at the headquarters of the League of Nations and its surrounding institutions. In June, she rents rooms for the Bureau which include a Baha'í Hall; by 1926 she's publishing a quarterly, *Massager Bahá'í,* in three languages. She, the Guardian, and two other ladies are funding the Bureau themselves, so Martha, to offer support, rents a small office for herself in the Bureau, though she prefers to work privately. She centers most of her efforts for the Bureau on Esperanto conferences.

Bucharest, January, 1926: Martha, a skylark who prefers being on the wing to being in the nest, has left Geneva to travel through Germany, Holland, Austria, and the Balkans. In Bucharest, Rumania, she's meeting with leading intellectuals and officials, but she won't be content until she meets the Queen.

Queen Marie is a world famous beauty, writer, patron of the arts, and dashing horsewoman, particularly admired for her nursing at the battlefront during World War I and her advocacy of her ruined country at the Versailles Conference. But she is mired in troubles and is not receiving anyone. Running a gamut of rejection, Martha finally succeeds in sending Queen Marie a letter, a picture of 'Abdu'l-Bahá and a copy of the book *Bahá'u'lláh and the New Era*. The Queen writes to Martha, inviting her to an audience at noon the following day, January 30, at Cotroceni Palace.

Martha dons a long white dress and a little hat given to her by Ella Goodall Cooper. It isn't quite the thing for the elegant palace in the dead of winter, but Martha has her own style. She refuses a wealthy American's offer of a private carriage and bottle of expensive perfume to bring the Queen, and goes to the palace in a hired hack, bearing an inexpensive bottle of scent which is, the wealthy American comments, the same kind used by the streetwalkers in Paris (and one wonders how she knew). Martha also brings Queen Marie a piece of chocolate wrapped in gold foil and a bough of white lilacs.

She also has more significant gifts, among them a copy of Bahá'u'lláh's mystical masterpiece, The Seven Valleys, and, since Marie was Princess of Edinburgh before her marriage, a report on an Education Congress there.

She will return to town in the Queen's coach, for Marie is charmed with Martha, and the feeling is mutual. They start on positive footing: Marie has stayed up all night reading *Bahá'u'lláh and the New Era,* and her first words to Martha are, "I believe these teachings are the solution for the world's problems today."[28]

In May, 1926, Marie writes in her widely syndicated newspaper column: "A woman brought me the other day a Book. I spell it with a capital letter because it is a glorious Book . . . I commend it to you all. If ever the name Bahá'u'lláh or 'Abdu'l-Bahá comes to your attention, do not put Their writings from you. Search out Their Books, and let Their glorious, peace-bringing, love-creating words and lessons sink into your hearts as they have into mine."[29]

On May 29, Shoghi Effendi receives word of this tribute while at Bahjí commemorating the anniversary of the death of Bahá'u'lláh and mourning the brutal murders of 13 adult Bahá'ís and a sixteen-month old baby in Jahrum, Iran. He sees in the Queen's conversion a sign of hope for the ultimate triumph of his Cause, and writes to Martha, in reference to the Marie's open letter, that it is "a well-deserved and memorable testimony of your remarkable and exemplary endeavors . . . It has thrilled me and greatly reinforced my spirit and faith."[30]

Queen Marie, allowed to express her beliefs minimally due to political constraint and oppression, publishes tributes through the years, the last one in 1936, not long before her death, and these are a source of hope to her Bahá'í brethren who also suffer constraint and oppression.

Warsaw, April, 1926: Martha, having met Lidia Zamenhof, the daughter of the founder of Esperanto, at an Esperanto conference, goes to Poland to speak at the dedication of a new monument on Dr. Zamenhof's grave, after which she spends two weeks at Lidia's house so Lidia can give her an intensive course in Esperanto.

Lidia becomes curious about Martha—why does she exhaust herself wandering around the world? Martha tells her why, and Lidia, being Jewish from a sense of secular identity more than from a belief in God, decides, "Well, I am not going to be a Bahá'í."[31] However, she finds that Martha knows "how to be patient, to be faithful—and to pray."[32] Lidia does become a Bahá'í, and is for many years the only one in Poland.*

Central Europe, the Balkans, Turkey, Egypt, 1927–1929: Martha, sensing and fearing the horror of coming war, is encouraged by Shoghi Effendi's assurance that war is not imminent, and, in case of peril she can take refuge on Mount Carmel. In Hungary she elicits a memoir of 'Abdu'l-Bahá for the Hungarian edition of *Bahá'u'lláh and the New Era* from Rustam Vambèry, who met Him in Budapest. Through all her travels, she finds translators and publishers for *Bahá'u'lláh and the New Era* and uses the book to follow up on her own teaching efforts.

She proceeds to Estonia, Spain, England, Finland, and Germany, traveling in unheated third class railway carriages, seated on wooden planks that she pads with her mother's white woolen shawl. The oppressed Bahá'ís of Iran, with Bahá'ís the world over, eagerly follow her progress, reported to them in letters from Shoghi Effendi. She makes a special tour of German universities, journeys rigorously through the Balkans, and has an audience with Zog, the self-proclaimed king of Albania. Feeling that "a match set to Albania would blow up Europe,"[33] she addresses prayers for the place to two Albanians in the next world: Constantine and St. Jerome. Then she heads east into Turkey, stopping in Istanbul and Ankara. Bahá'í activities are prohibited there, but Martha discusses religion with everyone and is invited to be guest of honor at the fifth anniversary celebration for the founding of the Turkish republic.

En route to her second pilgrimage in 1929, Martha is met at the train station in Cairo by a delegation from the nephew of King Fuad. The delegates search the first class compartments and fail to find her. They try second class, in vain. Then,

---

* During World War II, Lidia Zamenhof died in a Nazi concentration camp.

on their way out, they spot an old woman coming from the direction of the third class, carrying her own suitcase. This is Martha Root. The prince pays her homage, and treats her with tremendous respect.

Haifa, November, 1929: Martha meets first with the Governor and Grand Mufti of Jerusalem and the directors of the Jerusalem mosques, then arrives at the Pilgrim House in Haifa. She calls it Harry's House, because it was built by her friend Harry Randall, and she feels very much at home, especially because some of her family's household items, which she'd bequeathed to Harry and his wife, were in use: "Mother's table-cover is on the table, our butter knife on the butter plate, a tray cloth embroidered by my dear Mother on the tea tray, and our silver ware."[34]

She is welcomed by the Guardian and his Great-Aunt, 'Abdu'l-Bahá's sister, Bahíyyih Khánum, who is eighty-two years old and unable to walk. Martha remarks, "She is exquisite." She gives Martha a red ringstone, and one of the Bahá'ís, knowing Martha's propensity for giving things away, asks, "Should not Martha always keep the ring?" But Bahíyyih Khánum makes no restrictions: "I know if she gives it away it will be a great sacrifice for it is very dear to her."[35]

The Guardian is taken ill and his illness goes on for weeks. He insists that Martha stay in Haifa, telling the Bahá'ís, "Do not give her anything to do, she must rest."[36] Martha uses some of the fine tea Roy Wilhelm always sends her, and gives parties for the gardeners at the Shrine of the Báb and others.

Martha's next destination is Iran. Three days before her departure, the Guardian is able to see her. He urges her to stay, but a month was more than she planned. On Christmas Day, 1929, she leaves "Harry's House" with a copy of Shoghi Effendi's letter introducing her to the Persian Bahá'ís: "The enkindled handmaiden of God, the Glory of men and women believers, the Leader of the men and women teachers, Her Holiness Miss Martha Root is departing to the sacred land of Iran."[37]

Iran, winter, 1930: Martha, veteran of early auto marathons, third-class Turkish trains, and weeks on desolate, wintry seas, thinks that her trip from Damascus to Baghdád in a big car over a route with no signs, no paving, and, in some places, no roads, just wheel prints, is one of the easiest she ever took. After meeting with King Faisel in Baghdad and pleading for the Bahá'ís' repossession of Bahá'u'lláh's house there, she sets out for Teheran and reaches the Iranian border on January 9. The Iranian Bahá'ís, having received Shoghi Effendi's letter and his instructions to fête her royally, welcome her with ancient Persian instruments, dances and spring songs, though it is January, not exactly apple blossom time.

At Qazvín, birthplace of the Bábí martyr, the female poet, Ṭáhirih, Martha manages to visit her house, guided by a member of Ṭáhirih's family, which has previously opposed the Faith. It unnerves the Bahá'ís that five soldiers are permanently stationed in the hotel hallway, watching Martha's door day and night. Martha asks why they're watching and is told that everyone is Iran is watching her. When she leaves Qazvín the soldiers follow; she does not enjoy their vigilance.

Ṭihrán is rife with anti-Bahá'í rumors; newspapers report Martha as "the daughter of 'Abdu'l-Bahá, but she wears American clothes and speaks English to deceive the people."[38] The Bahá'ís hold great gatherings nonetheless, and Martha follows her usual pattern of journalistic and public relations work, interviewing government officials and writing articles for papers in Washington and Cairo.

Her tenderness and simple gifts are gratefully received by the Bahá'ís. Some even come to believe she can heal illness through prayer. Her boldness heartens them. In Tabríz, where the Báb was shot 80 years before, she sits beneath the window of the cell where He was imprisoned, and takes tea with an army officer. Her photo is taken with the women of Tabríz, and all who can get close enough touch her—her hands, her shoulders, her knees, even her feet—as if she is a talisman.

In May, in Shíráz, she visits the house of the Báb; at first sight of it, she falls to her knees and weeps, moved by its smallness, the idea that such a great Message came from such a little house. She takes her first plane ride to get to the port town of Búshihr, for spring rains have made the roads impassable, and the Islamic *mullás,* looking for her along the roads, are baffled because she does not appear. The Bahá'ís of Búshihr smuggle her aboard ship for India at 3:00 one morning.

During her four months in Iran, she feels she "lived a lifetime . . . Step by step was the inner drama. I do not like to say that I was sometimes afraid."[39]

India, Burma, China, and Japan, 1930: Martha again encounters restraints, this time because of political upheaval. She tries to meet Mahatma Gandhi, leader of the resistance to British rule, in Yeravda Prison near Poona, but it can't be done; in the prison, she does meet his disciple, Mrs. Sarojini Naidu. She continues on to Hyderabad, Bombay, Surat, Karachi, Lahore, Simla, Delhi, Veranasi, Lucknow, Patna, Bolpur, and Calcutta, speaking with everyone from Maharajas to tailors, Moslems to Theosophists. Many of her attempts to give public talks in universities are frustrated by picketing. She describes it: "The men and youth literally lie down in the walks and roads leading to the schools so that students and professors who enter must walk over their bodies."[40] She addresses a number of well-attended meetings in the Bahá'í Hall in Bombay, while, she writes, "one hundred thousand people in the political demonstrations . . . (congregate) each afternoon in the street below our windows."[41]

Lamenting of India, "Oh, I have left much undone,"[42] she proceeds to Mandalay and Rangoon, visits a Burmese Bahá'í village called Kunjangoon, and sails on August 7 for Singapore, then on to Hong Kong, Nanking, Shanghai and Canton. After two months in China she makes a whirlwind tour of Japan with Agnes Alexander, speaking in one instance to 2,000 people at a meeting arranged by a publishing magnate; she receives unprecedented publicity.

January, 1931, Hawaii and home: Hawaii, not yet part of the United States, is Martha's last stop beyond home shores after eight years away. In just over a week, she gives 25 lectures and four radio broadcasts. Then she sails for California. She spends a year in the U.S., making brief, special visits to relatives and friends like Roy Wilhelm and Agnes Parsons. She follows Shoghi Effendi's suggestion to speak in as many universities as possible. The quality of her love is something people have never encountered before.

Mignon Witzel, then a fourteen-year old living in California, describes it:

> I remember that (in the Los Angeles Bahá'í Center) they had a small table up front, and Martha Root was a very short woman. And she used to stand behind this little table and talk . . . She was extremely intelligent and she had a brilliant mind, (but) her talks were very simple. I remember sitting way in the back, and I remember thinking, 'Oh, I wish she'd finish.' Because, you wanted to get close to her.
>
> It was a long hall. But I could feel, clear in the back, the love that emanated from her . . . I don't know what it was, but you felt as if the whole world was cold, and the only warmth was around Martha Root, and you wanted to get close. And as soon as she was finished, as one person the

hall rose to their feet, everybody, and went down the aisles, and surrounded her. And I was timid, extremely timid, and they were around her in circles, and I was about the fifth circle out. I was tall, and I was afraid I was going to keep somebody from seeing her, and I could hardly see (her) head, with all those people around her—But I didn't care about *seeing* her, I didn't care about *talking* to her—I just wanted to get close and get warm, and *feel* this wonderful love that she had . . .

She taught by her *being*. And yet she wasn't this goody-goody, sweet-sweet type of person. It was a different thing.[43]

Central Europe, the Balkans, Edirne, Scandinavia, Iceland, 1932–1935: Martha is off to Europe again. In Central Europe and the Balkans she's tormented by pain, and writes to Ella Cooper: 'I massage it, bathe it, give it gymnastics!'[44] Yet it persists. In Vienna, she works with the young Marzieh Gail and her husband, Howard Carpenter. Marzieh, with an eye for style, is dubious about the effect Martha will have on the American Women's Club when she goes to speak there, for those women wear luxurious furs and high Russian boots, and Martha is wearing an ankle-length, pale blue satin dress topped by a straight, dark coat and a brown straw hat. Martha gives a simple address on Ṭáhirih, encounters with notable women and her own initially hesitant response to the Bahá'í Faith, and the club members flock around her adoringly at the end.

Marzieh notices how Martha finds time for homely and simple tasks as well as great ones: when she meets a gentleman who is desperate because his trousers are wrinkled and he has to look spiffy for an important appointment, she gets out her travel iron and presses his pants for him.

In autumn of 1933, Martha, with the pioneer to Bulgaria, Marion Jack, rides the fabled Orient Express to Edirne (then called Adrianople) Turkey, to find the places where Bahá'u'lláh lived during His exile there. In a mosque near the site of one of His houses, she is lost in ecstatic contemplation. Years later, the caretaker will tenderly remember Martha as the woman of rare devotion who prostrated herself and remained in prayer all day long, so that, when night fell and it was time to close the mosque, he had to regretfully ask her to leave.

Martha's pain grows worse, she has ceaseless headaches and has difficulty eating; in Stockholm she suffers a fall and in Oslo she becomes ill with flu, has fainting spells, cannot recover. She is nursed by Johanna Shubarth, whose laughter and gentleness remind her of her mother. Feeble as she is, she succeeds in having the new Swedish translation of *Bahá'u'lláh and the New Era* presented personally to the King of Sweden by the British conservationist, Richard St. Barbe Baker.

She at last leaves her bed to journey southwards into Greece, shepherding her large flock of luggage, leaning on a cane, her hair white, her eyes magnified by thick glasses, still skylarking, until, in July of 1936, she is home again.

* * * * * * * * *

Martha's friends were astonished at her physical frailty, and they had received instructions by Shoghi Effendi that Roy Wilhelm, Mountfort Mills and Horace Holley were to be his emissaries, his doctors assigned to monitor her: she was to rest and get well.

She refused to see medical doctors. She didn't want to hear what they would say, that she mustn't do anymore; she had decided she would just go on.

And so she did. On May 20, 1937, having taken just six months of "rest" to compensate for more than a decade of yeoman's labor, she boarded the *Tatsuta Maru* in San Francisco, bound for Japan.

Lucy Marshall, an old-time California Bahá'í, helped her pack, and reported that she had in her purse a second-class round-the-world ticket, and her seventeen pieces of luggage held, for the most part, Bahá'í literature: books, pamphlets, loose manuscripts enfolded in thin cotton cloth, radio talks, and photographs of rulers who had received Tablets from Bahá'u'lláh.

Each suitcase had its history. Martha told Lucy that a certain small leather one was her kitchen, for it contained her supplies for preparing her own frugal meals; it had been given to her by Lady Blomfield. She remarked of a spacious carry-all that Roy Wilhelm had had it made for her and it was very useful, for it held a lot.

On the deck of the *Tatsuta Maru,* Martha was interviewed by a newspaper reporter, and she gave him a red rosebud. She was photographed. Then she gave her friends red roses, anointed their foreheads with attar of roses, told them, "Alláh'u'Abhá" (God is Most Glorious), and kissed them. Once again, the Bahá'ís of the West Coast watched Martha sail away; this time they waved red roses instead of yellow jonquils, while Martha waved a turquoise scarf. They kept their eyes on that blue for a long time, till it disappeared over the blue horizon.

Martha went to Japan; she went to China and was caught in the bombing of Shanghai; she traveled through India for almost a year in India; she went to Australia; and she was heading home again when she died of cancer in Hawaii on September 28, 1939.

Martha Root during her last visit to Australia,
on board ship in Freemantle Harbor, 1939

The Guardian cabled that she was the "foremost Hand which 'Abdu'l-Bahá's will has raised up (during the) first Bahá'í Century."[45] In 1944, when he wrote his history of that first century, *God Passes By*, he concentrated salient facts and great events together with ruthless brevity, yet he dedicated 11 pages of pure tribute to Martha, calling her the "archetype of Bahá'í itinerant teachers."[46]

She is buried under a Rainbow Shower Tree, on a hilltop overlooking Honolulu and beyond, to the sea and the blue horizon, to a place where skylarks soar.

Chapter 4

Hyde Dunn

Clara and Henry Hyde Dunn

At around midnight in San Francisco, on October 1, 1912, as winds rich with sea mists blew in from the Golden Gate Strait, a cab coming from the train station stopped before a rented house and 'Abdu'l-Bahá alighted. He had arrived shortly before and, at His request, had been met by just a few Bahá'ís. That was why Hyde Dunn, a tall, slender, handsome British gentleman, stood discreetly on the curb across the street, watching from the shadows as 'Abdu'l-Bahá walked up the path to the house, mounted the steps and entered. With other Bahá'ís, Hyde had hoped constantly for 'Abdu'l-Bahá's visit; with some of them, he'd maintained an all night prayer vigil.

After observing 'Abdu'l-Bahá's safe arrival, he went to the hotel room he'd rented near the San Francisco residence; he had arranged his affairs so as not to miss a moment of 'Abdu'l-Bahá's visit to California. Day by day, he followed all of 'Abdu'l-Bahá's activities, benefiting by the contact so greatly that, in after years, he told the Bahá'ís of Australia, the land where he and his wife were the first Bahá'í pioneers: 'Abdu'l-Bahá's soul-quickening glance and animating words had sparked the flame of universal love in his heart and it burned so steadfastly that he wanted to do nothing else but devote his life to spreading that love. He fulfilled this desire to such a degree that Shoghi Effendi said future historians would hail him as the spiritual conqueror of a continent.

* * * * * * * *

John Henry Hyde Dunn was born in London, England, in 1858. His father was a consulting chemist—a pharmacist who attended patients and prescribed cures. He had some distinguished friends; Hyde remembered meeting Charles Dickens and the illustrator of many of the Dickens tales, George

Cruikshank. But Hyde didn't take up his father's profession and practice. He left England, went into business in Europe, then emigrated to the United States, which was still considered a brave new world, and settled in the newest part of it, on the dream coast, California.

That was the Golden West, and, in the 1890s, it was booming. One real estate pamphlet promised that buying land in Los Angeles guaranteed wearing diamonds. But Hyde, outgoing and not terribly interested in a settled existence, did not amass real estate or diamonds. He got married and worked as a traveling salesman.

By the time he was middle-aged, in 1905, California was described by the British Ambassador to the U.S. as a place of endless bustle, hurry, and tension, its people driven and restless. Hyde was restless too, yearning for something he couldn't name, and he found it at last while on a business trip.

He recalled that, in a tinker's shop in Seattle, his "hungry searching heart heard the penetrative utterance of Bahá'u'lláh from one just returned from the prison of 'Akká and the Presence of 'Abdu'l-Bahá."[1]

The speaker was Ward Fitzgerald. Deep in conversation with the tinker, he quoted Bahá'u'lláh, "Let not a man glory in this, that he loves his country; let him rather glory in this, that he loves his kind."[2] Hyde interrupted, exclaiming, "Surely, these words are a message from God."

Ward then briefly explained the Revelation of Bahá'u'lláh, and Hyde instantly became a Bahá'í. But even the explanation was superfluous to the words he'd first heard about the glory of universal love. Hyde said they clarified for him the meaning of Christ's life and its force. "That one glorious utterance magnetized the whole being; it appealed as a New Note sent forth from God to His wandering creatures."[3]

Hyde began combining business trips with Bahá'í teaching trips. His wife, Fannie, was not pleased. He had to subdue his eager, open nature to maintain harmony at home; he couldn't even host Bahá'í meetings. Nevertheless, he did a great deal while he traveled, and he became a well-known Bahá'í teacher. He spent as little money as possible on himself, so that he could give to the Bahá'í Fund and help the needy; his charitable acts were often anonymous. He was much admired for his consistent kindliness.

In 1911, when Lua Getsinger was in San Francisco, Hyde made a great effort to attend her classes. Sensing her depth and devotion, he also sought her out for private study. He later wrote that she gave him generously of her time and had a great effect on him. He also treasured the friendship of the first American Bahá'í, the man who had helped Martha Root decide to be a Bahá'í, Thornton Chase.

After meeting 'Abdu'l-Bahá in 1912, Hyde devoted more time than ever to Bahá'í teaching. When a Bahá'í Assembly was formed in San Francisco, he was listed as a member. His friends later noted, "In Bahá'í experience the San Francisco Assembly has indeed had its days of beginning, days of feebleness, when in very truth but two or three would gather together. But, whether in those days or these of greater fullness, none has woven more closely the bonds of love and steadfastness than Hyde Dunn."[4]

Around 1915, Hyde's wife became mortally ill. The Bahá'ís surrounded Hyde with help as she suffered a painful decline; they said she'd long been the object of his "yearning and devotion."[5] They held her in their arms and prayed with her. She was a Bahá'í when she died in March, 1916.

During the same year, the first of the "Tablets of the Divine Plan" were received in California by Helen Goodall. In September, her daughter, Ella Cooper, reported in the *Star of the West* that a student of Hyde's, inspired by the Tablets, had gone to Arizona carrying a supply of Bahá'í pamphlets, while Hyde himself had made a special trip to the silver mining town of Reno, Nevada.

About a year later, on the Anniversary of the Martyrdom of the Báb, July 9, Hyde remarried. Although he was fifty-nine years old, approaching the age when most people retire, his great life's work was about to begin. His forty-eight year old bride was Clara Holder Davis. He'd met her more than ten years before; in fact, he'd introduced the Bahá'í teachings to her.

* * * * * * * * *

Soon after Hyde became a Bahá'í, he and Ward Fitzgerald were both temporarily unemployed, so they decided to travel for their Faith. They arrived in Walla Walla, Washington, with empty pockets but no shortage of enthusiasm. They arranged an evening meeting, with Hyde at the podium. (Hyde often did the honors as speaker, for he had a fine voice and a distinguished accent which remained intact despite all his years away from England.) In the course of the day, while inviting people to their meeting, Ward and Hyde met Clara Davis, a pretty woman in her late thirties, with an Irish twinkle in her eye. "Are you interested in spiritual things?" asked Hyde. And Clara replied dryly, "I would be, if I knew of any spiritual things."[6]

Hyde told her about the Bahá'í Faith, and she attended the meeting. She had often thought, she later reminisced, that she would only join a religion if it was "for everybody in the world, of every kind and color."[7] At the meeting, she decided, "I'm sure it's from God."[8] She was also sure that Hyde and Ward were hungry, and she tactfully invited them dine.

Clara was a woman who had made her own way in a tough world. Born in 1869 in London, she was the youngest of six children. When she was small, her family moved to Canada and her father worked on the railroads. Home life was impoverished and unhappy; religion was an issue between her Methodist father and her Catholic mother. To escape, Clara married at sixteen. Three years later, her young husband was killed in a railroad accident, and she was left alone with their infant son. To support her child, she decided to train as a nurse, and she became a fine one.

After moving to the U.S. in 1902, she worked for fashionable doctors in Walla Walla and Seattle, and also was a volunteer nurse to the poor. Her son lived with her eldest brother and his family in Ontario. He was troubled, became a drug addict, spent time in jail, and Clara mourned all her life because she hadn't been able to raise him herself.

Soon after her encounter with Hyde Dunn and Ward Fitzgerald, Clara was the lone Bahá'í in Seattle. She told everyone about her new Faith, but no one responded, so, in addition to her worry about her son, she suffered agonies of self-doubt. Finally, she had a nervous breakdown and was hospitalized. When she came out of the hospital, she had no job and no money. A friend offered attic space. This friend, Clara said, "loved me as much as she could love her own daughter."[9] But, at the same time, the friend warned everyone that Clara was insane and wanted to convert the world to some crazy religion. In the meantime, an erstwhile suitor pressed Clara to marry him.

While living in that lonely attic, Clara received a telegram from a Bahá'í in San Francisco saying 'Abdu'l-Bahá was about to arrive. She decided she must go and see Him. She borrowed money for the trip from the man who wanted to marry her—although she had rejected him, he was magnanimous.

On October 24, the last night of 'Abdu'l-Bahá's stay in San Francisco, Clara arrived in the city.

With no idea where 'Abdu'l-Bahá was staying, other than that it was on Market Street, she boarded a trolley and asked the conductor if he knew where there were some Persians. He took her right to the house. Clara felt her deepest prayers had been answered as she hurried up the path and knocked on the door. But the door remained shut. She rang the bell. No one came. She knocked again. Still, no one came. She knocked and rang, rang and knocked—nothing. She was tired and hungry, and she began to weep. Then she got mad. She gave the door a shove, and it opened. It hadn't been locked at all.

Clara went inside and 'Abdu'l-Bahá greeted her, but He was exhausted, for He had just concluded a press conference. He asked her to wait, and He went off to rest. Twenty minutes later He reappeared, jovial and serene, and asked Clara to join the guests at His dinner table.

"Oh, His smile was so beautiful," she often recalled. And as He told a story, His eyes on Clara all the time, He was "radiant and glorious looking."[10] Years later, in Australia, Clara realized He'd been telling the story of her life to come with Hyde Dunn.

That night, after 'Abdu'l-Bahá went upstairs to His room, Hyde, who had been at the dinner table, said to Clara repeatedly, "I was the one who should have opened that door." She replied, "Thank God you left it unlocked, so I could get in."[11]

In the morning, Clara was present as 'Abdu'l-Bahá said His goodbyes. He came down the stairs carrying a large bottle of rosewater and bade each person farewell, anointing hands and heads with rosewater. Clara said she instinctively held out both hands and 'Abdu'l-Bahá poured the water over them. Then she looked around and saw Him anointing Hyde Dunn's head.

But she didn't feel she knew Hyde very well at the time, and she certainly had no inkling of their joint future.

* * * * * * * *

Five years later, she was Hyde's wife, and he immediately found himself able to fulfill his dream of opening his home to Bahá'ís and friends. The newlyweds—one childless, the other sadly bereft of her son, and both, in a sense, orphaned for many years by a lack of family ties—began to call each other Father and Mother, and soon their friends followed suit. They'd been married for two years when all seventeen of the "Tablets of the Divine Plan" were presented at that convention in New York from which Martha Root began her epic journeys. Hyde and Clara followed quickly in Martha's footsteps.

They weren't present at the convention, but were vacationing in Santa Cruz when they received copies of the Tablets. Hyde later wrote,

> Mother was reading 'Abdu'l-Bahá's . . . call to the United States and Canada, and His appeal was so penetrating and thrilling, it pierced our hearts. In one part He said, 'If I could only go in poverty and barefooted, and raise the call of Yá-Bahá'u'l-Abhá,* but that is not possible.' Mother looked up and said, 'Shall we go, Father?' 'Yes,' was my reply, and no further discussion took place. We returned to San Francisco, and after a few months my resignation was sent, everything given up, and arrangements made for our prompt sailing.[12]

---

*An invocation and prayer, "Oh Thou, the Glory of the Most Glorious."

Hyde described the feeling that accompanied this decision: "It was all very simple—a wave that came into our lives possessing us and satisfying every desire to serve our beloved Cause."[13]

The Dunns decided to go to Australia. This was a pragmatic choice. Australia was an English-speaking British commonwealth, so no new language would have to be learned.

And it was a young, raw nation like the United States; in fact, it was younger and more raw. Hyde had already made his way under such conditions, and it is possible that California already seemed somewhat jaded and played-out to him.

But as they began preparations to travel, Clara began to wonder if resettlement in a completely unknown land was such a good idea, after all. Hyde wrote to 'Abdu'l-Bahá. While awaiting His answer, they went ahead with their plans. "It seemed like ages," Hyde said, "before a reply came." At last, on a January morning in 1920, he and Clara were packed and ready to leave their cottage. "While the carriers were loading on our luggage," Hyde wrote, "and Mother waiting in the wee garden, a telegraph boy appeared with a *cable* from 'Abdu'l-Bahá containing these words, *'Highly commendable.'* Imagine our hearts' delight and joy. This made our future an open door to service on this continent."[14]

The Dunns set sail that day on the S.S. *Sonona* for Honolulu. They spent two months in Hawaii, making what Hyde said was "in the truest sense a real Bahá'í visit, with a lasting profit of understanding and consciousness of real love and service to God." Soon afterwards, they received a letter from 'Abdu'l-Bahá saying, "Praise be to God that even in the steamer ye did not sit silent but stirred and exhilarated some souls and met the friends of God in Honolulu."[15]

With an eye to earning a livelihood, Hyde bought coral jewelry in Hawaii to sell in Australia. He and Clara arrived in Sydney on April 10, 1920, and he was terribly chagrined when customs officials confiscated the jewelry. His health was already bad, and this final blow was too much. He fell ill, too ill to work.

There he was, ailing, some 15,000 miles from home, in the land of duckbilled platypuses, dingoes, and kangaroos, with strange types of flowers clustering in doorways among the bleeding hearts and roses, and the Southern Cross shining in the night sky while familiar constellations like Orion seemed to be standing on their heads. Australia was a continent of vast distances and wide skies, of rough and rowdy, hard-drinking white settlers clustered in cities and towns fringing the outback, which was a wilderness unlike any other in the world. Hyde was in Sydney, the big city, with its parks, Botanical Gardens, and bustling harbor at Botany Bay filled with ships.

Under the new sky, in the new land, he and Clara had the single, shared purpose of gladdening 'Abdu'l-Bahá by establishing the Bahá'í Faith at the heart of the continent. Everything else was secondary. All Hyde wanted to do was get started, and he couldn't do anything.

Clara thought it a very fortunate thing that a former employer of hers had been on the ship to Sydney and had offered her a job. She'd given up nursing long since, but she'd worked for some years as a sales representative. She was glad to earn enough to keep food on the table.

But Hyde didn't want her to go back to work; he felt protective of her. Though he was a decade older than she, he saw her as being delicate, and he always said that he had the strong constitution in the family. He didn't like the fact that she supported them during their first year in Australia, but he accepted it gracefully as a blessing. He and Clara were both greatly cheered by a letter from 'Abdu'l-Bahá in December, 1920: "This journey is pregnant with greater prosperity, because great results will issue therefrom. At present it is full of hardship, but later on favour, comfort and happiness will be bestowed."[16]

At the time of the Dunns' arrival, Australia had plenty of alternative religious and philosophical movements nourished by reaction against the traumatic and tragic Australian experience during World War I. Among others, there were Theosophists, Spiritualists, Socialists, followers of New Thought, and members of Radiant Health Clubs; there were also numerous women's groups for charitable work and self-improvement.

News of the Bahá'í Faith had arrived in Australia some years earlier, but had made only a mild dent on the surface of religious life. In 1904, Reverend Charles Strong preached on the life of 'Abdu'l-Bahá in his church in Melbourne. In 1912, Reverend H. Price told Robert Stewart, a dentist in Brisbane, something about the Bahá'í Faith. Shortly before that, news of 'Abdu'l-Bahá in London reached New Zealand and Australia via the *Christian Commonwealth* newspaper. In 1916, a New Thought magazine called *The Revealer* quoted 'Abdu'l-Bahá in an article. In 1919, Shoghi Effendi, acting as secretary to 'Abdu'l-Bahá and writing to Bahá'ís in America, referred to correspondence received from Australia. In short, the field was very slightly cultivated and wide open for Hyde and Clara.

* * * * * * * *

One evening, while setting the table for dinner, Hyde found himself thinking, "Now the time is ripe . . . to write to the firm in Melbourne regarding a position."[17] That night, he mailed a letter to the Nestlé Company. By return post, he received a reply saying his application was opportune, and he should make an appointment with the Sydney manager. By around September, 1920, the Australian springtime, Hyde was covering all of New South Wales as a traveling salesman for Nestlé. After a year, he'd topped the national sales record and the manager asked him what favor Nestlé could do for him. Hyde replied, "Make me an inter-state man."[18] That meant he could travel even more widely.

He later recalled,

> Mother was able to surrender her position and God made it possible for me to earn enough to travel all over the continent, taking Mother to the capital cities. . . . For two and a half years we remained in New South Wales. . . . Interest in the Cause continually increased and people . . . came at all times to see us. There was no breathing space at all. It was an incessant plowing ahead."[19]

Shoghi Effendi summed up the effort in *God Passes By:*

> A new continent was opened to the Cause when . . . the great-hearted and heroic Hyde Dunn, at the advanced age of sixty-two, promptly forsook his home in California, and, seconded and accompanied by his wife, settled as a pioneer in Australia, where he was able to carry the message to no less than 700 towns throughout that Commonwealth.[20]

Shoghi Effendi cited the introduction of the Bahá'í Faith in Australia as a direct result of the "Tablets of the Divine Plan," and he said it was one of the great achievements embellishing 'Abdu'l-Bahá's brilliant ministry.

The Dunns evolved their method of traveling and teaching: while Hyde was posted to a state capital for a few months, they rented a cottage and Clara kept house and invited people to meetings. Hyde visited rural towns during the week, doing his job and also bringing news of the Bahá'í Faith to those remote areas. Meetings were held on weekends. Hyde often did the honors as speaker, but Clara also gave excellent talks, though she'd rarely assumed the lecture platform before coming to Australia.

In 1922, Oswald Whitaker, an optometrist, became the first Australian Bahá'í. He met Hyde in Lismore, New South Wales, or, rather, he was brought by a group of businessmen to refute Hyde's arguments for the Bahá'í Faith. Hyde said Mr. Whitaker's "friends brought him in great triumph. He asked me one question and one question only, which they all thought would floor the Bahá'í Faith and Revelation. He asked me, 'Can you tell me what love is?' My reply was, 'Yes. The whole law and power of the Great Universe is formulated love in action.' He said: 'Is that what love is?' He never asked me another question." [21] Hyde gave him some Bahá'í literature, and he brought it back the next day; when Hyde asked him his opinion of it, he declared that every line evinced the truth.

Effie Baker, the first Australian woman to become a Bahá'í, met Hyde shortly after that in Melbourne. She and a friend, Ruby Beaver, were members of the welcoming committee for the New Civilization Center. Hyde attended a meeting, and Effie, seeing the mild and distinguished white-haired gentleman in the audience, decided he should be invited to speak. She didn't invite him at the time, but someone did, for, when she arrived at the next meeting, she saw a notice in the vestibule saying that Mr. Hyde Dunn was to speak about the Bahá'í Faith.

Effie later said he,

> . . . opened with a prayer and then prefaced his talk by a quotation from *The Hidden Words,* 'O Son of Spirit: Free thyself from the worldly bond, escape from the prison of self, appreciate the value of time for it will never come to thee again. . . . ' Having heard this I thought, 'I must listen to what this speaker has to say.' He then gave the principles given to the 'world of mankind' for the age by Bahá'u'lláh. The one that arrested my attention was, 'Investigate truth for yourself. . . . ' It suddenly dawned on me, 'Why! I was born a Christian, my forebears were Christians for centuries. I certainly have never investigated truth for myself . . .' After the meeting closed, I immediately went to Mr. Dunn and declared myself as accepting the Bahá'í Message.[22]

Shortly after Effie became a Bahá'í, her friend Ruby also did so that, when the Dunns left Australia to visit New Zealand, there were three Australian Bahá'ís. The Dunns assumed they would be the first Bahá'ís to set foot on New Zealand's soil. They were in for a surprise.

* * * * * * * * *

"We landed," Hyde wrote of his and Clara's arrival in Aukland, "not knowing one soul . . . The first night we met . . . a man and his wife. They took dinner with us—listened to the message then said, 'You must meet our friend, Mrs. Blundell.' The next night we both went to Mrs. Blundell's home."[23]

About twenty people gathered at Sarah Blundell's to meet Hyde and Clara. Among them was Margaret Stevenson. When Sarah introduced Margaret to Hyde, Margaret noticed the

Bahá'í ring on his finger. Margaret later reminisced, "I was also wearing one and turned my hand to him. His pleasure and astonishment when he saw my ring will always be something to remember."[24]

Margaret had been a Bahá'í since 1912. She first heard of the Bahá'í Faith in 1911 via a copy of *The Christian Commonwealth*, which her sister, who had heard 'Abdu'l-Bahá speak, sent from London. Margaret said, "I read the article about Him . . . but am sorry to say I did not think any more about it." A year later, a friend named Dorothea Spinney came to New Zealand to give recitals of Greek plays and, while she was in Auckland, she stayed with the Stevensons. She'd met 'Abdu'l-Bahá, and she told Margaret about Him. As she spoke, a spark was struck.

Margaret later said, "As a child, I used to wish I had lived when Christ was on earth . . . I remembered my childhood's wish, and the thought came to me that I too might have denied Him as so many others had done. It was this secret thought that made me seriously think of what I had heard from Miss Spinney."[25]

Margaret told others about the Bahá'í Faith. Mrs. Blundell, who had also read the article in *The Christian Commonwealth*, was the one who was most significantly interested. Margaret sent to America for Bahá'í books, and subscribed to the *Star of the West*.

After that first meeting at the Blundell home, a hall was rented for further meetings, and Hyde also spoke at the Higher Thought Center. Shoghi Effendi had cabled, "Friends in Holy Land waiting lovingly for news of friends in Australia."[26] So, the Dunns arranged a special gathering and had a photo taken; there they were, white-haired and enduring, in the midst of a cluster of twelve new Bahá'ís, including Margaret Stevenson and Sarah Blundell. They all sent a cable to the Guardian, and also a contribution to the United States towards building the Bahá'í Temple. Then Hyde returned to Australia and Clara stayed on for several weeks to guide a study group that met in the Stevenson home. That group continued regular meetings for a decade.

* * * * * * * * *

Soon, the Dunns began to garner a rich spiritual harvest in Australia. It certainly didn't come effortlessly. By July, 1923, Hyde had visited 225 towns since starting work for Nestlé, so he averaged a new town each four or five days. People entered the Faith from time to time, from town to town.

In November, 1923, Percy and Maysie Almond heard Clara and Hyde address the New Thought Society in Adelaide. Two days later, the first Bahá'í group in South Australia was formed in the Almonds' home. Percy was an accountant who used to load his little Renault with inquirers and take them to meetings at the home of another new Bahá'í in Adelaide. Since few Bahá'í books were available, Hyde would bring along typed copies of extracts from the literature.

Early in 1924, the Dunns took the Faith to Tasmania, described in the *Star of the West* as "an island in the Pacific Ocean which was settled by British seamen who married daughters of the people of Tahiti . . . This island . . . is covered with orange, lemon and other fruit trees and beautiful pines."[27] Effie Baker accompanied the Dunns, and Gretta Lamprill, a nurse, became the first Bahá'í in Tasmania. Like Margaret Stevenson, she'd encountered the Faith years before, some time between 1908 and 1912, when her mother pointed out a paragraph in a newspaper which said that the British Museum had in its collections scriptures by a man in the East who claimed to be the Prophet for this age. Years later, when Gretta heard Hyde speak passionately of his Faith, she felt it was what she'd been waiting for.

Back on the mainland, the Dunns traveled, again with Effie, to Perth, the capital of Western Australia. Hyde was equipped with the newly published book by John Esslemont, *Bahá'u'lláh and the New Era*. He met a Mrs. Miller, who had known Dr. Esslemont when he was a boy. She asked Hyde if he, also, knew Dr. Esslemont personally. Hyde, glad to have the wise and pithy book which relieved him of making all those typewritten extracts and carbon copies that he'd been carrying around for years, said, "No, I never met him—but, oh, how I love him!"[28] A Bahá'í group formed in Perth, and the Dunns were still there when Martha Root arrived in June.

They were greatly uplifted by Martha's visit, and she was uplifted by their love. She described them as "two Bahá'ís with beautiful gray hair and sweet young faces so filled with light and love that any stranger would say to himself, 'What makes them so happy?'"[29] She also said she knew the secret as to why they were such successful teachers: "People know they can come to Father and Mother Dunn . . . and they will receive that sympathy, that ineffable love, that knowledge of the Bahá'í Teachings that show them how to meet their difficulties with radiant acquiescence."[30]

Martha pointed out that it was also important that "Mother always fed them! Cups of fragrant tea and the most delicious little cakes . . . were always part of every meeting. This may seem a little thing, but it is what 'Abdu'l-Bahá always did. Later the friends came away laden with cakes!"[31]

She said, too, that the Dunns "always gave everything. No one could see their lives without realizing that all they possessed was for 'Abdu'l-Bahá and His Cause."[32]

The new Bahá'ís that Martha met in Australia and New Zealand recounted to her in glowing terms how the Dunns had touched their hearts. And yet, Hyde said to Martha, "Never mention us in writing about Australia. I wish that I could do something for Australia." While Clara wept, and made the astonishing remark, "I have failed."[33]

* * * * * * * * *

New Bahá'ís kept coming. Among them were Stanley and Mariette Bolton. At the end of 1924, they had just arrived in Sydney from Canada. Stanley met a Bahá'í who invited him and Mariette to lunch. Walking up the path to the house, the Boltons saw their host on the balcony with an impressive look-ing white-haired gentleman. On closer scrutiny, they noticed that the gentleman was wearing a lumberjack shirt with banded cuffs buttoned at the wrist, a cummerbund around his waist, and, at his neck, a bow-tie. This uniquely garbed person was Hyde Dunn, who proceeded, during the meal, to tell the Boltons about the Bahá'í Faith; he spoke of the need for a universal language and quoted passages from Bahá'í scripture by heart. A few years later, the Boltons became Bahá'ís and followed in the Dunns' footsteps, traveling and teaching throughout Australia.

So Clara and Hyde forged ahead, guided, like the prince and princess in a fairy tale, by the love and goodness of their hearts. Shoghi Effendi wrote to them: "What an encourage-ment and what an inspiration to be revived every now and then with a fresh breeze wafting from far away Australia and laden with the perfume of your love and devotion . . . A thou-sand times well done, my dearly beloved ones! Your warmth, your perseverance, your confidence, your faith will, I am cer-tain, establish our precious Cause in the very heart of that continent which in the future will ring with the Greatest Name and extol the glorious self-sacrificing labours of you who are the pioneers of His Cause in those far away regions. Your reward will be unexpectedly great and your efforts will be richly recompensed by 'Abdu'l-Bahá Himself in the world to come."[34]

In 1925, Hyde and Clara settled permanently in Sydney, but Hyde continued to travel. In February, 1926, at the age of sixty-eight, he reported to her from the Queens Hotel in Townsville that he'd been to visit the thirteen and eight-year old daughters of friends at their Church of England boarding school. He regretted that he'd missed seeing them perform in *A Midsummer Night's Dream,* and said he'd brought them gifts: "A dear little bottle of perfume, each—A pretty wee thing with a screw top and a plunger reaching into the bottle—Also some candies."

He philosophized that the troubles he and Clara were passing through were "a purifying process . . . that others may see the signs of Bahá'í in our lives, then will they come to the Bahá'ís and ask what is it that you possess, that sustains you in difficulties. On this account we must rejoice . . . When the supreme love—follows the supreme test — that love becomes the divine magnet to others." He told Clara, "It is your sweetness, after your tests, that has shown me so much of God's way for us poor atoms of nothingness."[35]

In March, 1926, Hyde wrote to Ernest Brewer from the Central Hotel in Hughenden, "This is hot country, everything you touch is hot, my machine (typewriter) is hot, chair is hot, table is hot . . . " He was sure to mention a mitigating factor: "But a fairly dry heat . . . " He was working on some "lecturettes," short radio talks for the Nestlé company. His manager was by then a Bahá'í, and the idea was to indirectly teach the Faith, or at least some of its principles. Hyde had long been interested in the Bahá'í teachings on a just economic system based on spiritual principles, and he was excited at "what it means to get such a Message before the commercial world." Ernest, a new Bahá'í, was a journalist, and Hyde wanted him to rewrite the lecturettes. Yet Hyde, in his fatherly way, worried about asking too much of Ernest, who had just been promoted to an editorial position. "This may look somewhat hard of me—knowing how hard your life will be with your new work—But just as my life is a hard life—I find service in (the) Bahá'í Cause a great help in every way and my health grows stronger each day—Business is softened and the world eased in one's life—when we are able to give out spiritual qualities to others . . ."[36]

In a subsequent letter, Hyde thanked Ernest for his help, saying his own "weak point" was "not being able to convey in writing the truths of my heart and soul . . . " The next month, Hyde, still traveling, generally by train, separated by desert and distance from his wife and friends, wrote to Ernest, "The work of this servant has always been pioneer work among people—In some way God uses me and causes hearts and souls to listen and to be attracted—then . . . Mother gives many finishing touches with her precious love."[37]

Ernest had said he had trouble comprehending spiritual teachings. Hyde counseled, "As we let go (of) conventional material meaning . . . the spiritual (will) arise in our hearts like the sun . . . Remember, Patience is the Bahá'í preserve and Meekness is its Conquering Power — so entirely opposite to the ways of the world—Yet *these are the spiritual powers God has given man for complete success.*"[38] Ernest had said he yearned for some of Hyde's enlightenment. Hyde replied: "The Light of Reality . . . is the Light of the Manifestation of God—the

Light of Oneness is His Light—for all humanity . . . Search for this full realization and you will find you are living in the greatest of all days and illumined with the Self of God manifest in your own sweet heart."[39]

Shortly after that, writing to Clara from Rockhampton in the rough country of Northern Australia, he mentioned how frequently he had to be away from her, and quickly, gallantly added, "But that is allright, you could not travel in this country."[40]

While Hyde traveled, however, Clara was never at rest. Shortly after he returned from Northern Australia, he was off again to Cairns, and Clara was occupied with nursing a woman who was exhausted by the care of a sick husband, and who had been informed by her doctor that she would probably die any minute, her heart was in such bad shape. Clara was also helping sponsor an orphanage. Hyde returned after a month to find Clara's patient fourteen pounds heavier and in the pink, while Clara was, he wrote, "down again and very tired from the exertion for which she had no real strength . . . Yet God gave her each day as many times before—now she is not writing or seeing anyone for a time until strong again."[41]

* * * * * * * * *

If Hyde had any hopes of retiring from his sales work, they were dashed by the Depression. It hit Australia harder than it hit the United States, and it began earlier. So, at seventy, in 1930, he was, of necessity, still on the road. He and Clara, long-suffering, gentle, and generous, glowed jewel-like on the dowdy bosom of Australian society, although the nation as a whole was completely unaware of them. And the Bahá'ís, who adored them, were not always able to surrender former beliefs that didn't agree with Bahá'í teachings.

This situation wasn't peculiar to Australia; it existed all over the world. So, in 1931, Keith Ransom-Kehler, a stellar speaker and firebrand teacher, was sent, at Shoghi Effendi's request, by the American National Spiritual Assembly to deepen understanding of Bahá'í administration in Asia and Australia. When she disembarked at Thursday Island, the outpost of Australia, a letter awaited her from Hyde, "We need you and need you badly . . . Conditions in Australia at the present time are far from satisfactory. The Bahá'í Message is badly needed from a public platform. Most of our best work as pioneers has been done in home Groups and Meetings—with loving hospitality—We have many beautiful souls, but suffer from the same frailties belonging to the human family."[42]

Hyde, casting a genial eye over the vagaries of his Bahá'í children, was disturbed by Australia's general condition. But Keith's task demanded that she awaken the Bahá'ís to the spiritual potency of their Administrative Order, and, to do that, she had to break the news to them that they couldn't continue to be Spiritualists or Theosophists or Christian Scientists or anything else if they wanted to be Bahá'ís; they could only have one avowed allegiance. People who couldn't reconcile themselves to this were no longer calling themselves Bahá'ís when they left Keith's meetings. It was hard on them, and harder on their saddened friends, who nevertheless remained to form Australia's first real Bahá'í community. And it was, perhaps, hardest on Keith.

She had arrived, utterly spent, from about two months in Japan and China and then a long, hot trip over tropical seas. She wrote in her diary, "The Dunns are like two heavenly angels. Their perfection could never be described." And, "Mr. and Mrs. Dunn have cared for me like a baby. This afternoon she took me to see (the film) 'Skippy,' and a good cry was had by all."[43] Clara, whose charitable interests abounded, also took Keith to visit a soup kitchen. Soon, Keith was calling Hyde and Clara "Father" and "Mother" like everyone else did; she particularly enjoyed prayer sessions with them.

However, she sometimes felt overwhelmed by the Dunns. Their purity was a challenge to her. Clara's unwavering conviction was more than an attitude; it was a state of being. Keith admired Clara's faith and identified personally with her pain, for Keith, like Clara, had suffered over loved ones with a grief that never really healed. Her amazement increased when she learned that Clara, although constantly up and doing, was battling severe illness. She called her acquaintance with Clara a "stirring contact."[44]

Hyde, on the other hand, challenged Keith's patience. She had a disciplined mind, was astute and articulate, and Hyde was not analytical or precise. Anyway, Keith tended to have more patience with women than with men. The time came during her visit when she was very tired and irritable, and she lost her head and harangued Hyde about the uselessness of vague generalizations. As she discoursed she said, "Of course, I'm arrogant and conceited."

She expected him to tell her that she was nothing of the kind. However, Hyde agreed that she was arrogant and conceited. "But," he added kindly, "you'll get over it." Later, Clara, alone with Keith, looked at her and remarked dryly, "Well. Pop went the weasel."[45]

Reviewing the incident in her journal, Keith enjoyed it— she always liked poking a pin in her own balloon, and Hyde had done it for her. Later, she wrote fondly of him that he had eyes like a fallow deer. That's a beautiful, small, European type of deer, pale yellow, with white spots during the summer that give it the camouflage of dappled sunlight. And, in an article called "In the Footsteps of the Pioneers," she wrote of the Dunns: "Mr. and Mrs. Dunn . . . are of singular beauty both of person and character. Mr. Dunn has the rarest and most charming disposition: loving, forgiving, genial . . . Mrs. Dunn . . . lives in the Presence of God with a kind of awe and candor that assure men of His Power and Benignity."[46]

Keith, Hyde and Clara, living and working under intense and fatiguing conditions, overcoming personality conflicts and personal biases for a cause greater than themselves, embodied the virtues of mercy, justice and altruistic love, without which the Bahá'í Administration—and they were, themselves, building it with their every action—could not function.

* * * * * * * *

Clara made her pilgrimage to Haifa a year after Keith's visit, in 1932. Hyde wasn't able to accompany her. He wrote to the Guardian to thank him for the "wonderful love, care, kindness and many privileges" bestowed upon Clara, and said he could only show his thankfulness by the "attempt to release more love and effort (in the remaining years of my life) imparting the true teachings of Bahá'u'lláh in Australia and New Zealand and perhaps the South Seas—this is my desire."

With deep humility, he then outlined his own understanding of the Bahá'í teachings and said, "My heart and soul yearn to know if these fundamental teachings are the correct essentials. Deep down in my being these realities have dwelt for the past twenty-five years. Working hard and striving to spread the Blessed Revelation, whatever there may be wrong, I can only pray for the truth of correction."[47]

No wonder Shoghi Effendi wrote that the names of Hyde and Clara Dunn were "graven in letters of gold" upon his heart.[48]

He gave Clara instructions on how to elect the first National Spiritual Assembly of Australia and New Zealand, and this was done at the first Australian National Convention, in Sydney, May 15–18, 1934. Robert Brown, of Adelaide, opened the convention with a tribute to Mother and Father Dunn, expressing the gratitude of all their Bahá'í children.

In 1936, Hyde, now a member of the National Assembly, but with failing health and dimming eyesight, could not see his typewriter keys, yet wrote to Gretta Lamprill in Tasmania,

Don't be worried, Dear, about having a home. Mother and this servant have no home but are blessed with friends like you. Nestlé Co. considered me too old to give my services to them any longer and I had to leave them two years ago. Next year sees me in my 80th year. Mother is younger, not the strong constitution of this servant, but keeps fairly well. Our blessed friends have been most kind and hospitable to us. We are staying with our dear friends, Mr. and Mrs. Brewer, at Penhurst, just outside Sydney. Both Mother and I fortunately got the old age pension. It is not much, but such a blessing to have a little coming in. So see how beautiful and good God has been to us, but above all and everything the National Assembly for Australia and New Zealand is established—nothing else matters or counts.[49]

The next year, an Australian Bahá'í named Ethel Dawe returned from Haifa with a precious gift for Australia, a lock of Bahá'u'lláh's hair arranged to look like a calligraphic ink stroke and set in a frame by Bahíyyih Khánum. The Guardian said he wanted it in Australia because Australia was so distant from Haifa, and he especially wanted Mother and Father Dunn to touch it.

When, in 1939, Martha Root passed through Australia again, she noted: "Mr. and Mrs. Dunn are truly angels, and their work in twenty years is like a great romance of religion."[50]

On February 17, 1941, when Hyde was eighty-three, he attended a meeting at the Sydney Bahá'í Center, where he was his usual wise, cheerful self. But, shortly after returning home, he fainted. He recovered and seemed fairly well for a few days, but then he became unconscious again, and, after two more days, he died. Clara was calm and smiling at his funeral, and when she spoke she imparted to the mourners a message of hope and joy; it was what she knew Hyde would have said to them.

Shoghi Effendi sent a cable extolling the "magnificent career" of the great-hearted John Henry Hyde Dunn, "veteran warrior" of the Faith of Bahá'u'lláh. He said that Hyde, as one who had helped spark the growth of the "far-flung spiritual dominion" the American Bahá'ís were "commissioned (to) establish," was one with his sister pioneers—Keith Ransom-Kehler, who died in Iran in 1933; Martha Root, who died in Hawaii in 1939; and May Maxwell, who died in Buenos Aires in 1940.[51]

In a letter written in April, 1941, to the Bahá'ís of Australia, he said, "The truly remarkable services of Hyde Dunn will never be forgotten. They have added a golden page to the history of the formative period of our Faith. The whole-hearted response to 'Abdu'l-Bahá's call, raised more than twenty years ago, when he and Mother Dunn made their quiet and unassuming sacrifices for the Cause; the wisdom and permanence with which he laid the foundations of the work in Australia and New Zealand; and the faithfulness with which both of these noble souls tended the growing institutions of the Faith— all constitute a landmark in the victorious progress of the Faith

. . . The influence he has exercised will . . . continue to live and the example he has set will inspire the rising generation to perform deeds as great and brilliant as those which will ever remain associated with his name. Our dear friend, Mr. Hyde Dunn, will, from his exalted station intercede on your behalf, and you should, on your part, strive to emulate one whom Bahá'í historians will recognize and acclaim as Australia's spiritual conqueror."[52]

In 1954, Hyde Dunn was posthumously named a Hand of the Cause of God by the Guardian, and Clara Dunn, still pioneering and traveling when she was nearly ninety, was also named a Hand of the Cause, so that she redoubled her efforts and influence.

Clara died peacefully at the age of ninety-one, in 1960, and was buried beside her husband under a monument in Sydney raised for them by the Bahá'ís. Above them opens the wide Australian sky; before them rolls the Tasman Sea; around them, forever, breathes the continent.

Chapter 5

Keith Ransom-Kehler

Keith Ransom-Kehler

On September 13, 1931, while on board ship sailing from China to Australia, Keith Ransom-Kehler wrote in her diary, "Twenty years ago to-day I met 'Abdu'l-Bahá, the beloved of the world. 'Be very happy,' were the first words addressed to me by Him Who knows the end from the beginning; and He has bestowed upon me that precious gift. To have seen 'face to face' the . . . pivot of (the) Covenant, what destiny could be comparable to this? To have felt the pressure of His Hand and have His Command is an eternal blessing."[1]

Keith was not a Bahá'í when she met 'Abdu'l-Bahá. She was one of the seekers who flocked to Him in London, in 1911. A restless Christian, crusader for many causes, she was thirty-five, petite, pretty, highly educated, opinionated, and often mercilessly direct, with an inquiring mind and great charm. The exact circumstances of her meeting with 'Abdu'l-Bahá may never be known. If the brief diary entry written so many years after the event had not come to light, perhaps the information that she met Him would have been lost, for, when she died, the Bahá'ís were so overwhelmed by the loss and by the stature conferred on her by the Guardian that her obituary consisted only of reports of the last two years of her life; no biographical information was included. Now it is time to make amends.

****

Keith Ransom-Kehler was born Nannie Keith Bean on Valentine's Day, February 14, 1876, in Dayton, Kentucky. Her father was Colonel William Worth Bean, her mother was Julia Keith Bean, and she had one brother. Her father's military title was not bestowed by any institution; it was that of a so-called Courtesy Colonel, peculiar to southern gentlemen whose fathers had fought for the Confederates during the Civil War.

When Keith was about thirteen, the Colonel took his family north to the twin cities of Benton Harbor and St. Joseph, Michigan; but Keith always retained a slight southern accent which was, in later years, particularly admired in Australia. Colonel Bean, originally a schoolteacher, became a self-taught engineer and brought electricity to the twin cities, installing a trolley line. He was crusty and quick-tempered, and Keith was just as fiery as he was, so, they didn't always get along. In fact, Keith had a low opinion of herself because somehow she'd never been able to win his approval. She was always grateful for the warmth received from her maternal grandfather.

Keith went to Vassar College, famous as one of the world's best women's colleges, majored in child psychology, and graduated in 1898; then she took graduate studies at Albion College and the Universities of Michigan, Arizona, and Chicago. When she was twenty-five, she married Guy (Ralph) Ransom and accompanied him to Paris, where he studied painting. They returned to the United States around 1906, and their daughter, Julia Keith Ransom, was born in February, 1907. Keith later had another daughter who was stillborn. There's a little marker for her near the memorial stone that Ralph Ransom's family erected for Keith under an old pine in the St. Joseph cemetery.

The young couple, with their infant daughter, lived for a time on the Colonel's fruit and chicken farm, and Keith was properly impressed forever by the depressing exigencies of chickens. A Ralph Ransom painting, now at the International Bahá'í Centre in Haifa, shows Keith wielding an artist's brush beneath the fruit trees. She didn't pursue painting, but she had an educated eye for composition, form, and detail; she was an aesthete.

Ralph, not a great painter or chicken farmer, became a professor at Albion College, and Keith taught French and English Literature there. She was well-liked by her students, always the life of the party. Sadly, Ralph died in his mid-thirties of tuberculosis.

Around 1910, Keith married James Howard Kehler. She always called him Jim. With him, she went to live in New York, where he became one of the city's most expensive advertising men. He moved in exalted circles: Keith remembered celebrities she met through him, among them the great architect, Frank Lloyd Wright.

Keith and Jim enjoyed a romance of equals. They were both powerful personalities, and in New York they maintained separate apartments, but not separate lives. Keith could be devastatingly outspoken, and Jim liked to compare her to a gun; whenever she leveled an opponent—usually a man, for she had pity on women—Jim would remark compassionately that the poor fellow must not have known it was loaded. Nevertheless, she had a dazzling smile, multitudinous interests, and tremendous *joi de vivre;* men were charmed by her.

Keith led a liberal Christian Fellowship that was centered in Chicago from 1918–1922; she was a star speaker. In May, 1921, she enrolled as a Bahá'í. The year after that, she chaired a session of the North American Bahá'í National Convention in Chicago.

In 1923, she went south with Jim to nurse him through a mortal illness. She wrote to May Maxwell: "Pray for me, May. It is my only refuge. . . . Through this bitter storm of trial in which every attribute of light is obscure or withdrawn, you still stand, a dazzling presence on the further shore toward which I struggle, a gift and evidence lent me by the Master."[2] Keith was devastated when Jim died. She could never forget the sound of the earth falling on his coffin. The agony of her separation from him numbed her heart; she thought, for the rest of her life, that she was somehow separated by an inner coldness from warm humanity, and fancied that she was incapable of love, even while she was doing everything for it.

Keith returned to Chicago, took a course in interior design, and worked at Carson Pirie Scott, the prestigious Chicago department store. She wrote an article on "The Questing Soul," published in *The Bahá'í Magazine* in 1924, and took a leading role in various Bahá'í events. Then, in 1926, she went on pilgrimage and met the Guardian. The visit set the course for the seven brief years that remained of her life.

* * * * * * * * *

Keith was fascinated by the orient and by oriental ways. Alone at dusk on the steps of the quaint old pilgrim house at Bahjí, she wrote:

> Venus is the evening star. I sit . . . entranced with her magical beauty: in this latitude and through this atmosphere she is bright enough to cast a shadow and light seems incessantly to brim up and overflow the beaker of her brilliance. . . . Twilight encroaches; the silence is vaster than any sound; something at the base of one's soul stirs like an unsuspected titan. . . . Now the shepherds on two distant hills start piping to their flocks, a plaintive, poignant testimony, like all Oriental music, to the ineffable home-sickness of the soul. . . . Then, and as from the portal of para-

dise, a mystical beautiful chant arises. It is the voice of a woman, broken with sobs, tragic with longing, rich in praise. . . . It is Laila, the cook, who in her humility has not even entered the Shrine, but is kneeling on the garden path outside. Surely in her reverence, her obedience, her lowliness, her longing, she carries up to God, in that beatific wail, something of the desire of our tortured hearts to reach Him. The wide beds of stock begin to loose their fragrance with the coming of night, mingling with rose and jasmine. Laila passes me alert and smiling, restored completely by her abandonment to the Spirit.[3]

Keith could appreciate Laila's passion, for she herself was, she told the young Marzieh Gail, just as dramatic with God as she was with people; she said that when she prayed "They know there's something doing in heaven."[4] One day at Bahjí, in one of the two rooms in the Shrine of Bahá'u'lláh, thinking that she was alone, she was kneeling, sobbing, and crying out, as was her wont, when she suddenly looked across into the other room and saw a whole group of Persian men quietly observing her.

She was a bit nonplused, but she never minded creating a little stir and, besides, she felt very much at home, at one with the spirit of the place.

She particularly reveled in the chance to be with some of the oriental Bahá'í women, especially the eighty-year old Bahíyyih Khánum: "Exquisite, fragrant, imperturbable, assured, she walks among the fluctuating conditions of the world."[5] She noted that, although Bahíyyih Khánum made no overt attempts to reform people, she ennobled them by her mere presence; her constant, unselfconscious kindliness was in itself a state of grace.

But Keith was most moved by the Guardian. She perceived that he wanted the Bahá'ís to go out and teach, and immerse themselves in a sea of light rather than in a sea of troubles, but countless individuals wrote to him about personal problems and petty disagreements; he answered each one, and he became exhausted. Keith saw that his energy was needed for greater work. She wrote a letter to the American Bahá'ís gathered at a national convention, and related a conversation she'd had with him, during which he'd said, "The most essential thing in all matters is for the friends to work in harmony, for if they do not work together there is no need to teach—there is nothing to teach. What we need is not so much devotion to the Cause, for this has already been abundantly proven and is being proved, but this love for God and for the Master and for the Cause must be translated into love for one another. If this Cause cannot unite two individuals, how can we expect it to unite the world?"[6]

With great tenderness, she described the Guardian:

> . . . This youth under thirty, laboring day and night for us, sacrificing every human desire and tendency to further our efforts, deprived for our sake of all those natural satisfactions so significant to an alert and sensitive nature; with no more personal life than a graven image, no more thought of self than a breeze or a flower, just a hollow reed for the divine melody. Any one of us is ready to die for him, but can we conscientiously number ourselves among those who are willing to live for him?"[7]

Longing to fare forth on his behalf, Keith was yet reluctant to leave Haifa, until 'Abdu'l-Bahá's widow remarked, "You should be very happy, for you have the opportunity to go out into the world and give to others these glad-tidings."[8] Keith said, "Then a great peace poured into my soul." She felt, "Nothing can ever happen to me now that can thwart me, in imagination, from burying my face in the jasmine-strewn threshold at Bahjí and knowing as a definite part of my spiritual equipment, forever, that 'God will assist all those who arise to serve Him.'"[9]

****

Keith went home to New York City, where she lived at the Vassar Club, which she referred to in letters as her only address. She had a small income of her own and an extensive and lovingly preserved wardrobe by famous designers like Chanel and Lanvin. She once said that, if she had to visit Buckingham Palace at a moment's notice, she had the clothes. But her elegance and independence certainly weren't synonymous with ease and indolence. The evening of the day she arrived in New York, she took the leading role in a teaching campaign.

Orcella Rexford, a traveling Bahá'í teacher, had been giving a series of lectures in New York. At her last one, called "The Golden Age," she asked Keith to come up to the platform and told her audience of 500 that Keith would teach classes starting the next day, in the ballroom of the Majestic Hotel. Keith then addressed a series of meetings, and at the last one asked only people who considered themselves Bahá'ís to stay. The result was thirty-five new Bahá'ís—thirty-one women and four men. This was an unheard of mass enrollment for that time and place, and the Guardian sent thirty-five ringstones as gifts.

In January, 1927, the *Bahá'í News* reported that Keith's success had encouraged the New York Spiritual Assembly to lease a larger space for a Bahá'í Center and launch an ambitious teaching program. Keith was also Field Secretary for World Unity Conferences, and she participated in regular firesides in Harlem. She faithfully subscribed to Bahá'í periodicals, and sent money to Fanny Knobloch to ease her way as she pioneered in South Africa.

She wrote to Fanny: "Due to the offer of a winter trip I am about to set sail for the West Indies, especially Barbados where they have been asking for a Bahá'í teacher for some time . . . I am starting off on a new mission and implore your prayers. You are in mine I assure you everyday. I have put the beautiful blue flowers you sent in the case for my glasses and think of you warmly and lovingly every time I read anything."[10]

At the end of her life, Keith was also comforted by some blue flowers, forget-me-nots that she found growing at the site of one of the Bábí martyrdoms in Iran. But when she embarked for Barbados in February, 1929, she didn't know she would have no home-coming except for one more visit to Haifa, and no rest until her eyes closed for the last time, in Isfahán.

Of her visit to the conservative, provincial, small world of Barbados, Keith later said she felt, the whole time she was there, that all her effort would be in vain if she allowed herself to lose patience, even for a moment. She touched on the northern coast of South America and was the first Bahá'í to visit some Caribbean islands, but mostly she concentrated on Barbados. She had a long article on the Bahá'í Faith published in fifteen newspapers, covering twelve countries, in four languages; and she spoke in packed halls, schools, churches and theaters. Despite, or perhaps because of several public attacks on the Faith, her last lecture drew eight times as many people as the first.

Almost immediately after returning to the U.S., she toured seventeen cities in the Midwest, dashed back to New York to teach more classes, and by 1930 was in California, traveling continuously, also making forays into Arizona, the Northwest and Canada, enjoying the new low-priced air passenger service.

In Washington she addressed large meetings of the I.W.W. labor organization. The crowds, all-male, contained hecklers who tried to rout her, but in the end they applauded her enthusiastically. She gave forty-five public talks in Seattle alone.

She had so many interests and such a wide range of knowledge that she could deliver a convincing address on almost anything. In a lecture hall at the University of California at Los Angeles she spoke on "Drama Types in Cinema Production." Like a great actress on tour, she received rave reviews and left a definite gleam of excitement in her wake. While she visited a place, no one wanted her to leave; and after she left they wrote to her asking when she'd come back.

Nevertheless, she was lonely. She missed Jim. And the very qualities that entranced people, her beauty, brilliance, and forthrightness, also brought criticism. She always did and said what she believed to be right, even in the face of possible objections, and even though she feared rejection and was painfully sensitive to every ripple of thought around her and every mood. As she intently followed her path of service, it was as if she walked with bare, uncalloused feet over sharply stony ground. Yet she went bravely on. In May, 1931, the Bahá'ís of San Francisco reported that Keith had spoken 329 times in eleven months.

For a month, Keith stayed with the Holley family, and Marion Holley Hofman later remembered how she used to sit with Keith during the mornings while Keith rested. Marion was going through a period of doubt, and Keith wisely never mentioned the Bahá'í Faith to her. In the evenings, Marion attended Keith's lectures; she said they resolved her questions, after she thought about them for a year.

She enjoyed Keith's style, how she always wore splendid jewelry and would gradually remove bracelets while giving a talk and stack them on the table in front of her; and she never forgot the dashing silk ensemble Keith wore when she lectured several clergymen. At night, she'd help Keith raid the refrigerator, for Keith was always ravenously hungry after she spoke. Marzieh Gail later told Marion that she'd found a note in one of Keith's diaries recalling how she pulled Marion up by her bootstraps. Keith had prayed hard for her young admirer, while maintaining an appearance of chic detachment.

****

From the Pacific shore of the U.S., Keith sailed to Japan. Her twin duties continued to be to proclaim the Bahá'í teachings publically and to educate her fellow Bahá'ís about how to manage their administration. 'Abdu'l-Bahá had said that Iran was the cradle of the Bahá'í Faith and North America was the cradle of its administration. As the American Bahá'ís rose to meet that challenge, they were able to establish and incorporate their institutions according to civil law, without opposition. They could also champion their fellow Bahá'ís in other nations when pogroms erupted against them.

By 1931, the National Spiritual Assembly of the United States and Canada had succeeded in drawing up by-laws for Local and National Spiritual Assemblies and, when the Guardian asked them to send a representative abroad to teach the pattern of Bahá'í Administration, they chose Keith. So, she also represented the Guardian.

She arrived in Japan on June 25, 1931, and was greeted by Agnes Alexander. Activities began immediately. After her third day in Japan, Keith wrote in her diary that she'd been to "a fashionable Japanese tea given by Mrs. Kuroda, wife of the famous virtuoso who is a member of the Society of Connoisseurs and passes on the authenticity of art objects for the museums of the world."[11] She was charmed by the highly refined household and the elegant gathering, but particularly by Mr. Kuroda's eighty-five-year old mother, though she found it taxing to return the deep bows with which everyone, including the old woman, effortlessly greeted her. She was thrilled to note a connection with Jim: Mr. Kuroda, a philosopher as well as collector, had inspired the writer of an essay called "The Gods of Tea." Keith admired this essay and had given copies of it to many people; Jim had been the one who first showed it to her.

The next day, among her various meetings was one with a Japanese Christian minister. She was pleased when he remarked, "Between me and my next door neighbor there is a wall of formality but I seem to have been friends with Mrs. Keith for many years."[12] That evening, she spoke at the University of Commerce, and then the whirlwind of activity grew more intense. She spoke to numerous students at universities, two Buddhist gatherings (one in a temple), and women at tea parties at their houses or in Agnes' room. When an American lady bubbled to Agnes that she simply couldn't express how much she'd enjoyed entertaining Keith, who was so different from everyone else, like a being from another planet, Keith was amused and recorded the dubious compliment in her diary.

During her travels Keith developed a routine of taking a rest-day once a week. On her first day off in Japan, she got her hair done at the Imperial Hotel and then browsed through shops on the Ginza all afternoon, fascinated by oriental life. On another solitary jaunt, she visited the Great Buddha— "a bronze figure over forty feet high measuring some thirty-five feet between the spread of the knees, the eye a yard across. . . . Surely the serenity and peace of this figure are worthy to rank with the enkindled majesty of the maimed and broken face of the Sphinx which so impressed me with its heroic spiritual ardor. The hands of the Great Buddha are turned upward in the lap, the thumbs and forefingers forming two circles and touching. In Buddhistic lore this represents 'firm faith,' but it also signifies life as the moment between two eternities, each moment being the only contact between all that is past and all that is to come."[13] Keith knelt and said her Bahá'í prayers ardently before the Great Buddha.

Keith's rest-days refreshed her for her public talks and her troubleshooting tasks among the Bahá'ís but, nevertheless, she felt tired as the day approached for her departure to China and she took up the hideous chore of packing. The silks and laces of her stunning wardrobe were not wrinkle-free, and each garment had to be carefully pressed, folded, scented, wrapped in tissue paper and optimally placed in trunks and suitcases. No wonder Keith referred to her luggage as being mountainous. It usually took her two nights running to get it all in order. When she was finished, she wept as she bade farewell to Agnes and other friends. Then she received a cable from Shoghi Effendi, in answer to one Agnes had sent, consenting to an extension of her stay.

Agnes and Keith spent six more weeks together, and it wasn't always easy. Agnes was a day bird, and Keith was a night owl. Agnes insisted on fixing meals for Keith, though Keith loved dining out and all the little pleasures that went with it—"Remembering the old days in Paris, I stopped to have my portrait painted by a street artist for ten cents."[14] Agnes thought Keith's mental processes were too complicated, while Keith found Agnes' mind to be distressingly vague. When Keith and Agnes worked together on a speech for a radio broadcast, the result, in which Keith's ideas were watered down to meet the demands of the Japanese censor as well as by Agnes' desire for simplicity, didn't please Keith. She began to feel frustrated, and confused as to her role as a Bahá'í.

Still, her *joi de vivre* remained intact. One day, she discovered it was Agnes' birthday, an anniversary that Agnes was modestly concealing, and she immediately organized a party. She also particularly enjoyed a Bahá'í meeting in the home of a Miss Eto, where a traditional ceremony was underway to honor Miss Eto's deceased mother: "We left the car at the head of a street too narrow for any passage save by foot and walked between quiet houses, little shops, enclosed gardens, taking one mysterious turn after the other, through mud and water until we came to an open gate and lighted entrance. Entering a small lobby with a very high step we had to leave our galoshes and shoes and proceed in our stockings. The house became more and more spacious as we passed by several rooms, at last entering the main . . . gathering place, from which the sliding rice paper doors had been almost entirely removed. . . . As we entered it presented a beautiful sight: in the Tokonoma a rich table was spread, an alter, as it were, with every form of offering, for within this year Miss Eto's mother has passed away and this was her first official visit to her family since her departure."[15]

Keith loved the flowers, the candles, the lanterns, the piled dark green pumpkins, bananas, and other fruits, the copper gong people rang and the candles they lit as they bowed in prayer before the shrine. She spoke for half an hour, at Miss Eto's request, on immortality.

As her real leave-taking approached, she was thrilled to finally view Mount Fuji, which had been hidden for weeks by rain and mists. She was also charmed with a temple in Masuyama Park, where she admired the poems on hanging paper streamers, left from a feast in honor of the annual conjunction of two stars. Which stars? She said that nobody seemed to know. But as she sailed out from Yokahama for China, over the vast swell of the sea, she copied into her journal a two line poem by a five-year old girl: "Heavenly river! Heavenly moon!"[16]

* * * * * * * *

On August 12, 1931, Keith arrived in Shanghai and was greeted by the resident Bahá'ís bearing huge bouquets of flowers. She addressed the Bahá'ís, gave a newspaper interview, and found time to view traditional Chinese theater before reembarking. Then, on August 15—"All morning we sailed along the rugged coast of China and between islands, at last entering the narrow channel that separates Hong Kong . . . from the mainland. We came to dock at Kowloon on the China side with Ling (Fung Ling Liu) in the Chinese costume of peach-color waving welcome from the dock."[17]

Ling Liu and her brother Chan Liu had both become Bahá'ís through Martha Root while they studied at U.S. universities; they both now headed Chinese colleges. Keith and Ling took a train to Canton, where Chan met them. Because of Keith's mountain of luggage, crowned with the basket of flowers (now battered) from Shanghai, it wasn't easy to transport her to his house. As they alighted from a taxi, rain was pouring down, and it was only then that Keith learned there was no road. To reach Mr. Liu's house, her nine pieces of luggage would have to traverse two sets of railroad tracks, a golf course, a vacant lot, a deep ditch, and a fortification. Mr. Liu, a target for bandits in the rain and the moonless dark, stood guard over six suitcases and the wrecked flowers, while Keith and Ling, dragging three pieces of luggage, went to get the servant. They practically swam the train tracks, the golf course, the vacant lot, the ditch and the fortification, and also had to wander far afield due to some hazard that Keith did not care to describe in her journal. She felt awfully embarrassed. But at last everyone and everything was home, and tired goodnights were said.

The next day, Chan Liu, his young wife, Ling, and his elderly mother entertained Keith by taking her to visit the Flower Pagoda; among the eighteen Djinns represented as fine gilded figures, Keith bemusedly recognized Marco Polo. She found herself ravenous, and relished dinner in a restaurant by a lily pool. The food, including lotus root, cucumber and bamboo, was perfect for her, because she was seriously fond of vegetables.

She was charmed with the Liu family and with China, but she noted jarring preparations for civil war: "The other day our bus was stopped and we were searched for guns. There is a sham battle and drill under our windows every morning; propaganda banners line the streets and the papers are full of the reasons for revolt. 'All that China needs now is peace,' says Mr. Liu wistfully . . . 'Now instead of going to public improvement and necessary equipment, all is blown-up in gunpowder.'"[18] Keith also felt "an anti-foreign sentiment."[19]

She was appalled by the poverty and hardships under which most people labored, muscles straining as they lifted huge loads.

She admired their fortitude and strength, but commented, "This aching body of man cries for its new God-sent freedom."[20] She at first thought the Chinese demeanor meant the people were in despair, but after long conversations with Chan Liu she concluded, "What I took for despair is philosophic calm. China is the comprehender, not the comprehended. Civilization after civilization has gone against China and been absorbed: nothing could absorb China."[21] As for Chan Liu, he asked her shyly if Shoghi Effendi had ever spoken of China. "With what thrilling joy," Keith said, "I was able to tell him that on several occasions Shoghi Effendi had spoken . . . of the vast importance of work in China; of his pleasure at Martha's visit."[22]

Keith kept up a full schedule of speaking engagements and felt she learned as much as she taught, especially in the arena of patience. She resolved to be philosophical, like the Chinese, and daily that resolve was tested. One evening she was to broadcast from a radio station, then address the Esperantists. Her self-scheduled departure time for the station was delayed because Chan, her interpreter, only rose from his chair as she headed for the door, and then he had to go to his quarters and dress. She was further delayed when she and Chan saw Ling crossing the golf course as they left the house, and waited for her. They got to the entrance of the station five minutes after the time when Keith was to speak, and another five minutes passed as they crossed the courtyard and much of the large building. Keith thought by that time another speaker would have preempted her, however, she was served tea, and she found that she wasn't expected to deliver her address for another hour or so. "This is China," Keith told herself. "In the meantime, let the Esperantists tear their shirts."[23] But the Esperantists were doing no such thing. They were placidly awaiting her with a banquet. Both her talks were very well-received.

The next day, she left Canton—not very elegantly. She wrote, "We formed a quaint parade, the gardener, maid, Ling, Mr. and Mrs. Liu, a neighbor's servant and I carrying the mountainous luggage, minus the spectacular flower basket, back across the golf links to the taxi."[24] At the station, Keith gave Chan money for a second-class ticket to Kowloon, and he went to buy it, but he came back with a first class ticket, having paid the difference himself, and settled her in state, in a compartment all to herself. She was touched and gratified.

* * * * * * * *

From Kowloon, Keith embarked on a Japanese ship over tropical seas to begin what she called her Australian adventure. The ship went slowly, meandering through the Philippine islands, making frequent stops. On the sea around Mindanao, she wrote to her "home-folks" that the ocean was "a gorgeous lapis, the sky pale, the sunlight deceptively mellow, the clouds thick and very white, the breeze kind," while the screaming of the monkeys among the dense coconut thickets that crowded the water's edge made "a pandemonium of meaningless energy."[25]

Wherever Keith went, she enthusiastically bought souvenirs to send home; as the ship wended its way south, she wandered through island bazaars, buying hand-crafted batiks and noting, "No American can travel far enough to get away from Standard Oil and Camel cigarettes."[26] Everyone on the ship spoke only Japanese, so Keith had plenty of time to add to her diary impressions of Japan and China, and to feel homesick; she wrote a particularly touching description of a little boy she'd seen on a train in Japan who reminded her of her nephew, so that she could barely resist the urge to hug him, and she still missed him. She managed to complete an article on Bahá'í Administration for which she'd had many requests, and she said she felt extremely grateful for her trusty deck of cards with which she played Solitaire.

On September 3, after nearly five days of nonstop sailing, the ship reached Thursday Island, a bleak place, where she received Hyde Dunn's letter of welcome telling her to join him and Clara in Adelaide. So she sailed on, down the Queensland Coast, through the Coral Sea, observing that the south was the shady side of the hills, the north the sunny; just the opposite of how it was in the northern hemisphere. The white beaches reminded her of Barbados, and a gauzy morning mist reminded her of the air through which she'd seen Mount Fuji.

But she lamented, "I have begun to feel extremely old on this trip, and old is one thing I never feel: futile, depressed, inexpressibly weary from time to time, but never old."[27] She had no one to talk to, no one to dress up for, although she followed the tradition she and Jim had established of dressing for dinner. Fortunately, she soon had to be on her toes again among friends in Australia.

At Brisbane, in pouring rain, with tears in her eyes, she embraced the lone Bahá'í at the dock and after getting herself some Australian currency at Cook's travel bureau, she bought her welcomer a festive bouquet at a flower stand. She managed to visit two more Bahá'ís and two newspapers, then went on to Sydney, where she met nine Bahá'ís and addressed two meetings. That night she took ship for Melbourne, a rough and cold passage, and was met by three Bahá'ís who accompanied her to the train for Adelaide. She found the train very uncomfortable, so she was far from rested when she was met on the station platform by the Adelaide Bahá'ís, who piled her arms with flowers as newspaper photographers snapped her picture with Hyde and Clara Dunn.

Despite her fatigue and feeling of age, Keith couldn't have looked younger and more radiant; she never spared a smile. A week later she reported that the Adelaide papers had called her calm, beautiful, and well-dressed, and wryly remarked, "If you see it in the paper it must be so."[28]

Keith's clothes were much appreciated in the frontier atmosphere of Australia, where women longed for a little refinement and splendor. After one lecture she noted, "I wore my white satin ensemble to the satisfaction of all concerned."[29] Because of the hectic schedule of public meetings and Bahá'í gatherings, Keith's diary entries became less frequent, but, with every entry, she caught up on reporting what she'd worn for each event. She must have been trained as a young girl to do that, for a lady never bored society with repetitious costumes. "At the first lesson I wore my ruffled taffeta and blue velvet coat, at the second my red chiffon and purple velvet, at the third my Lanvin satin with the loops and white brocade, Monday night my rose silk and velvet with my white brocade coat and Wednesday my purple crêpe with the purple coat—also my court earrings. In the afternoon at Mrs. Murray's I wore my orchid silk suit and wisteria hat, in the evening my silver and black lace with the white coat."[30]

For her part, she appreciated the custom in South Australia of presenting flowers. "In this they actually rival Hawaii," she said. "Everywhere I speak I am presented with beautiful and tastefully arranged bouquets by perfect strangers. As the lectures become more popular the nosegays increase, so that at the last lecture I seemed literally lost in a wilderness of flowers. The platform is always a bower: knowing my love of calla lilies they are the predominating feature."[31] She also enjoyed the kindness of the Bahá'ís and their love of music; their custom was to have group singing, and to feature a soloist, at every gathering.

However, an old jaw injury started aching, and she felt irritable, and disgruntled with her herself and everyone else, for she had to minister to some tender egos while presenting the demanding standards of real Bahá'í belief. She said, "The people who are serving on the so-called Assembly are not Bahá'ís at all; they have all sorts of reservations and evasions, so that now the real Bahá'ís resolve themselves to about five."[32] Whatever her feelings about her work, she noted, "The precious Dunns seem pleased with the results."[33]

* * * * * * * *

Soon after that she went to bed for three days for a complete rest, and then was off for New Zealand, "in a little peach of a craft," she enthused, "that rides the ocean like a duck."[34] Her first week was crammed with engagements and the Bahá'ís were "inexpressibly sweet and kind."[35] November 20 found her in a hotel in the thermal region, Rotarua, armed with a letter of introduction from the Maori Society in Auckland to the Maori Chief Mita Taupokei.

The Maoris were the original inhabitants of New Zealand. There were 80,000 of them in 1840 but, just a few decades later, settlers had wrested their land from them and their numbers had sadly declined. The hot springs area, where most of them lived, was regarded as a wasteland; but they had managed to survive.

Within days of her arrival in Rotarua, Keith donned her "black lace" and went to the village of Wacka. "Chief Mita Taupokei arranged a meeting for me at the central meeting house," she said. "When I arrived a little boy was sent to ring a bell through the streets and in they pressed, grandmothers and infants-in-arms, Chief, guide, and college students, with great cordiality and curiosity. The old Chief (age 85) arose and spoke in his native tongue asking Rangi (Keith's guide, a young woman) to interpret. He welcomed me heartily . . . 'To what great matter are we about to listen? A subject of such urgent importance that this stranger traveling over many seas and abandoning her native land has come to share with the Maoris, obscure and forgotten, her valuable news. We await impatiently the unfolding of her purpose.'"[36]

Keith spoke, stressing unity in diversity, and the value of Maori culture, then many questions were asked and she spoke again at length. "In the meantime," she reported, "Rangi's aunt had interpreted to Chief Mita. His voice rang out, 'Congratulations, congratulations, you bring good news to my people . . . This is the first time any white woman has ever come to speak to us, and the first time we have ever heard this Message of kindness and peace.'"[37]

Keith bade the Chief good night and went with Rangi to her home, "a typical Maori house, beautifully carved but furnished in modern style."[38] A Maori man who was an Episcopal minister accompanied her to the hotel and several of the women went along for much of the distance.

Soon after that, Keith went to the Maori settlement at Oraki, near Auckland, for a *hangi,* a traditional Maori dinner. "When we arrived at the settlement," Keith wrote, "we were kept waiting a little till the elders of the tribe were lined up and ready to receive us."[39] Then, at Keith's request, each member of the welcoming party grasped her hand and pressed noses with her in the traditional Maori greeting of *te hangi*. They proceeded to the *hangi*, a small pit dug in the ground, with wood and stones piled neatly in it. The pit, with layers of pork, potatoes and fish laid over the hot stones, and baskets of shellfish on the sides, became an oven, and water was poured in to make steam. All was covered over with a large pan, some gunny sacks, and earth until no steam could escape.

The food would be ready in an hour, so Keith went to the meeting house, where quite a large audience awaited her. The village spokeswoman, Waiata (Song of My Grandfather), greeted her. Waiata wore two flax skirts, one around her waist and the other over her shoulder. Speaking in what Keith described as "musical liquid tones," she said, "The Maoris rejoice that one from afar has come to share with them her knowledge of the great world. But you have come to a deserted home, where only a tale and a recollection can speak to you: the Maoris have departed! You must seek for them beyond. The affairs of those far removed are echoed here amongst us, nor are we so remote that we can escape the cares that burden mankind. We would know if you bring comfort and peace."[40]

Keith tried to give comfort and peace, but with her usual frankness emphasized the need for unity and decried the fact that allegiance to various Christian sects had divided the Maoris. In thanking her, the Maoris sang a song that she described as "a plaintive minor."[41] Then all went outside and snapshots were taken. Keith had one taken of herself and Waiata, pressing noses. The women, in the meantime, had been weaving baskets of New Zealand flax, which was, Keith recorded, a kind of lily with healing properties in its roots. Each guest received a flax basket and it was loaded with the feast from the *hangi* oven. They took the high-piled, steaming baskets back to the hall, to a table spread with more food—"all kinds of fancy cake and *parkiah* (white man's food)," said Keith, "but the native cooking was delicious."[42] Pressing noses one last time, taking her leave, Keith wondered what would become of the Maoris, "a gifted, an ingenious and socially-minded people."[43]

She went on to a grueling schedule of further engagements, and remarked, several weeks later as her visit to New Zealand drew to a close, "Well, Mother's coming down the home stretch again under whip and spur."[44] She was dubious about her effectiveness but, before she left, felt "a sudden confirmation," so the tour "seemed to end in a blaze of light."[45] The New Zealand Bahá'ís were not at all dubious. In a letter to Hyde and Clara Dunn, Sarah Blundell's daughter, Ethel, wrote, among a forest of exclamation points, that she couldn't find words to adequately express the wonder and beauty of Keith's work.

Back in Sydney, Keith continued her wearying pace, and at last went by train to Newcastle, where she stayed overnight and delivered an address to a room full of hecklers, complete with "a very officious man with a dog." The dog came to the lecture platform and sniffed Keith before retiring to its master's side. The whole scene resembled something out of *The Adventures of Huckleberry Finn*. Keith spoke for fifty minutes, although she'd only slept a few hours the night before, and there were interruptions and exclamations and comings and goings all during her talk. At question time, people arose and made their own speeches, so that the chairman finally said, "Put your questions briefly," and, turning to Keith: "Make your answers brief." Keith asserted, "I shall answer to suit myself as adequately as possible to the question."[46] And she proceeded to do so, to the tune of guffaws and challenges from the crowd, for another hour and a half. Finally, several people, including the man with the dog, lyrically expressed admiration and gratitude.

On January 21, Keith was on her way to Singapore aboard the S.S. *New Zealand*. "We are just getting into open sea after a day at Brisbane," she wrote. And she added that she looked forward to "another glorious oriental adventure."[47]

* * * * * * * * *

The adventure came, but only after a tedious voyage during which the exhausted Keith fell into an abyss of self-doubt, convincing herself that none of the other passengers liked her, and lamenting, "I am bearing witness throughout the world to a light I cannot see."[48] She kept to herself, playing Solitaire in the smoking lounge. She felt "stranded without centre, enthusiasm, desire or energy . . . I read the prayers, try to meditate, wring my hands, cry aloud to heaven but 'the skies are brass.'" She'd read of "the mystical experience of the 'dark night of the soul,'" and commented, "What hell could be more tormenting?" However, her inner conviction in the existence of God's love remained, and she said, "Even as I have written the words that I am too small for God to know . . . there stirs somewhere in the depths of my withered soul a faint assurance and protest." At last she recollected the simple maxim of Ralph Waldo Emerson's that she'd pondered as a girl, "To be loved, one must be lovely." And she came to her "right senses." She "set to work . . . quite mechanically" to try to obey 'Abdu'l-Bahá and attract people to herself for the sake of her Faith. She said, "The atmosphere changed almost immediately." She "developed a spirit of real fellowship" with certain people who had been cold to her.[49]

By February 18, she was writing, "Oh! the joys of Mandalay. Its glories have never been told in song or story."[50] She spent three exceedingly full weeks in Burma before going on to India.

Her arrival in Calcutta on March 3 was less than thrilling. There was no one at the dock to meet her. "As usual," she said, "the only address I had was a post office box. After waiting on board I had a coolie take my luggage ashore and there sat waiting for another half-hour." The heat was broiling. At last, feeling "rather forlorn," she summoned a taxi and was about to get in when "a little man in a huge white turban" addressed her, in a quiet and dignified voice. "Are you Mrs. Ransom-Kehler?" He was Professor Pritam Singh, Secretary to the National Spiritual Assembly of India and Burma. Keith said he had a "beautiful gentle face."[51] It turned out there had been a mix-up about the time of the ship's docking. Now a young man, chairman of the Bahá'í Spiritual Assembly of Calcutta, rushed up, handed her a huge bouquet of roses, and welcomed her to India.

That night, she attended a banquet in her honor, given by the Bahá'ís of Calcutta. She wrote, "It was then that I came to understand something of their faithfulness and devotion in the midst of destitution and great misery." They were all of Moslem background, of humble status, and had suffered much persecution. A successful Iranian Bahá'í businessman had rented a hall where they could gather freely, and a Bahá'í from Bombay had bought land so they had a place to bury their dead. "There seemed to be such a great happiness among them," Keith commented, "in spite of such untoward conditions."[52]

After giving several public talks in Calcutta, Keith learned to ask (in commanding tones) from the podium, if all who felt bored would please leave. She found this caused amusement and immediately put her *en rapport* with her Indian audiences, which tended to be, she said, "kaleidescopic," with "groups wandering in and out of the balcony, the Bahá'ís themselves talking at the sides," and, outside the open doors and windows, "hawkers and paper boys crying lustily, motor horns honking, the ceaseless din of traffic."[53]

Keith's itinerary included Varanasi, Lucknow, Aligargh, Agra, New Delhi, Amristsar, Lahore, Karachi, Bombay, Hyderabad, and Pune. She was accompanied by Pritam Singh. In Varanasi, on the banks of the holy Ganges River, she was fascinated with the spectacle of diverse humanity swarming by the river and coursing through the streets. She marveled at a funeral procession—with all the mourners, and the corpse in its winding sheet, sprinkled with ceremonial pink stuff—closely followed by three wedding processions. She said, "We in our drab colorless lives cannot begin to grasp the spectacular motion and beauty of oriental pageantry. Large parties marching with bands and orchestras through the streets, draped in garlands with brilliant headresses, a riotous explosion of color. . . . The bride, smothered in flowers and finery, born on a golden litter, the groom surrounded by his friends riding with his best man on a richly caparisoned horse. . . . As night falls great acetelyne torches are borne aloft on the heads of servitors lighting the scene near and far." She rose at dawn to go with Professor Singh and view the Ganges from a hired boat, and was so fascinated that she went again the next morning, before train time, "for another view of the phantasmagoria."[54]

She was happy in India but, after awhile, her stomach wasn't, and by the time she reached Aligargh she could eat nothing but shredded wheat and boiled milk. She was to go on to Delhi, but public speaking was forbidden there because of anti-government demonstrations. Indeed, it was a time of great unrest; later, in Hyderabad, a young lady lamented to Keith, "You have come at such an unfortunate time. All the most interesting people are in jail."[55]

By the time she reached Agra, Keith felt deadly ill and could eat only rice water and papaya. Nevertheless, she went to see the Taj Mahal. She found it disappointing, passionless and glacial, but she admitted that her reaction might have been due to her own fatigue. She felt the Indian Bahá'ís were passive and suffered from lassitude; Shoghi Effendi had told her they needed stimulus, and she was giving it to them. She said, "I feel that I must exlaim, excoriate, protest furiously. Again and again I have felt as if I had a lash of fire and light in my hand."[56]

She continued, never resting, through waves of sickness, finding the Bahá'ís in various states of activity and inactivity. After she gave the Bahá'ís in Karachi a piece of her mind, she feared they might be offended but one remarked admiringly, "You certainly put your whole being into what you said. We could feel the force and power coming out of you like a whip." Keith concluded, "So that's where my energy goes."[57]

In Bombay, the Bahá'ís didn't respond as favorably; Keith said she was "about as popular as the income tax" until she allowed some Assembly members to read the Guardian's letters saying the Indian Bahá'ís needed to be reawakened. She suddenly became, she said, "a kind of Jeanne d'Arc sent to save Bombay."[58] She was being ironic, but the lash of fire and light was ever more firmly in her grasp and, no matter how it burned her, she would not complain, and she would not let it go.

In Pune, Keith signed autographs, as she had everywhere in India. She remarked that it seemed to her she'd written in 10,000 autograph albums, and she quipped, remarking about the fickleness of fame, that her fans would always have to explain to people who she was unless the Guardian decided at some point that she was an international figure. She didn't dream that he would do just that, nor could she know how soon and with what sorrow he would place her star forever in his firmament of heroes.

In Bombay, she was stunned when the Bahá'ís told her they'd decided to cable Shoghi Effendi and ask if she could extend her visit five more months. She'd been looking forward to her next stop—Haifa. She went through agony thinking she might have to miss her pilgrimage, because the Guardian always consented to extensions of her visits, but she managed to resign herself, "for after all I am trying to serve the Cause and not secure satisfaction."

Soon after that, she took a rest-day, her first in many weeks, went out to do some errands, and came back to find a man who was not among her favorite people waiting for her. She snapped at him, "I'm having a rest-day." He replied, "Yes, but there is a cable from Haifa." She opened it and read: "Feel urge request you proceed promptly Haifa preparatory extended summer tour Persia. Preferable revisit India autumn. Cherish high hopes your future services. Cable reply. Shoghi."

Keith was, she wrote, "thunderstruck." She said, "In the first place it had never seriously occurred to me that I was any part of the Guardian's plan. Of course he had written encouragingly and had directed me only I thought because he did not want to dampen my ardor and was encouraging my volunteer effort. But to find that I entered into his scheme of things was really astonishing. . . . My next surprise was Persia for he had already written that he was planning a European campaign for me; and my third surprise was his refusal of Bombay's request."[59]

She couldn't book her steamer passage because travel agencies weren't open that day, so, since it was still her rest-day, she went to the movies. Thus, in a seemingly very low key, began her life's crowning mission.

* * * * * * * *

In May, 1932, Keith arrived in Haifa to learn that her task in Iran was very important and most delicate: to petition Reza Sháh to remove the restrictions on bringing Bahá'í literature into the country.

Reza Sháh had had himself crowned king, the first of the Pahlavi Sháhs, in 1925. He came to power as Reza Khan the Cossack, after heading a *coup d'etat* in 1921. The Bahá'ís hoped his reign would be friendly to them, for his original impetus in government had been more secular than religious, but, in April of 1926, he joined forces with the mullás against the Bahá'ís in the Jahrum massacre, during which fourteen Bahá'ís were bludgeoned, stabbed and hacked to death in their houses and in the streets; after that, about twenty were killed in other towns.

However, by 1932, Reza Sháh found it expedient to be tolerant towards the Bahá'ís. Some of their progressive principles had become fashionable. Also, following Bahá'u'lláh's injunction, they were obedient to government, apolitical, so they were trustworthy, and the Sháh, while appeasing the mullás by forbidding the employment of Bahá'ís in the civil service, appointed them to government posts, particularly those involving finance. He allowed them certain civil rights, sent his offspring to Bahá'í schools, and relaxed an edict against the publication of Bahá'í literature. People who weren't Bahá'ís began to greet their Bahá'í friends with the Bahá'í salutation,

"Alláh'u'Abhá," as they openly discussed the Faith in public. The ban on importing literature was viewed as one of the last restrictions facing the Iranian Bahá'ís.

However, the tolerance was a façade, and it was already crumbling. The Sháh had begun as an anti-monarchist, but he was increasingly enamored of his own kingship, and it annoyed him that the Bahá'ís, following Bahá'u'lláh's law instead of his, wouldn't kiss his hand as court protocol required. He also had a constant fear of being overthrown, and if he became too friendly with Bahá'ís the mullás would incite the populace against him. So, things were not as hopeful as they seemed.

The Guardian felt that Keith could meet the challenge, for she was, as he told Marzieh Gail, "very frank, very sensitive, and very brave."[60] He gave her books on Islam, and she stayed up all night studying them. His great aunt, Bahíyyih Khánum, very old and frail, showered Keith with love, so that she felt "dissolved by her sweetness," and said, "To come into her presence was to hush and exalt the soul."

Bahíyyih Khánum would cup Keith's chin in her hand, or soothingly stroke Keith's hand, and chant a prayer or poem. Once, when Keith asked an attendant, "Does she remember me? Does she know who I am?" Bahíyyih Khánum herself replied with a title that meant "Teacher. " She continually referred to Keith by that name. When departure time came, Bahíyyih Khánum, despite Keith's protestations, insisted on being lifted to her feet by her niece to enfold Keith in her arms, and told her: "When you are come to Persia, I want you to give my love to every Bahá'í in all that land, to the men the same as the women. And when you reach the holy city of Teheran enter it in my name, and teach there in my name." Keith later wrote, "How blind I was not to realize that she was sending her last message to Persia."[61]

The Guardian blessed Keith with a smiling farewell, and remarked that she should be grateful to have such an opportunity for service. His smile and his simple statement sank deeply into her heart.

* * * * * * * * *

Keith entered Iran from the western frontier and visited the Bahá'ís in Kirmánsháh, Hamadán, Tabríz, Qazvín, and other spots before going to Ṭihrán. She was welcomed with tremendous love and enthusiasm. In the village of Sísán, where there were 1,000 Bahá'ís with their own Bahá'í Center and schools, the Bahá'ís built a road five miles long for her car to pass over, and they donned holiday garb to greet her.

She had her first meeting with the Ṭihrán Bahá'ís, 150 of them, on June 29, 1932, in a Bahá'í garden twenty-five miles from the city. Her second reception was that afternoon, outside the city gates, at a Bahá'í's home. The house was packed with people and Keith, ill and tired, spoke briefly; the Bahá'ís felt the power of her spirit, they reported, even before her words were translated. The next day, there was another reception, and Keith met with the Ṭihrán Assembly.

Because she wasn't feeling well, she moved from the Grand Hotel to the home of Raḥmatu'lláh and Najmíyyih 'Alá'í, for Najmíyyih was a nurse. At the Guardian's request, the couple accompanied Keith throughout her stay in Iran. She loved them and affectionately called them Raḥmat and Najji.

While lying on her bed one morning in their home, she suddenly burst into tears and wept for half an hour. "It seemed so unreasonable," she said, "for I had not any idea what I was weeping about." The next day, a telegram arrived announcing the death of Bahíyyih Khánum, and Keith realized the flood of tears had broken at the hour of her passing. "How greatly I prize the ringstone, a coin from the pocket of

Bahá'u'lláh, some rock candy and a broken phial [not broken when she presented it] of attar of roses that she had given me," said Keith. And she prayed Bahíyyih Khánum to intercede before God, "that the priceless gift of love which you so consistently taught us may descend into my cold and untenanted heart."[62]

Keith's mission in Iran unfolded largely under the sheltering wing of a nine-month mourning period for Bahíyyih Khánum, with nine consecutive days of memorial services in Teheran, ten memorial suppers, and services in her honor every nineteen days. Keith spoke at many of these gatherings and also gave a lot of public talks with emphasis on the equality of men and women. She developed a great love for the Iranian Bahá'ís, so that she doted on their faces, saying they were among the loveliest on earth.

She was thrilled to visit Mázindarán, province of nightingales, wild mountains, and meadows where Bahá'u'lláh had roamed as a child. It fulfilled her sense of destiny, for she had seen it before in dreams and reveries. She wrote to a friend, "A profound inner delight and agitation coupled with scene after scene of my well-remembered fantasy assured me that this was the place of my visions."[63]

She visited Bárfurúsh, where one of the greatest disciples of the Báb, Quddús, had been killed, and went to the place of his martyrdom in the village square. She journeyed to nearby villages on horseback, Raḥmat 'Alá'í walking beside her, balancing her all the way with his hand. After the aridity of Teheran, she was thrilled by the green countryside, and she said that the ferns, grasses, shrubs and trees brought back the landscape of her childhood and, with it, a glad nostalgia.

For the first time in years, she heard the nightingale sing, and the remembered notes sweetly stirred her heart whenever she read the Tablet of Aḥmad—"Lo! The Nightingale of Paradise singeth upon the twigs of the Tree of Eternity."[64] Yet, she said, the welcoming chorus of men's voices singing as she neared a village was sweeter to her than the nightingale's song. The Bahá'ís tossed flowers in her path; at the turn of the road, school boys were singing, and then a chorus of school girls which particularly delighted Keith. Women carrying brass trays loaded with fruit, perfume, flowers and incense sprinkled Keith with rose-water and flung fragrant spices before her. Of all this beauty, she found the welcoming faces to be the most beautiful.

In November, Keith made a special pilgrimage to Fort Tabarsí. At that place, about eighty-five years before, a hard-pressed group of 313 Bábís led by Mullá Husayn, who raised the black standard prophesied by Muhammed, took refuge from the king's army and, starving and in rags, resisted the soldiers. When the defenders of Fort Tabarsí finally fell, it was not to force of arms and not to famine, but to trickery.

Keith, with Rahmat 'Alá'í beside her, again journeyed by horseback. She jogged over winding, rough roads for six long miles which included fording a river. On the steep riverbank Keith learned, "It was in this very spot that . . . Mullá Husayn implored those who were unprepared for the unprecedented difficulties that lay before them to turn back. Those who finally crossed with him remained to the end."[65]

Mullá Husayn died at Fort Tabarsí and is buried there. Keith's meditations at the site were profound. She recalled how he had been the first seeker to find the Báb, yet had two times watched the Báb choose another disciple, Quddús, over him for enviable missions; and how he had, as he lay dying, handed the command of the group at the fort over to Quddús. She recollected the description she'd read of Mullá Husayn standing on a threshold, with his arms folded across his breast "like a servant to the man (Quddús) who had been twice preferred before him," and how, with his last breath, he "rose from the dead, as it were," to insure that Quddús, taking over his leadership, would receive all due attention and respect.

She said, "No one could kneel upon the Shrine of . . . Mullá Ḥusayn and arise the same person. The world is still resounding with his challenge. . . . 'Are there any who will assist me?' . . . As I knelt there, something bouyant and eager in me seemed to answer 'Here' to his muster-call, while ringing down in a forgotten vista in my heart I heard the marching order, 'Mount your steeds, Oh heroes of God!'"[66]

But all was not ineffable ecstasy. Keith, as Marzieh Gail observed, upheld her standards of dress—curling her hair prettily and wearing, when she addressed the Women's Progress Committee, a pink dress with a long necklace of pink and lavender beads—yet she felt somehow broken, and told Marzieh, "In future when I'm in my resting grave and people ask what I was like, it is your mission to tell them how I suffered in Persia, Bahá'u'lláh's country . . . There were battles every step of the way."[67]

The Ṭihrán of Keith's day was a city in the throes of modernization, with torn up streets filled with trucks and debris, noise and disorder everywhere, the people hopeful of a new capital rising out of the old. Keith met quite a few people who weren't Bahá'ís and who professed indifference to religious preference; the daughter of a diplomat told Keith that her religious adherence was to *Le Lion et le Soleil.** The spirit of new pride in Iran as a progressive nation carried over into Keith's first interview with a Minister of the Crown.

She went to see him in August, right after her arrival in Ṭihrán, and he told her the book ban would be lifted immedi-

---

*"The Lion and the Sun," ancient symbol of Persia.

ately. She happily reported this home. But by January, 1933, it was clear to Keith that his promise wouldn't be fulfilled. Bahá'í books sent to her from Beirut had arrived in Iran, customs officials had inspected them, and Keith had been told she couldn't receive them. She wrote to the Minister but never received an answer. He had disappeared. Marzieh Gail later wrote that he'd probably been taken to a certain walled building outside the city where people suspected of disloyalty to the regime were summarily relieved of the burdens of existence via a so-called remedial shot, administered by a doctor.

Meanwhile, the Crown issued edicts against the Bahá'ís which removed the recently granted civil rights, and the press virulently attacked the Faith. Thus, under Reza S͟háh Pahlavi, conditions became worse than ever for the Bahá'ís because occasional pogroms were augmented by State-supported, consistent discrimination.

Keith, as this tragic wave began to swell, rise and rush towards the Iranian Bahá'ís, fought against her own growing physical weakness and raised her "lash of fire and light" to defend them. "How strange the ways of God," she said, "that I, a poor, feeble, old woman from the distant West, should be pleading for liberty and justice in the land of Bahá'u'lláh, who has given to the world its most advanced standards of humanitarianism and enlightenment."[68]

She sought audiences with government officials. Not all of them would consent to meet with her but, with those who did, she was as Shoghi Effendi described her, frank, sensitive, and brave. They were far from frank, but their manners were perfect, suave, and charming; no emotionalism marred their constantly shifting presentation of the reasons, apparently improvised on the spot, why Bahá'í literature could not be imported into Iran.

Besides meeting them personally, Keith wrote them eloquent letters, rational, but deeply felt. She also wrote to the Sháh more than once.

In July, 1933, she addressed him, "To my horror and grief I have just heard of the burning, on the part of Your Majesty's officials in Kirmánsháh, of the sacred photographs of 'Abdu'l-Bahá. I am fully convinced that such a sacrilege has been committed without the knowledge of Your Majesty . . . The Bahá'ís of the world as a body . . . are willing to endure any degree of injustice and persecution themselves, but when it comes to regarding with other than outraged sentiment a gratuitous indignity offered to that illustrious example of human perfection, 'Abdu'l-Bahá, the Bahá'ís of the world arise in the full strength of their solidarity to utter a vehement protest."[69]

Marzieh Gail has pointed out the little known fact that the Sháh was illiterate, and it is likely that Keith's passionate appeals never reached him at all. The only reply she received to any of her letters, and to the petitions from the North American National Spiritual Assembly that she forwarded to authorities, came from the Minister of Education, and it offered no hope of lifting the literature ban. Finally, the Guardian instructed Keith to depart Ṭihrán at the beginning of autumn, travel through Iran and leave the country from Búshihr around December 21.

The night before she left Ṭihrán, the Bahá'ís gave a large meeting in the Bahá'í Center, and on Friday, September 22, numerous friends escorted her to a Bahá'í village on the road to Qum, where refreshments were served, many pictures taken, and last farewells spoken. In Qum, she met with the Bahá'ís and also with local government officials. (She did that in as many towns as she could, clearly setting forth Bahá'í precepts.) So she wended her way southwards, addressing Bahá'ís— who gave her festive banquets— inquirers, and authorities, till she reached Iṣfahán on October 6. The next day, she visited Bahá'í sacred spots, including the tombs of two brothers called by Bahá'u'lláh the King of Martyrs and the Beloved of Martyrs.

Keith had made pilgrimages: to Fort Ṭabarsí; to Zanján, where she astonished passersby when, on her knees in the ruins of the house of a hero named Hujjat, she prayed and wept; to the house of Quddús in Bárfurúsh, and to the village square where he'd been killed and mobs had mutilated his body. The place where he fell was an enclosed garden, and there Keith knelt and picked one of the blue forget-me-nots that starred the grass. Like those blue flowers, sent her so long ago from South Africa by Fanny Knobloch.

After addressing the Local Spiritual Assembly of Isfáhán and its committees in the Bahá'í Center on October 7, she spent the 8th addressing an afternoon women's meeting and an evening men's meeting. On the 9th she called on the governor in his home, met with the heads of the telegraph department and the police, and, in the evening, received and addressed a group of Bahá'ís who had traveled from villages around Isfáhán to meet her. After they left, she went to bed with chills and high fever. The next day, she could not get up.

Rahmat and Najji Ala'i did not leave her side. On October 11, the illness was worse. A Bahá'í doctor diagnosed it as measles. It became more severe, and a cable was sent, at Keith's request, to the Guardian, asking for prayers. Then the doctor made another diagnosis: smallpox. After an anxious week and a half, Keith seemed about to recover. On Monday, October 22, she was able to dictate a cable to Shoghi Effendi saying that his prayers were overcoming all difficulties.

In her cable she stated her plans to make her return visit to India, and travel through Europe, as the Guardian wished.

But, an hour or so after dictating the cable, she suddenly became almost entirely unable to speak. The doctor said a nerve center was paralyzed. For four hours, she could still say "Yá-Bahá'u'l-Abhá," and "Alláh'u'Abhá," and she motioned those at her bedside to pray. Bahá'í doctors labored around the clock to save her; but she died at 4:10 P.M., Tuesday, October 23, 1933.

Najji 'Alá'í, with another Bahá'í woman, washed the body and placed it in a casket. A cortege of 600 Bahá'ís followed the flower-laden hearse down one of Iṣfahán's main avenues to the cemetery where the King of Martyrs and the Beloved of Martyrs were buried, and there, not far from their tombs, Keith was laid to rest.

"The intrepid defender and illustrious herald of God's Cause," the Guardian cabled Iran, "has risen triumphant from the depths of darkness to her heavenly home; her magnificent deeds were hidden from the negligent in that land; the Supreme Concourse knew her worth; she possesses the rank of martyrdom and is one of the Hands of the Cause." He called upon the entire Local Spiritual Assembly of Ṭihrán, along with delegates from other cities, to go on pilgrimage in his stead to "her venerated grave."[70]

He cabled America that "Keith's precious life" had been "offered up in sacrifice . . . On Persian soil, for Persia's sake, she encountered, challenged and fought the forces of darkness with high distinction, indomitable will, unswerving, exemplary loyalty." He said she was a "valiant emancipator" of "her helpless Persian brethren," and she was the "first and distinguished" American Bahá'í martyr; her rank among the Hands of the Cause of God was, he said, "eminent." He lamented his "earthly separation from an invaluable collaborator, an unfailing counselor, an esteemed and faithful friend."[71]

In accordance with the wishes of the Guardian, on November 23, 1933, the Bahá'ís made a pilgrimage to her grave. There is a photo of the cemetery as it was then, a desolate spot—dusty, rocky ground with flat stones lying over the graves, a line of jagged mountains beyond. Keith's grave is covered with desert flowers, brought by her mourners. One of the Bahá'ís sprinkled the grave with rosewater from the house of the Báb in <u>Sh</u>íráz. They placed a large photograph of her on the grave and wreathed it in flowers.

The photograph had been made in Ṭihrán. Keith, daintily and beautifully dressed in full ensemble with a little hat, faced the camera with elegant and erect posture, and a bright, if somewhat tremulous, smile. A friend later wrote that, just before the photo was taken, Keith had been weeping over the failure of her mission; she held back the tears for the photographer.

In one of her final diary entries, Keith wrote,

I have fallen, though I never faltered. Months of effort with nothing accomplished is the record that confronts me. If anyone in future should be interested in this thwarted adventure of mine, he alone can say whether near or far from the seemingly impregnable heights of complaisance and indifference, my tired old body fell. The smoke and din of battle are to-day too dense for me to ascertain whether I moved forward or was slain in my tracks.

Nothing in the world is meaningless, suffering least of all. Sacrifice with its attendant agony is a germ, an organism. Man cannot blight its fruition as he can the seeds of earth. Once sown it blooms, I think forever, in the sweet fields of eternity. Mine will be a very modest flower, perhaps like the single, tiny forget-me-not, watered by the blood of Quddús, that I plucked in . . . Bárfurú<u>sh</u>; should it ever catch the eye, may one who seems to be struggling in vain garner it in the name of Shoghi Effendi and cherish it for his dear remembrance."[72]

It was so hard to say goodbye to Keith that, a year after her death, the Guardian requested the Bahá'ís to make another pilgrimage to her grave, to lay flowers on it which he had sent.

And it is still hard to say goodbye to her. It would be good to travel with her forever, warmed by her smile, amused by her wit, entertained and inspired by her eloquence, and strengthened and defended by her lash of fire and light. But it is comforting to picture her traveling in her full ensemble— hat, dainty shoes, string of pink and lavender beads, and bright smile—traveling, in ecstasy at the beauty, across the astonishing light fields of heaven.

Chapter 6

Susan Moody

Dr. Susan I. Moody, with Bahá'í women and children in Iran

Susan Moody spent only three days with 'Abdu'l-Bahá in 'Akká in October, 1909, but she always felt that those three days comprised her entire life: everything led to them and everything afterwards was nourished by them.

The circumstances of her pilgrimage were unique. She was a doctor and 'Abdu'l-Bahá had asked her to settle in Iran and help the women there, so she came to Him en route to her new home.

'Abdu'l-Bahá, whenever he could, sent western Bahá'ís into Iran. In 1875, He'd written a treatise called *The Secret of Divine Civilization,* widely disseminated in Iran, which was a plea to the land of *Le lion et le soleil* to free itself from xenophobia and allow the sort of education, technology, and hygiene that would lead to development of resources and equitable distribution of wealth. He also summoned Iran to look further than mere self-advancement and establish a place in the world community by advocating peace.

His feelings about the country were deep: a few years after Susan Moody met Him, He was in America speaking at a conference on arbitration for peace at Mohonk Mountain House in New York and, despite the fact that He'd been an exile from Iran since the age of nine and had suffered intensely due to Iranian opposition to His Faith, when He signed the Mohonk guest book He gave His address as Persia.

However, He had no false hopes as to the response to His treatise, and He knew its precepts could best be demonstrated by human example. In 1908, when a group of American Bahá'ís visited Iran, doctors told them that Moslem women, since they wouldn't unveil themselves before men, desperately needed female physicians. Those Bahá'ís suggested to 'Abdu'l-Bahá that Susan Moody go and work in Iran, and He immediately wrote to her.

Susan had not imagined such a destiny, but she wasn't surprised. Several years before, in private prayer, she'd vowed, "I hereby devote, consecrate and sacrifice all that I am, and all that I have and all that I hope to be and to have, to Thee, O Divine Father, to be used in accordance with Thy Purpose."[1] At that time, she felt inspired to take up medicine. When 'Abdu'l-Bahá's letter came, her family and friends raised loud objections: why should she, a woman who was almost sixty years old, cast aside a medical practice in the United States to go to a country where her life would be endangered by strange diseases and fanatical opposition?

But Susan had no such doubts. She said she now knew why she had "felt the urge so strongly to study medicine," and, furthermore, she wrote, "My vow had been recorded and 'Abdu'l-Bahá had summoned me. I was ready."[2]

In describing her visit to Him, Susan wrote to her friend Eva Russell of standing in a window overlooking the courtyard of His house, after breakfast on October 12: "There are many sparrows twittering. The blue, blue sea is covered with ripples. There is a low fringe of light clouds. Mt. Carmel's point is in the distance. A row of olive trees are laden with fruit, with very few leaves on the side toward the house. In the court on the other side are two tall date palms, with three large bunches each, which have been sewed up in burlap to protect them from the weather until fully ripe. . . . A climbing vine with many purple blossoms, three-petaled, covers the side of a long flight of stone steps. . . . And another shrub with a dozen or more large white lily-shaped blossoms, each at least six inches across. . . ."

She watched 'Abdu'l-Bahá "walking up and down a shady walk—His favorite one in the garden. . . . A beggar had wandered into the courtyard. 'Abdu'l-Bahá went toward him and put His arms across the trunk of a Soria tree (. . . a shrub with feathery foliage and pinky plumes). Leaning His head on His arm. . . . He talked, making a beautiful picture. He stood there for some minutes, then moved up into the court, calling aloud to someone."[3]

As 'Abdu'l-Bahá gathered some of the oriental pilgrims and went with them into a little house in the garden, Susan enjoyed observing "the love and reverence of the Eastern believers shown in His presence."[4] She didn't know that, with tender concern, 'Abdu'l-Bahá spoke to those men of her own mission in Iran, asking, "Do you think she can stand the privations there?"[5]

Later that morning, He met with her and said she would, at first, "find things difficult—the conveniences are not the same. Many of the people are poor and sleep on the floor, as they have no beds." He instructed her, "You must not look at their circumstances, but at their hearts. They will love you very much and I want you to be happy there. You must have patience and try very hard to be faithful; lose sight of yourself entirely; work only for the love of God and you will succeed."[6] Susan asked Him to pray that she "might be separated from the self" so she could "fulfill His command."[7] He promised, "I will often pray for you—you are never separated from Me."[8]

They discussed how she should set up her home and practice in Ṭihrán. Then she gave Him messages of love from America and He told her, "You are a worthy messenger."[9] When He stood to close the interview, He put His hands on her shoulders and drew her to His side.

On October 13, Susan rose at dawn and looked out at the sea until it was time to join 'Abdu'l-Bahá for morning prayers, when, as she took her place on the divan, she felt an "instant consciousness" of "being absolutely nothing, weak, ashamed" of her former self. While the first prayer was chanted, she felt herself "melt and melt" until tears poured down her cheeks. She said, "I realized my unworthiness and His great love. When I thought that this was my last day, I had to exert myself to restrain my longing to kneel there at His feet. Gradually my horizon cleared and, through the chanting, I became tranquil again."[10]

She even managed to chant a prayer in Farsi, and felt happy when 'Abdu'l-Bahá congratulated her with a smile and "Very good."[11] She knew He was ending her pilgrimage quickly only so that she could avoid crossing the Black Sea when it was very cold and stormy. Her mission in Iran was dear to His heart, and He wanted Her journey to proceed as comfortably—and as quickly—as possible.

Before the final leave-taking, He reiterated that she must have "Patience, patience, and more patience," and said that, living or dead, He would always be with her.[12] From Istanbul, nearing Iran, Susan wrote to Eva Russell, "While I write I hear His voice. There is none other like it. Its ring is individual."[13]

And it seems the bell of His voice had rung in her life even before she became aware of it, guiding her surely towards her destiny.

* * * * * * * *

Susan Isabel Moody was born November 20, 1851, in Amsterdam, New York, to Protestant parents, members of the Scotch Covenanter sect. Amsterdam was very conservative, and Susan's family was considered one of the best in town, so her religious and secular education went forward accordingly.

After graduating Amsterdam Academy, she taught school until, in a daring departure, she entered the Women's Medical College in New York City.

Nursing had only recently attained respectability as a female domain, and it was very rare for women to become doctors. Unfortunately, the dissecting room was too much for Susan's nerves, and she left medical school. After her parents died in the 1890s, she moved to Chicago, lived with her brother, and studied voice. At that time she met some Bahá'ís. But she moved away to concentrate on art. She eventually apprenticed in New York with William Merritt Chase, a famous painter of still lifes and portraits, and took classes in Paris.

It wasn't until 1903, in New York, that Susan became a Bahá'í after studying with Isabella D. Brittingham, who was such a successful teacher that 'Abdu'l-Bahá called her "our Bahá'í-maker."[14] And then, when Susan was fifty-two she braved the dissecting room and reentered medical school, saw it through to graduation, and went to work as a doctor.

She also became an eloquent teacher of the Bahá'í Faith. She began the first Bahá'í children's classes in Chicago, for she was always fond of children and they reciprocated the affection, and she was also one of the group of women who walked the suburban terrain north of Chicago in search of a site for the Bahá'í House of Worship.

Although outwardly, the gentle, white-haired Dr. Moody might have seemed unsuited to the task 'Abdu'l-Bahá assigned her in Iran, she was actually very apt. Her friend Miriam Haney said that she was uncompromisingly selfless, detached, and humble, with a keen sense of justice and a rare capacity to equably and fairly approach situations. Susan also had the wonderful and comfortable gift of instantly adopting new acquaintances as old friends, indeed, as family. She was definitely a person who could successfully manage what is now called a social and economic development project.

A photograph taken during her journey from Haifa to Iran shows her standing in the midst of numerous Bahá'í men in the port town of Baku, Azerbaijan, in November, 1909; she was round-faced, serious, wearing a flower-bedecked hat. From Baku she crossed the Caspian Sea to Bandar-e Anzalí, where she entered Iran. She journeyed by horse and carriage on the post road that ran from Rasht through the Elburz Mountains to Ṭihrán.

Although by today's standards the trip looks short on a map, it was an epic journey, involving fast galloping through high-altitude passes with quick stops to change horses, and many joyous Bahá'í gatherings. Ten of the stops for carriages, camel and donkey caravans were run by Bahá'ís and, in fact, Susan discovered as she traveled that the manager of the post road, also a Bahá'í, had paid her expenses.

Susan described the road from Rasht going towards the mountains: "The roadsides and fields were just beds of pale violet crocuses. There were . . . mulberry forests, then rice fields and hundreds of donkey caravans going and coming. It took a continuous yell from our driver to get them out of the middle of the road, and as there are deep ditches on either side, their drivers were running and screeching, yanking and pulling to keep the poor little things from tumbling into the ditch. One did slide over the bank with his load, but was hauled back by the collar before he went to the bottom. About 11 o'clock we were nearing the mountains. The air was dry and bracing and almost intoxicating. We followed the course of a large river. The road was often at the edge of a precipice. The mountains came into view, peak after peak, as we rose, and the king of them all was our companion all day."[15]

When Susan's party, which included a young boy 'Abdu'l-Bahá sent home to Iran with her, stopped for almost an hour at a station house to have tea with the Bahá'í keeper, he played some airs on his *tar*, a stringed instrument which Susan thought "talked like a banjo."[16] She was able to minister to the very ill wife of the stationmaster for the next post, and, as twilight fell, she said good-bye to the king of the mountains, admiring it "swathed in the sunset glow which had left the lower peaks and valleys blue-gray and cool."[17] Camel caravans were at rest at caravansaries full of barefoot people in colorful ragged garb sitting on their haunches, drinking tea and gossiping, and in sheltered places in the rocky terrain Susan saw forests of ancient wild olive trees. Under a half-moon that rode high in the sky, they reached their lodging place.

The journey went on for nearly a week, the horses pulling the carriage up to the snow line and heights that made the little boy accompanying Susan dizzy and turned his lips and nails blue, then plunging it down again to cross plateaus and plains. Susan cared for the child and anyone else in need, maintained her steady good humor and health, and observed the land. Few places were unpopulated, no matter how remote; flat areas were cultivated with oxen pulling primitive plows, and there were flocks of sheep and goats even when they could graze on nothing but furze. Susan, aware of untapped mineral wealth and other resources, said she "became more and more conscious of the great needs of Persia, to bring to her aid the right kind of help, to develop her riches."[18] Looking up at the British built Iran-India telegraph line, she "often thought of the world flashing by us, while below were the most primitive conditions."[19] Like other egalitarian westerners, she had great hopes for Iran: the 1905–1909 revolution was drawing to a close and a parliament had been elected.

However, the Bahá'í poet, translator and diplomat, Ali Kuli Khan, who was in government service in Iran in 1906, observed that people's motives were so unclear, it was impossible to distinguish between wolves and shepherds. British and Russians jockeyed for power, revolution and anarchy constantly threatened, and the Bahá'ís were always at risk. On October 18, 1909, just after Susan left Haifa, five Bahá'í men in the province of Khúrasán were killed and four Bahá'í women were assaulted and wounded.

Nevertheless, intrepid as always, the Bahá'ís turned out in force to meet Susan, and she was overwhelmed by their love and kindness. In Qazvín, she also became aware of the great need for her help: women flocked to her for treatment. "They had never had a doctor," she wrote to her friend Eva, "would rather die than show their faces to a man, and now—well, all the breakfast I got was a snatch now and then. The next day I worked from 6 A.M. to 11:15 P.M. What a clinic! Neglected cases become chronic. Hearts all out of whack on account of altitude, etc., etc. Many women doctors are needed in Persia."[20]

Susan admired the women, especially when they came to her for a special women's meeting, all wearing "white veils back from their faces. The costumes showed many bits of pretty color, velvet, gold lace, etc."[21] When they asked Susan to pray, she sang a hymn, and when they asked if she knew a prayer in Farsi, she chanted "Alláh'u'Abhá." Then they looked at her Bahá'í photo album, which was to be her "open sesame" with all groups. The women poured over the faces of their fellow Bahá'ís in America like lovers, commenting on this one's gentleness, that one's intellectual qualities. As the sun set, the women kissed Susan good-bye, and, she said, "*flitted* away. They don't seem to walk."[22]

From Qazvín it took two days, crossing barren desert, to reach Teheran; the only great sight was towering, snow-capped Damavand, over 18,000 feet high. By the time she reached the Hotel de France, Susan's green traveling dress was, she said, reduced to rags, but she was swamped by callers, and barely had time to change into a blue suit before going to a meeting in her honor. There, she was astonished at being greeted by Ḥájí Akhund: he was a hero whose face she'd seen in a photograph taken when he was a prisoner, in chains. Large, fearless, prepossessing, he was one of the Hands of the Cause of God appointed by Bahá'u'lláh. Then she met another man whom she had seen enchained in the photograph, Ḥájí Amín: almost eighty years old, a homeless wanderer, trustee of the Bahá'í Funds, he traveled back and forth from Iran to the Holy Land with the appearance of utmost poverty, bearing thousands of Persian *tumáns,* or gold pieces. Susan said his face was "brim full of sincerity and kindness."[23] She also met Ibn-i-Abhar, also a Hand of the Cause appointed by Bahá'u'lláh, who had accompanied Lua Getsinger's protégé, Harlan Ober, to India a few years before. With these men sat Vali'u'lláh and Azizu'lláh Varqá, the two surviving sons of the martyred poet whose story would so affect Martha Root when she heard it in 1912 from 'Abdu'l-Bahá in a townhouse in New York City.

It was November 25, so Susan regarded the banquet at that meeting as her Thanksgiving feast. She reported home that she partook of it "in Persian style, sitting on the floor. There were many rich dishes and most delicious melons. They seem to keep like squash or pumpkin does in America—dozens of them are stuck up on the rafters of the shed. . . ." She added that her hotel bed "felt good that night when we got back after running a gauntlet of barking dogs and policemen. One is required to carry a pass card after ten o-clock and show it to every policeman. As we leave one he whistles shrilly to the next and this sends every dog in the street and on the roofs, chained and unchained, into a fury."[24]

Susan had a steady stream of visitors at the hotel, but women were forbidden by custom from coming out, so she went to them. One who made a great impression was named Táhirih, after the bold Bábí scholar, poet, teacher and martyr, and she was, like her namesake, an audacious soul. She wrote for newspapers, urging Persian women to educate themselves and establish schools. But she was frustrated in her dreams of traveling and teaching, and she saw in Susan a hope and a friend. "She gave me such a warm greeting," Susan wrote. "I feel her arms around me yet."[25] At one women's meeting, Susan made everyone happy by refusing the table and chair which had been placed for her and sitting on the floor beside Táhirih to partake of the banquet. She loved the food, and said, "I must confess that it was more of an effort to get up after eating than it was to get down before."[26]

Susan made a special visit to the widow of the poet Varqá, the mother of his son Ruhu'lláh; bereft of both of them because they'd given their lives for their Faith, she had "a sweet look," Susan said, "born of sorrow."[27] In Varqá's house, which was beautiful, with fine Persian rugs and Japanese embroideries adorning the walls and fruiting lemon trees and flowering plants in the drawing room, Susan had "one of the deep experiences" of her life when Varqá's family showed her mementos of the Báb, Bahá'u'lláh and 'Abdu'l-Bahá, along with relics of their own loved ones. "My dear . . ." Susan told Eva, "I cannot describe them. It is impossible. Enough to say we were sobbing together. It was a long time before we could again converse." Tea and some "real sponge cake," the first Susan tasted since leaving America, helped restore calm.[28]

* * * * * * * * *

Within days of coming to the capital, Susan leased a house at 10 Avenue Aladauleh, and, a month later, she moved in. Soon, her physician's shingle was swinging over Aladauleh street. "Imagine me hanging there in both English and Persian," she bemusedly observed.[29] With five other doctors, she also planned to open the Unity Hospital, but that took some time, so she was happy that she'd immediately opened her practice in her home, as 'Abdu'l-Bahá had suggested.

Ṭihrán in 1909 was as it had been in Biblical ages: unhurried, the hours unmarked, time told only by a cannon fired at noon from the citadel. It was a city of houses and gardens hidden behind dun-colored walls along winding lanes with, here and there, tall gates adorned with bright mosaics showing scenes from Persian classics, and green tree-tops waving above the walls. The women only went unveiled in the women's quarters, or *andarún,* and they wore lavish make-up—pale powder, red rouge, exaggerated, arched brows. No one had gray hair; men and women kept their hair dyed black. And rural and elderly people followed the old custom of using henna to make their palms and soles red. Few people could read, so there were no billboards, printed wrappings, or ubiquitous magazines and newspapers. Women spent long hours preparing food, enlivened by weddings, funerals, births, feast days, parties, all with ablutions and ceremonies. Daily visits took a long time, and ran according to set etiquette, with tea from the samovar, sherbets, cakes and candies, cigarettes or a shared hubble-bubble pipe, and an endless exchange of compliments, witticisms and gossip. The only really bustling places were the bazaars, which were always open; a closed bazaar meant total upheaval, such as revolution. In this dream-like setting, Susan Moody, efficiently learning Farsi, her hair frankly white, her face bare of make-up, cared for patients with health problems the likes of which she'd rarely seen.

Her days were endless; she often had to leave her consulting room, jammed with patients, and go off alone for a moment to pray for the patience 'Abdu'l-Bahá had enjoined upon her. She wrote home: "I wish you could have seen into my house to-day—crowds, and when a hurry call came from a distance where a woman had been poisoned—I had to turn away five women and three men and rush off in a carriage. In these homes I must do the work myself, and so little to do with; not a piece of flannel, nor rags enough to put on a compress; they know so little about nursing that they think I should stay and do everything day and night. I just have to break away when I feel the patient is out of danger. Wouldn't your tender hearts ache if you could see some of these homes? One room, the only sign of furniture is the 'corsi'. . . a table covered by a quilt, beneath is a brazier of charcoal; it is about two feet or 18 inches high and they sit or lie with feet under it. The walls and floor are mud, the ceiling is rafters. In the better class homes they still use the 'corsi' and sleep on the floor. I was called the other night to a wealthy home, the owner of the electric light plant here. Several courts and several separate dwellings enclosed within the grounds. The wife, who was ill, is a beautiful woman; her mattress was on the floor, but there was a fire in the chimney place. Everything showed wealth. This dear woman has hysteria, besides physical ailments, and her brother, who talks French, told me he knew it came from her living in the harem. No exercise, no outside interests. . . . Well, my American sisters, I am sure your hearts would ache in this home as well as in the other. Nothing but education can free them and it cannot come too soon."[30]

Susan needed a nursing assistant, and tried to teach hygienic measures to midwives, but thought younger women would be better able to understand. Yet, as her friend Táhirih pointed out, "How can they do efficient nursing while wrapped in these veils and afraid to let men see their faces?"[31]

By January 10, Susan happily wrote home that she and the other Bahá'í doctors had settled in a building to be outfitted as a hospital, and she'd be keeping morning office hours there and afternoon hours at home. She also associated with doctors who weren't Bahá'ís, and one had requested her help during an operation. She sent along a photo of some of her women friends, saying it must be published in *Star of the West*, as she'd promised them it would be, and she felt it was important that the promise be kept, for the photo marked "an important event in their lives; they have thrown down one rule, *for once* . . . (in showing) their faces to the world."[32]

A few weeks later, she wrote about the extravagantly emotional commemoration of the martyrdoms of Imam Hassan and Imam Husayn.

A very bloody time for three days. . . . The streets are filled with processions and they have crude music, carry banners, metal hands on the tops of spears, emblems made of feathers, cones of glass containing lighted candles, the cone being about six feet in circumference at base and proportionately high. It is wonderful to see them balanced on the head and to see the bearers change from head to head as they did under my window. In the midst of the line of each 'dasteh' or *bunch* is a group of flagellants. I would not go to the square on the day called 'Murder Day,' but I saw one squad pass whose backs were raw and still they were beating themselves with the chains. Riderless horses, covered with blankets full of arrows, are led in memory of the two (Imams), and on another horse is a child to represent one who was murdered. Tomorrow will be the last public exhibition, but for two months the people are supposed to mourn. When I mentioned the names in the home of a patient, all began to wail and weep."[33]

After the long hours of daily work and the total immersion in sights strange to her, Susan was reinvigorated by frequent Bahá'í meetings and by visits from the Bahá'ís. Upon moving to her house she'd hired a cook, and she took great pleasure in hospitality. In one letter she reported, "Today I had to turn away ten patients, time and strength could not be stretched further. . . . (But) tonight I had a call from six Bahá'í friends whom I had not met before. My little room is often thus illumined before and just after sunset, and I assure you it is the best of the day. Some sweet voice chants a Tablet, data concerning the Bahá'í work is brought up or discussed, they ask about America, and before I know it my material cares have fallen away and I find myself perfectly rested and refreshed."[34] Many of Susan's callers came from significant distances to meet her, such as the man from Shíráz who brought her a small fruiting branch from the orange tree growing in the courtyard of the Báb's home. Susan consumed the orange and sent the seeds to her friends in America.

* * * * * * * *

While Susan and the other doctors were founding the Unity Hospital, a movement was underway to start a girls' school. (The Tarbíyat School for Boys was already established.) In April, 1910, Susan wrote home that, during Ridván, the commemoration of Bahá'u'lláh's first public declaration of His Mission, "three meetings were held in various gardens and about 600 *tumáns* were collected. . . . The *young* men took charge of this matter. . . . This is a great sum for these times, and shows how eager the people are to progress. . . . It makes one hold one's breath to see the faith of these grand old teachers and their fearlessness in going forward. The Constitution is really making them able to act like free men. They are, at the same time, careful not to arouse public prejudice, which is strong still. . . . The girls' school is assured. They will start with accommodations for fifty pupils, and they think as the girls are not yet educated in Persian that they should not ask to have an English teacher sent just yet, but wait a few months and see how many will want to take up English. There are a few who have been in the American school and can talk very well. Please tell any who want to help that it will take only $1.50 per month to educate a girl. There are many here too poor to pay and this is the way to help lift Persia from her otherwise hopeless condition. . . . Think of it, since we arrived they have started a hospital, a girls' school and a (Temple Fund)! *Come over and help us. COME!*"[35]

Susan's plea—or pleas, for this one was followed by others—brought contributions through the Persian-American Educational Society. It also brought three persevering helpers to her side: Elizabeth Stewart, who was the niece of Susan's influential Bahá'í teacher, Isabella Brittingham; Lilian Kappes, not yet twenty-one, described by Marzieh Gail as being young, pretty, gay and lively; and Dr. Sarah Clock, like Susan a middle-aged woman dedicated to medicine. In 1910, Dr. Clock arrived, and in 1911 Elizabeth Stewart came to help with nursing and Lilian Kappes to run the Tarbíyat Girls' School.

Susan was the superintendent for women's health at the Unity Hospital, and she was loved and appreciated outside the Bahá'í community as well as within it. A Teheran newspaper printed an article, "Doctor Moody—American Lady," saying, "We give the utmost thanks and gratitude to such a noble woman, to such a respected person, whose presence here is a great privilege to the country of Persia. On account of the great care of this blessed person, the sick of all nationalities, Moslems, et. al., become healthy and well. We beg of God to keep this blessed and respected person with us."[36] As for the Bahá'ís, when one of Susan's fellow doctors, Yunís Khán, wrote to America about her, he referred to her as Amatu'l-A'lá, which means Handmaid of the Most High.

That title was conferred by 'Abdu'l-Bahá when He saluted Susan in a letter: "O Thou Amatu'l-A'lá, I address thee with this blessed title that it may attract for thee the confirmation of the Kingdom of Abhá and the cause of the glorification of the people of Bahá."[37] Susan sometimes put the title after her name in the Persian, with the English transliteration, for 'Abdu'l-Bahá had told her there was "no sweeter name."[38] However, she usually signed her name "Susie."

Shortly after Lilian Kappes reached Iran, she wrote home, "You cannot imagine how beloved Dr. Moody and Dr. Clock are."[39] Lilian plunged into work at the school, while Elizabeth Stewart managed to take up her nursing work fairly quickly, after she recovered from what Lilian called "a light case of typhoid,"[40] with which she'd been stricken upon arrival. As time went on, Elizabeth became an invaluable right hand to Susan.

Gruesome diseases and worse horrors were ever-present threats. In 1912, while the American Bahá'ís joyously prepared to greet 'Abdu'l-Bahá in New York, Susan wrote that, because of conflict with Russia, bazaars, schools, and businesses had been closed for a month, and she had just heard of a famine near Hamadán: fathers were eating their children, and the children each other. The famine was the result of the sacking of the area by an uncle of the deposed Sháh. The Bahá'ís gathered and took up a collection to relieve the distress, but it wouldn't be enough; people had to be sustained till harvest. Susan said she couldn't sleep, thinking of the suffering.

She was also deeply grieved because her friend, Táhirih, had passed away. Elizabeth Stewart fell ill again, and Lilian Kappes had been sick, but was recovering.

In an earlier letter, Susan had described a public hanging. "I passed through the square in coming from the hospital and saw the empty gallows, also had to cling to a young sapling to keep from being swept from my feet in one of the mad rushes of the crowd. I learned afterward that the hook on the scaffold had broken, the victim had fallen to the ground and the people broke in a panic."[41]

Susan was tender-hearted, compassionate and deeply empathetic. She never became inured to tragedy, but she gained nobility through it. She wrote home about the murder of a Bahá'í in a village, after which "five grand and gentle, though rough-looking, men . . . came to seek justice from the government." In this case, their petition for redress, presented to the Prime Minister, was granted. Then the widow, "sick, but with a wonderful strong character," came to Susan, who said, "I ought to take on some (strength) myself by contact with these suffering ones."[42]

By 1912, Susan was a member of a Bahá'í women's assembly which looked after poor families. She wrote to Agnes Parsons, "When I get an extra hour I attend one of the women's meetings, where my heart is always warmed and strengthened."[43] She also went to Bahá'í women's study classes on *The Book of Certitude* and *Some Answered Questions,* given by Ḥájí A<u>kh</u>und, and, she wrote home, "I look into their faces, full of love and full of earnestness, and wish you could all share my privilege." She also told of a day after a class when, as she crossed the court to leave, two little boys came running with open arms, calling, "Dr. Moody! Dr. Moody!" and she "got the most loving hugs and kisses."[44]

It was around this time that Susan received a tablet from 'Abdu'l-Bahá saying, "Praise be to God, that in service thou art successful. . . . Thou art educating the maidens of the Paradise of Abhá and healing the sick and the ailing. . . . Thou didst choose to live as a stranger because of thy love for the Best Beloved."[45]

* * * * * * * * *

Susan's charity to people in need of medical help and students in need of tuition and school supplies knew no bounds, and, from 1912 onward, she also devoted a great deal of time to finding scholarship sponsors for the Tarbíyat Schools. Working through the Persian-American Educational Society, run in Washington, D.C., by Joseph Hannen, she kept up correspondence with individual donors, sent photos of prospective scholars, and encouraged correspondence between donors and students. In the raising and distribution of funds, her wonderful equanimity was invaluable, especially in the occasional cases when persons entrusted with money proved unworthy of the trust. In a letter to Joseph Hannen, after describing the facts of a situation when, because of one individual's dishonesty, teachers at the schools received no pay for five months, Susan said, "I am myself withholding *any* adverse criticism until he has had ample time to '*make good.*'" She said she hadn't "told these facts to Dr. Clock nor Miss Kappes, nor talked them over with any of the school people. It would do no good."[46] But she had spoken strongly to the thief, giving him a deadline for repayment. Joseph Hannen was also equable and firm, so he and Susan made an admirable team.

They had the unquestioning support of 'Abdu'l-Bahá. He did everything possible to promote and assist the schools. In Paris, in the spring of 1913, a woman offered him 500 francs; following His usual practice, He wouldn't accept the gift for Himself; but, when she insisted, He told her to send the money to Dr. Moody for the Tarbíyat Schools.

Students at the Tarbíyat Schools were highly motivated and standards were high. Joseph Hannen published a letter from Susan in *Star of the West:*

> The annual examinations are something to talk about. From boys' Tarbíyat School, thirty-three students were examined at the Government University, before the Board of Education. *Thirty* received certificates. From all the other boys' schools (in Ṭihrán) three hundred boys went before the Board, of whom only ten passed satisfactory examinations and received certificates. . . . In the girls' schools, I don't know which to praise most, teachers or scholars. . . . These teachers, who were totally untrained, have produced great results. This is notably true in Miss Kappes' school, but the same is true of (another) school, where at first all teaching was voluntary. Now they pay a French teacher and

their own native teachers are paid a very meagre salary. This school has made a wonderful struggle. . . . I attended examinations in this school three afternoons, and in Miss Kappes' five afternoons, and without exception from beginners up, the American students (pupils with scholarships paid by American Bahá'ís) stood well in their classes."[47]

Susan adored attending school events, such as graduations, and always relished sharing, as a family member, the lives around her. She described the passing of an eighty-year old Bahá'í craftsman who had been in the presence of Bahá'u'lláh, had made and decorated pen-holders for Him, carved one of His seals and made illuminated borders and bindings for Bahá'í tablets. When he was dying, he told his wife he had three requests: that she shouldn't grieve, that she should bury him in a nearby graveyard, and that only Bahá'í hands should touch his body. After the Bahá'í burial ring was put on his finger and about fifty Bahá'í men had carried him away, Susan went with Elizabeth Stewart to sit with the widow. She showed them two Tablets that her husband had received from Bahá'u'lláh, talked of their long life together, and told how he had come to be a Bahá'í. Three days after his death, there was an afternoon meeting of about 200 women. As the women were going home, they met the male Bahá'ís arriving to pay their respects, and numerous men came and went reverentially until midnight. Up and down the street, people wondered that this humble artisan received so much devotion.

Soon afterwards, with no relish at all, Susan wrote of the martyrdom of a noted Bahá'í in Mashhad: "The assassin shot him in the back and the body lay where it fell in the bazaar for some days. The animosity against the Bahá'ís had reached the point where none dared to move it for fear of a general slaughter. A photograph of fifty Bahá'ís was posted in the bazaars and they were boycotted in all the shops. . . . A few days ago news reached Teheran . . . that the wife of the martyr has died in childbed; the child also died. No midwife would attend her, nor would a Mussulman prepare the bodies for burial. It was forbidden to bring them to the graveyard, so the grandmother washed the bodies and had them buried in their own garden."[48] 'Abdu'l-Bahá had foretold the man's martyrdom, but that didn't diminish the terror, pain, and sadness—and it still doesn't.

* * * * * * * *

World War I made life in Iran even more difficult, because mail was disrupted and imports cut off. Susan wrote of examinations for students in Bahá'í classes for girls, held in her home. "We take them in small groups. . . . They are given simple gifts, as a remembrance. . . . Miss Kappes loans out a beautiful medal sent by Miss Holmes, which is worn by each graduate in turn during one session of the class. We serve sherbet and tea, the pupils chant prayers and poems from memory and the atmosphere is just what one desires, nearness to each other and to the Beloved."[49]

These little graduations exemplified the golden edge of sweetness that selflessness can bring to the most impoverished situation. But shortages increased. "I suppose it is difficult for the west to realize how far we are from *every* necessity," Susan wrote to Joseph Hannen. "The thing we feel most is lack of remedy for the sick."[50] Bahá'í school funds were dwindling as less and less mail got through, and the Iranians, scared of the situation, hoarded their own money—until 'Abdu'l-Bahá asked that 1,000 *tumáns* be given on His behalf, whereupon one man contributed the whole sum, and another topped him.

After that, almost no mail got through until after the Armistice in 1918, when Elizabeth Stewart wrote to Isabella Brittingham, "We are nearly at the end of everything. All things are high in price. . . . Bread very poor and so high that I have made it for a long time, under very difficult conditions. . . ." The schools had been forced to drop many pupils and struggled to keep others on at no charge. But, said Elizabeth, "We are now in a state of rejoicing over the news of peace," and she told of a banquet given by one of the Bahá'ís at his house for an American government commission. (One of the commissioners had seen 'Abdu'l-Bahá at the Hotel Ansonia, in New York.) "It was made a freedom meeting," said Elizabeth, "where every Persian man brought his wife. A long table was arranged. About twenty sat around it. . . . We (she and Susan) felt so happy to be there, helping to carry forward the work of freeing the women. . . ."[51]

Following the war, the schools continued in debt, but they grew. In the spring of 1920, they sustained a blow with the sudden death of Joseph Hannen, and the threat of persecution was so grave that 'Abdu'l-Bahá advised small gatherings, so the Bahá'ís had to refrain from convening a large memorial for him. Susan, with compassion and wisdom, wrote to Joseph's widow, Pauline, of the meetings held in his honor, and described them in detail so Pauline would have a feeling of participation. She also enclosed many letters of condolence, including one from Hájí Amín, trustee of the Bahá'í Funds. He had recently had a cataract operation on one eye, which was bandaged, and Susan pleaded with him not to write and strain the other eye, but, she said, "his love would express itself."[52]

Despite the risk, the Bahá'ís taught their Faith enthusiastically and the women strove for more expression, with regular teaching events at fourteen different locations in Ṭihrán, one being Susan's home. On Saturdays, at sunset, a men's meeting was held at Susan's—that had been occuring consistently for seven years.

Then, in December, 1920, one of the women's bright stars, Lilian Kappes, not yet thirty years old, died of typhus. She "literally went to sleep," Susan said, "to awake in the Holy Presence."[53] She was buried in the garden beside the tomb of the martyred poet, Varqá, and the Bahá'ís planted violets on her grave.

'Abdu'l-Bahá was generally extremely sad when valuable workers like Lilian passed away, especially at such a young age, so it was unusual that He cabled, "Miss Kappes is very happy. I invite the world to be not grieved."[54] He then revealed a long requiem for her, in which He said, "She left her native land and remained apart from family ties . . . enduring every trouble and distress . . . content to accept the bitterness of separation for the love of teaching the children . . . She was patient in every difficulty. . . . She gave her hand unwearied every night and day and at even-tide and morning-tide to the service of the friends. . . . Then, supported by Thy favor, she returned to Thee . . . the sublime Refuge."[55]

About a year later, He Himself "returned...to...the sublime Refuge," and the brightest star fell from every Bahá'í's life. At the same time, conditions in Iran worsened; Alí Kuli <u>Kh</u>an's wife, Florence Breed Khan described the country's situation as "life-breaking, nearly soul-breaking," and said, "Every man active for the general good is checked on all sides here, by intrigue, jealousy, and money poured out against him."[56]

Susan, seventy years old, went on; it was as if her dedication to 'Abdu'l-Bahá's spirit and her own years of selfless service had built a bulwark for her soul. Her little team of American women workers was further depleted when Sarah Clock died of pneumonia in January, 1922. But Dr. Genevieve Coy, a psychologist, came to run the Tarbíyyat girls' school. However, the confiscation of Genevieve's Bahá'í literature at the port of Bandar-e-Anzalí was a bad omen: over 300 people gathered, hoping to burn the books publically.

By 1924, persecution threatened even the venerable Dr. Moody, so that she was considering leaving Iran for a time. After a vicious mob gathered in the street outside her house one night, she and Elizabeth Stewart sought help at the American Consulate. She wrote home, "Our new Consul, Major Imbrie, immediately telephoned the Chief of Police and said if the two Americans suffered any discomfort or danger, he would hold the Persian government responsible, and they must send us protection. This was done and we have had peace. We learned that the same night they (the rioters) were here, they were all over the city, yelling and even doing damage (at Bahá'í homes). They banged on many doors and put an effigy of our Master on a donkey and drove about with it. If they had not been stopped, the next night there would have been looting and probably murder. There are now interesting rumors, such as 'America sent cablegram,' 'the Consul went to Reza Khan,' etc., etc. I told Major Imbrie of a plot which had been confided to me on the quiet, against (another Bahá'í doctor) and myself."[57]

Robert Imbrie was a friend of an American Bahá'í educator, Stanwood Cobb, and he and his wife readily befriended

Susan and Elizabeth. He hoped to be their protector, and he stayed in Ṭihrán although, with xenophobia rife and Islamic feast days coming up, the rest of the American legation had decamped to a small town. The aging Susan felt great tenderness for the young, dauntless Consul.

Then, a week later, on July 21, she brokenly wrote: "How can I go on—Major Imbrie was assassinated on Friday, July 18th. They were coming here for tea." (A simple calling card from Major Imbrie's wife, found among Susan's affects after her death, attests to the depth of her feeling for these friends.) She said, "We sat awaiting them, when a servant came from the Consulate with the shocking information. Elizabeth had heard two hours before that (an) American had been killed because he took a photo of the place where alleged miracles were performed. Twenty minutes before the servant came, I received the impression that it was Major Imbrie, and I got my prayerbook and read the prayer for the dead."[58]

The murder was particularly horrible because, after a street mob with knives had attacked Major Imbrie and several people who tried to defend him, he was taken to a hospital, and the mob rushed into the hospital and killed him ("killed" is really too gentle a word for what they did) in his bed.

Ṭihrán was placed under martial law, patrolled by police and Cossacks (soldiers), on foot and mounted. There was a regal funeral with Iranian government and religious officials. But Mrs. Imbrie lost the baby she was carrying, and when she left Iran under military escort in a sad procession that included her husband's coffin being transported home for burial, she wouldn't allow any Iranian officers except for one Bahá'í to approach her; he came to her car a few times a day, brought her tea, spoke to her in English, and supplied flowers to lay on the bier.

Even this bitter event didn't dim Susan's love for Iran. Lilian Kappes, shortly before she died, had bought silk to make an Iranian flag with the idea of having it raised at Green Acre Bahá'í School in Eliot, Maine. The director of the Tarbíyat primary school sewed the flag, and Susan sent it to Agnes Parsons, asking, "Will you unfurl it there and lovingly suggest free will offerings (for the expansion of Tarbíyat) in memory of Miss Kappes."[59]

* * * * * * * * *

But it was Susan herself who unfurled the flag at Green Acre. She and Elizabeth Stewart left Iran in November, 1924. On the way to America, they stopped in Haifa to pray in the Bahá'í Shrines and meet the young Guardian. He wrote to North America: "Our untiring and devoted sister Dr. Moody (the handmaid of the Most High), has had to her profound regret to discontinue for a time the invaluable and unique services she has been rendering to the Cause in Persia."[60]

In January, 1925, Susan and Elizabeth arrived in New York and were greeted by the Bahá'ís at a reception at the Waldorf Astoria Hotel. Dr. Moody spoke to them all about her experiences in Ṭihrán, and remarked later, "To return to America and receive such love from the friends is worth more than any sacrifice one could make."[61]

She traveled and attended various events, enjoying herself greatly, but Shoghi Effendi began recommending that she find a companion to accompany her and return to Iran. (Elizabeth Stewart was in a convalescent home, and, sadly, never recovered her strength.) The Guardian said, "Whoever steps into this field will find, as he settles down to his work, that the environment is extremely disheartening, that restrictions are oppressive, that the amenities of social life are lacking, that forces of opposition are determined and organized. But let him realize also that, however tedious and exacting his labors, however precarious and thankless his task, the pioneer services it is his unique duty to render in this time of stress will forever live in the annals of God's living Faith, and will prove a source of inspiration to the countless workers who, in happier times and with better means at their disposal, will consummate the spiritual regeneration and material rehabilitation of Bahá'u'lláh's native land."[62]

Susan could not immediately comply with the Guardian's wish. However, she spent much of her time on the road mustering support for the Bahá'í schools, while also serving as a public speaker for Bahá'í teaching efforts and enthusiastically attending Esperanto classes. In 1927, in California, she took her first airplane ride, and her picture was in the paper: she stood smilingly beside an aviator who sported the goggles, leather cap, and jacket that were *de regeur* for young flyers in the '20s. Susan commented to the reporter that, having entered Ṭihrán in a coach and four, and exited it fifteen years later in "a flivver of doubtful vintage," she saw no reason why aerial transportation should hold any fears for the modern woman.[63]

* * * * * * * *

On November 17, 1928, Dr. Moody, accompanied by Adelaide Sharp of San Francisco, went home to Iran. Adelaide was a wonderful pioneer: she was a schoolteacher who took hold of the Tarbíyat work and kept at it for almost fifty years, until her death in Ṭihrán at the age of eighty. She also did valuable translations and was the first woman member of the National Spiritual Assembly of the Bahá'ís of Iran.

When Martha Root came to Iran in 1930, she found Susan recovering from pneumonia, visited her as often as possible, brought her gifts, and even had a beautiful blue silk robe made for her because she felt the color would raise her spirits and speed her recuperation.

Two years later, the eighty-one year old Susan, youthfully ardent and selfless as ever, made a great sacrifice when she sent a photograph of her friend from long before, Ṭáhirih, to a Bahá'í in the U.S. who requested it. Susan treasured the portrait and didn't think it would be possible to get another, because, she said, "In one of the terrible uprisings here years ago (the photographer's) studio was raided and every negative smash-ed . . . I am sending you my copy. At first I wondered how I could spare it—then came the thought from the Dawn Prayer 'of the recompense to those who give up what they have in Thy Cause . . .' and the *mist* all cleared away."[64]

By 1933, Susan rarely left her home, but welcomed visitors daily. She spoke Persian, even with Americans, and her great happiness was to hear about Bahá'í progress. Keith Ransom-Kehler wrote:

> Foremost amongst the Western pioneers in this sacred land must ever stand the name of Susan Isabel Moody, M.D. . . . Although very feeble and partially bedridden, so unconquerable is her spirit, so cheerful her disposition, so intense her eagerness for the Cause and its welfare, that young and old throng to see her and her presence is a blessing to every meeting that she finds strength to attend. She always reminds me of the lines of Stevenson:

'I knew a silver head was bright beyond compare,
I knew a queen of toil with a crown of silver hair;
Garland of valor and sorrow, of beauty and renown;
Life that honors the brave crowned her himself with the
    crown.'[65]

In the autumn of 1934, Susan's heart began to fail, and on October 23 she quietly passed away. Hundreds of Tarbíyat students, all bearing flowers, followed her cortege through Ṭihrán to the Bahá'í cemetery. Shoghi Effendi cabled that her "indomitable spirit (and) ceaseless services" had earned her "unique distinction," and had "forged (the) first link" in the "chain uniting (the) spiritual destinies" of the Bahá'ís of Iran, the "cradle of our Faith," and the United States, the "community of its stalwart defenders." He said that Susan's "sacred life" had shed "imperishable lustre" on the American Bahá'í community.[66]

Susan would never have dreamed that he would say such things about her. Shortly before her death, when one of her many visitors asked her to say something about her life, something that could be preserved for posterity, all she said was, "Let it go. Let it pass into the infinite."[67]

Chapter 7

Dorothy Baker

Dorothy Beecher Baker

When Dorothy Baker's grandmother took her to meet 'Abdu'l-Bahá in New York City in 1912, she was a thin thirteen-year old with a pale face, a sweet mouth, and blue-gray eyes which she hardly dared lift to the faces of the people who crowded the room. And, overcome with shyness, it was her wish that 'Abdu'l-Bahá wouldn't look at her, wouldn't speak to her, wouldn't notice her, or call any attention to her.

Seated and quiet, with His air of being at once a shepherd and a king, 'Abdu'l-Bahá was the center of all activity, the focal point in that crowded room. Somehow, without giving Dorothy the feeling that He was making her conspicuous, He motioned her to a footstool beside His chair. Then He addressed the assemblage.

Dorothy never could remember what He said that day. Sheltered by His nearness, her eyes downcast, she felt her shyness towards Him become an intense longing. She loved Him and wanted to be with Him forever. Without knowing that she was moving, she turned on her little footstool like a flower towards the sun, so that when He finished speaking she was looking directly up at Him, her elbows on her knees, her chin in her hands.

His face, His eyes, and voice stayed with her. Finally, she wrote to Him asking to be allowed to serve Him and the Cause of Bahá'u'lláh. He replied in His own hand, "Dearest child, Your goal is great and God is All-Bountiful. My hope is this: that you succeed in your desire."[1]

Shortly afterwards, He sent for Dorothy's grandmother, Ellen Beecher. When she reached Him, He was surrounded by people, deep in discussion, but He turned from them to tell her: "I called you to say that your grand-daughter is my own daughter. You must train her for me."[2]

* * * * * * * * *

Dorothy King Beecher was the child of Ellen Beecher's son, Henry, and Luella Gorham. Ellen Beecher was seventy-two in 1912. She had become a Bahá'í shortly before 1900, when she found in the Bahá'í Faith the realization of her personal visions and the fulfillment of her life-long Messianic quest.

But Ellen was the only Bahá'í, in fact, the only religious person in her family, although, through her husband, she was connected to the Beechers, the famous family of male Christian preachers and orators. (But the most famous member of the family was a woman, Harriet Beecher Stowe, author of *Uncle Tom's Cabin*.)

Ellen's son, Henry, was a lawyer whose views on women radically belied his mother's independent spirit, as well as his distant cousin Harriet Stowe's and his own wife's. His daughter would have some hard choosing to do, because of that.

Luella Gorham Beecher had been hoping for a daughter when her son, Chauncey, was born in 1896, so she was happy when Dorothy was born on December 21, 1898, in Maplewood, New Jersey. Dorothy adored her parents and her dashing older brother. She was torn between their so-called enlightened materialism and Ellen Beecher's mysticism.

Like her parents, Dorothy was a high achiever. At sixteen, she convinced her father to let her take her senior year of high school at Northfield, a fine boarding academy. She was interested in academics, but Henry only let her go because the school also taught etiquette and housekeeping. She graduated with honors and announced that she wanted to study law. Her father did not approve. They finally compromised: she attended Montclair Normal School, a two-year teacher-training college.

Ellen Beecher, far from Dorothy, traveling and teaching and helping to edit the *Star of the West,* never forgot 'Abdu'l-

Bahá's injunction to train Dorothy for Him. In fact, she profoundly affected Dorothy's spiritual development through letters, example and instruction. Dorothy, no longer the shy child who met 'Abdu'l-Bahá, had a dazzling and vivid personality; she was elected class president during her second year at Montclair Normal School and edited the yearbook. Decades later, a classmate recalled that she was not only witty and bright, but had great spiritual values, so that her friends felt unable to speak an unkind word, or even think a mean thought, when in her presence. She found many of these values in her grandmother's responses to her youthful questions and thoughts expressed in correspondence.

After graduation in 1920, Dorothy taught grade school. She was the belle of her circle of friends, with an ethereal and piquant beauty, a robust good humor, and a streak of daring. She was also the belle of her classroom of seven and eight-year old students in a Newark slum. They came from such poor families that their mothers, many of them immigrants who knew no English, hoping to keep them alive during the bitter winter, sewed them into their clothing: if the school hadn't initiated a shower program, they wouldn't have bathed till spring. Dorothy sang children's songs and pop hits to them, and they were fascinated with her wardrobe, especially one outfit consisting of a hot pink blouse and an orange skirt. They had trouble reciting the names of colors from a color chart, but they shouted out the names when asked to identify what Miss Beecher was wearing.

Dorothy also fascinated Sara and Conrad Baker, two children who regularly came with their widowed father, Frank, to dine at the boardinghouse where she lived. Sara's adoration, in particular, drew Frank's attention to Dorothy. He was a tall, stout, quiet man in his early thirties. Dorothy had only recently been courted by a clever young Boston lawyer, and she had been greatly attracted to him, yet, when he asked her to marry him, she told him no. Why? Years later she said simply that a force greater than herself restrained her. Now, at twenty-one, she had a brilliant career ahead of her; she'd just been offered a job at the prestigious Ethical Culture School in New York City. Yet, nothing held her back when Frank Baker, the slow-spoken, plain son of German Lutherans from Zanesville, Ohio, proposed.

Frank had been born November 21, 1889. He spoke only German until he started school. Despite his conventional outward appearance, he was sensitive. As a child, he used to stand at his window, pondering Biblical prophesies, thinking he might be living at the time of Christ's return. When Dorothy told him about the Bahá'í Faith, before their marriage, it fulfilled his expectations, and he quietly accepted it.

* * * * * * * * *

The newlyweds went to live in Buffalo, New York, where their daughter, Winifred Louise, was born in May, 1922. A few years later, they had a son, William King. They lived in a big brick house, Conrad and Sara went to fine schools and did very well, and the babies flourished. Dorothy loved her family and enjoyed golfing and playing Bridge, but Frank traveled a lot and she was often lonely. She was refreshed by visits from her grandmother.

Ellen, at eighty-five, was still on the road, without a permanent home, giving talks on the Bahá'í Faith all over the United States and Canada. Dorothy didn't think of herself as a speaker for the Faith; it was her grandmother, known to the Bahá'ís as

Mother Beecher, who was the legend. Dorothy saw Ellen not only as a phenomenon but as a fragile old woman. The little white-haired woman, with her white shawl and the small cane chair she brought with her wherever she went, was inexpressibly dear to Dorothy, and she wrote her mother that she and Conrad took turns guiding Grandma into the den on the maid's day off, so she wouldn't notice the kitchen and insist on washing all the dishes.

Meanwhile, Grandma was trying to guide Dorothy out of her own den in the brick house, to get her out among the Bahá'ís. Dorothy told her children hero tales from Bahá'í history and hosted many Bahá'í events at her home, but she didn't formally address any gatherings. However, one evening she spoke spontaneously at a meeting which she attended with Ellen Beecher at the home of Grace and Harlan Ober. One of the guests, Doris McKay, who met Dorothy for the first time there, was unforgettably impressed by Dorothy's eloquence and bearing. She recalled that Dorothy was wearing a wine-colored velvet dress that stunningly set off her height, slenderness, pallor and gray eyes as she told a story with the moral that we are all God's children.

Dorothy was twenty-seven years old at the time. Since her early teens, people like Grace and Harlan Ober, friends of her grandmother's, had been watching her, praying with Ellen for her, waiting for her to publically fulfill the promise 'Abdu'l-Bahá saw in her. But Dorothy had to fill great needs in her family. Soon after she attended that meeting at the Obers, her brilliant and sweet step-daughter, Sara, became ill and was diagnosed as having leukemia. Two weeks later, she was dead.

Sara had declared herself a Bahá'í shortly before the illness struck, and, after she died, Dorothy had more than one affirmation of her immortality. Spiritually moved, she became more ardent in her Faith. In November, 1926, she was elected to the Local Spiritual Assembly of the Bahá'ís of Buffalo.

However, Frank had lost his mother while he was in his teens, and then he had been widowed when Sara's mother died at a young age, so he had great difficulty recovering from this third devastating loss. He needed a change. In 1927, he opened his own wholesale bread bakery, named Plezol, in Lima, Ohio.

****

For Dorothy, the move to Buffalo from the New York metropolitan area had been a move to the wilderness. Ohio was desolation. She and Frank and their three children were the only Bahá'ís in Lima, and they were very private about their religion. They joined a country club and the Lutheran Church (this was before Shoghi Effendi made it clear to the Bahá'ís that they couldn't have other affiliations), and Dorothy threw herself into reforming the Parent-Teacher Association (PTA) at Louise's school by getting fathers as well as mothers involved.

When eighty-eight year old Ellen Beecher arrived at Dorothy's house for her yearly visit, Dorothy decided she was too frail to continue traveling, so she and Frank asked Ellen to live with them, and Ellen was thrilled.

She was also worried about Dorothy. Sara's death and its aftermath had taken its toll: Dorothy was thin and tired, and the doctor found a spot of tuberculosis on her lung. Her love for her family tore her heart, for she thought she would die and leave them, striking Frank with yet more sorrow; she also felt she hadn't lived up to her Bahá'í responsibilities. She studied daily with Ellen and longed to render great service, but she couldn't see herself as a traveler and speaker. She wanted to write children's stories about Bahá'í history, and she wrote to Shoghi Effendi asking where she could get information, for, in 1929, not much history had been published. The Guardian responded that material was forthcoming but not yet available, and added that he would pray at the Shrines for Dorothy to be able to serve the Cause with distinction. Ellen Beecher, anxiously watching over her charge, wrote to a friend in 1930 that she thought Dorothy, if she lived, would become "a great teacher as well as writer—for she is a chosen instrument without doubt."[3]

Dorothy gave a public talk at the Foundation Hall of the not-yet-completed Bahá'í Temple in Wilmette, and her eloquence and knowledge so profoundly impressed everyone that she found herself flooded with speaking invitations. After the threat of tuberculosis was past, and after she'd weathered an attack of food poisoning which brought her definitely to the brink of death, Dorothy threw herself into Bahá'í study and teaching. She decided her duty was to give forth living, spirited thoughts, so, she developed speaking techniques: breathing, posture, elocution, a fund of humorous stories, a well-directed glance. But the unique quality she had that she could not have learned anywhere—for it came from the depths of her soul—was a singular and constant sincerity. When she began giving classes at Louhelen Bahá'í School in Michigan, her students adored her.

****

Margaret Ruhe recalled that Dorothy "just burst upon us." Margaret was fifteen when she first met Dorothy. She had been a Bahá'í since infancy, but she'd never experienced anything like Dorothy's classes: "She was poetic, she was picturesque, she was graphic. The words just flowed from her mouth. We used to sit spellbound at her feet."

Dorothy was in her early 30's, and her good looks, glamour and jauntiness were bracing to her students, while her kindness gave them a sense of security. Margaret said, "Dorothy was a free spirit. She was an untrammeled spirit, a liberal soul who possessed a magnanimity that permeated every act and every thought. She possessed a sin-covering eye that almost never saw fault with anyone. She always saw the good in people."

Dorothy wanted her young students to call her "Dorothy," not "Mrs. Baker." That was a radical departure back in 1930. And, she drove big, fast, new cars. She'd arrive at Louhelen (then called Davison) in a Buick, a Cadillac or Pontiac, and she'd let the youth drive her car, not for joy-riding, but to do errands for her. "Dorothy had confidence in all of us young people," Margaret Ruhe said.

She also noted that Dorothy "believed in prayer with a tenacity and determination that was remarkable. She often stayed up very late at night to be alone and pray, and would rise at dawn, very tired, to pray. She had to have her dawn prayers."[4]

To prepare for these summer school sessions, Dorothy studied for hours, day after day, in a small room in her family's stone house on Elm Street in Lima. When Louise and Bill got up to go to school, they used to see their mother sitting on the floor of her little room, her open books, bristling with bookmarks, spread out around her. She kept an eye on their progress, and when they were done washing and dressing, they'd find her in the kitchen, fixing breakfast. But, when they came home from school, they knew she'd be in her study, among her books.

Dorothy once told Margaret Ruhe that the reason she threw herself so ardently into Bahá'í tasks was that she hated housework. Like every humorous remark, that one had a grain of truth. How could housework compare to the passion and drama of Bahá'í history and the poetry of Bahá'í scripture? Dorothy memorized passages and prayers from the Bahá'í Writings and stated them in her beautiful voice with clarity and precision; she made their gem-like qualities apparent, so her hearers could receive them with reverence.

And certainly the fun of getting to know many and varied people made housework look bleak. Dorothy adored going to Bahá'í events. Margaret recalled, "She loved people, and people loved her. She talked a blue streak, and always wanted to know everybody's last name, profession, course of study, parents' names, etc. I can remember at meetings and conferences and conventions and institutes, frequently, after the formal part of the meeting was over Dorothy was off in a corner talking with a person who needed special help, or visiting with someone who needed to gain more knowledge of the Faith. She was very, very sensitive to people's personal needs."[5]

However, Dorothy didn't discuss her Faith with friends in Lima. If anyone did that in the Baker household, it was Ellen Beecher. At ninety-two, Ellen was brilliant and lucid, powerful and straightforward. She had always been a refuge for Dorothy and now even her room was a haven. It was a bower, full of bouquets, and the most beautiful flowers were always arranged around the picture of 'Abdu'l-Bahá. Ellen herself was ensconced there like a full-blown rose, faded to little more than finest silk and fragrance, among her books and papers.

Dorothy asked Ellen if, after her long life of work and service, she wasn't a little tired? Ellen replied simply that, at her advanced age, she couldn't help being little tired, and added that she was also very happy.

Soon afterwards, Ellen fell and broke her hip. Too fragile to survive the injury, she died a week later. Until her final hours, she was visiting with friends and family members who gathered around her bed, and she forced herself to stay conscious and graciously shower love upon all until her son, Henry, arrived and she could have a final glimpse of him. Then, she slipped into a coma and slipped away.

Dorothy wrote five articles on Ellen Beecher's life, "The Evolution of a Bahá'í," and they were published in *The Bahá'í Magazine* during 1933–1934. The Guardian wrote a sweet note of condolence to Dorothy, containing his prayer that she would be enabled to follow the example of Mother Beecher.

* * * * * * * * *

Dorothy's career as a "Bahá'í-maker" (to borrow 'Abdu'l-Bahá's epithet for Isabella Brittingham) really began after her grandmother's death. Frank came home from work one day shortly after Ellen died and announced that he'd invited fourteen people who were studying a philosophy called Unity to come and hear about Bahá'u'lláh's teachings on unity. He assumed Dorothy would do the honors.

She had four days to prepare and, despite her years of study, she read, indexed and annotated for some thirty hours so that, when Sunday came she was nervous, but she was armed with newly memorized quotations, thoughts vivid with imagery, and stories. Dorothy always told stories. And she always prefaced her presentations with ardent private prayer.

She achieved her goal of giving forth thoughts that breathed; on February 2, 1933, she wrote to the Guardian that there were eighteen Bahá'ís in Lima and a second study group had been formed for new inquirers. Dorothy spent twenty to forty hours preparing for each class. On April 21, 1934, the first Local Spiritual Assembly of the Bahá'ís of Lima was elected. Frank was voted Treasurer, and he held that post for some twenty-five years. He also frequently served as delegate to the National Convention.

But it was Dorothy who was the star, and Frank wholeheartedly supported and encouraged her, even when she began to travel extensively and he and the children missed her, and she missed them. He once told her, "We both love this Faith, and neither of us wants you to give only your gray hairs to it."[6] He and Dorothy had tremendous mutual respect, appreciation, and tolerance, and neither of them had any false vanity. Frank's long work weeks made him weary, especially during the rough Depression years and, quite often, while the elegant Dorothy stood and addressed a large gathering at the Elm Street house on Sunday night, Frank fell asleep on the couch at the back of the room, and he snored. Dorothy smiled and said that if he was bothering anyone, wake him up but, otherwise, let him sleep.

By 1935, Dorothy longed to make her pilgrimage and meet Shoghi Effendi. She'd received a small inheritance and her mother, Luella, had become a Bahá'í; they thought they'd go together. In 1920, she'd tried to make a pilgrimage but it had been deferred and, the following year, 'Abdu'l-Bahá died. But Dorothy was torn between visiting the Shrines and contributing her money to the construction of the Bahá'í House of Worship in Wilmette. She wrote to the Guardian, and he responded, "You truly deserve to visit Haifa and lay your head in thanksgiving on the sacred threshold."[7] However, he asked her to contribute her money to the Temple Fund.

She did so, and threw herself more intensely into her Bahá'í work as a storm of persecution hit the Bahá'ís of Lima. Attacks from the pulpit had begun soon after the Lima Bahá'í community was born. The significance of upstanding church members leaving their pews to gather in home meetings to follow the teachings of an Iranian who claimed to be the return of the Christ Spirit was not lost on Lima's clergy. In 1934, Dorothy wrote to the Guardian about the attacks, and he said that the enmity would not quench the fire of faith in new Bahá'ís' hearts; rather, adversity would fan the flame. That proved to be the case, but the process was arduous.

In 1937, persecution in Lima peaked. On just one Sunday morning, three ministers denounced the Faith from their pulpits. On another occasion, a minister told a new Bahá'í that Mrs. Baker was stealing all the best people from the churches. An elderly schoolteacher who had begun attending Bahá'í gatherings was threatened by her superiors with the loss of her pension if she should become a Bahá'í. Another minister announced in church that people only became Bahá'ís because Mrs. Baker hypnotized them, luring them with her beauty and intellect. Dorothy told a friend, "I thought I had achieved detachment, but the agony this is causing me shows I haven't become free of self."[8] She grieved that the attractive power of the Baháí Faith was mistaken for her own personal power, and that her labors stirred up such acrimony. Things got so bad that Frank's income, which had remained relatively good because people always needed bread, and which had enabled the Bakers to help many people during the Depression, now plummeted as Lima citizens boycotted his products.

In the midst of all this, Dorothy's responsibilities to the U.S. Bahá'í community suddenly multiplied when she was elected to the North American National Spiritual Assembly. Stunned, she exclaimed to Margaret Ruhe, "Why, I never thought such a thing could happen to me."[9]

* * * * * * * * *

Dorothy took her seat on the National Assembly when it was embarking on the task of piloting the Bahá'ís through the Seven Year Plan, the first of Shoghi Effendi's teaching campaigns calling on the North American Bahá'ís to make a collective effort to reach the goals set by 'Abdu'l-Bahá in the "Tablets of the Divine Plan"; previously, efforts had been scattered, individual.

In 1937, when Shoghi Effendi launched the first Seven Year Plan, he perceived World War II approaching and foresaw the coming attacks on the Bahá'ís in North Africa, Iran, Germany, and Russia, along with repression in other parts of Europe. He called upon the Bahá'ís of the U.S. and Canada to take advantage of their freedom and establish assemblies in every State, Province, and Central and South American country.

As the National Assembly grappled with its new tasks, Dorothy was challenged by the attitudes of its male members. May Maxwell had been one of the few women on the Assembly before Dorothy. Amelia Collins was on the Assembly with Dorothy and, although she was a woman of great courage and achievement, she was also a lovable little old lady with a motherly tolerance for the foibles of the men. Dorothy had no such tolerance. She found the Assembly to be like a men's club, particularly during breaks when the fellows relaxed with ribald jokes. The men didn't appreciate her efforts to elevate the plane of the gatherings.

Dorothy used to repeat the long, powerful prayer, the Tablet of Aḥmad, nine times in a row as she drove to Wilmette for Assembly meetings. She always picked up hitch-hikers, but she wouldn't give anyone a ride till after she said her prayers. She would also rise at dawn, even after a meeting that extended far into the night, to say her Long Obligatory Prayer and the Tablet of Aḥmad. A friend who saw her praying remarked that she seemed to incarnate the prayer. Dorothy told this friend that she prayed her fellow Assembly members through the meetings.

Meanwhile, enmity against the Faith in Lima became so rancorous that Dorothy sent her two teenage children away to school. She longed for the solace of a pilgrimage and a meeting with the Guardian. But Frank's business was suffering so much because of boycotting that she decided she had to use any extra funds for traveling expenses as an Assembly member and teacher; so, for a third time, she deferred pilgrimage. This postponment hurt Dorothy more than the others. She wrote to May Maxwell, "Somehow I can't bear it that I did not go to the Guardian."[10]

Dorothy was strengthened during that difficult year by her friendship with Martha Root. Doris McKay brought Martha and Dorothy together in Jamestown, New York. Doris always remembered Dorothy, tall, youthful, and regal, hurrying forward with outstretched hands to greet the tiny, gray, fragile Martha. Then Dorothy, usually so talkative, sat contentedly silent, listening to Martha, and Doris rejoiced in the shared incandescence of the two great women. Martha later stopped in Lima while making her final trip to California to sail for the orient. When Dorothy took her to the train for Chicago, she found it very hard to say goodbye. And she wondered at that. She wrote to Martha that great people usually were a bit of a strain, and so it wasn't very hard to bid them farewell, but Martha, in her humility, caused no strain; rather, she risked others becoming proud before her.

Dorothy had intently observed Martha's detachment from material conditions, her ability to turn any circumstance to the advantage of her Faith. Operating on Martha's principles, Dorothy went to a Lima clergyman and asked to be allowed to speak from his pulpit. He said yes. After she spoke, the tide began to turn.

A Bahá'í who was reporter on a fifteen-minute radio news program sponsored by the Frank Baker's bread company arranged for the Bahá'ís to use a fifteen-minute slot following his news report. Soon, one of the ministers most opposed to the Faith moved away. The young clergyman who took his place read from *Bahá'u'lláh and the New Era* during his first sermon and made favorable comments.

The Lima Bahá'ís emerged strengthened from their ordeal. Dorothy learned a great deal about selfless love from it, and she always credited Martha Root for being an example of that kind of love—a love which does not wait, but rushes forth to serve and never misses an opportunity to extend its helping hand, bestow its enlivening touch.

* * * * * * * *

Dorothy's value to the North American Bahá'ís grew by leaps and bounds along with her service to the National Assembly and the Lima Assembly, and her work on committees, such as the Inter-America and Race Unity Committees. The Guardian wrote to her in 1938 that he admired and felt thankful for her noble qualities; he encouraged her to persevere and be confident.

During that year, the first Local Spiritual Assembly south of the U.S. border was formed in Mexico City. In 1939 the first Bahá'í of Mexico was welcomed at the North American National Convention; the Central American teaching campaign was launched; and some of the Guardian's letters were published under the title, *The Advent of Divine Justice*. In them he called upon the North American Bahá'ís to leave their homes and become pioneers of the Faith. "Unrestrained as the wind," they were to "carry the word of God to the uttermost end of the Continent." The appeal came, as Garreta Busey wrote in her article, "Uniting the Americas," at a time "of tension, of ominous stillness before the storm of violence and terror moving across the earth."[11] Soon after that, Hitler invaded Poland and World War II broke out.

The Bahá'ís of North America were increasingly pressured to win the goals of the first Seven Year Plan by 1944. The Guardian wrote that the American Bahá'í community had been "preserved through the inscrutable dispensations of Divine Providence for a destiny which no mind can as yet imagine," and its members were "the inheritors of the shining grace of Bahá'u'lláh" upon whose teaching activities their oppressed brethren depended for their "welfare and progress."[12] To anyone looking through other than a Bahá'í lens, it was the worst imaginable time to leave home and loved ones, all for a vision of peace which seemed a cruel chimera. And yet the Bahá'í pioneers went forth.

Dorothy admired the pioneers above all others. She wrote to Elizabeth Cheney, who was going to Paraguay: "You have been born in the Day of God, heralded for centuries. . . . *You* are conscious, and you have bowed down before its splendor, saluting its mighty King, and risen up to call in His Name to the sleeping nations. . . . That you may have the greatest joy in every passing moment . . . I want to make sure. I have only two rules to give you. One is this: look not to the creatures. Let your heart be supremely attached to our Beloved, then you can serve *all* his children with detachment and joy. . . . The second rule is this: make a joyous thing of the *little* services, because you can never tell which is little and which is big in God's sight. . . . And now . . . if I never see you, touch you, speak alone to you again in this world, soldier, know now the comfort you have brought me, and know that the march is all that matters: THE MARCH IS ALL THAT MATTERS! And when the march is over, through all the worlds of God, the miracle of it all will be continually unfolded before us, and there will be no separation."[13]

By 1940, there were Local Spiritual Assemblies in Mexico City, Bahia, and Buenos Aires; and groups in Havana, Tegucigalpa (Honduras), Guatemala City, Montevideo, and Panama City. The march had required sacrifice: May Maxwell died in Buenos Aires; Matthew Kaszab, who went to Nicaragua, got sick there and then died alone in Texas; others suffered untold trials. From 1940 to 1942, while the U.S. was drawn into global war, the Bahá'ís intensified their struggle to give their message of global peace. By April 1942, there were nine Local Spiritual Assemblies in Central and South America, including one in the southernmost city in the world, Punta Arenas, Chile.

The Bahá'ís, especially the pioneers, attributed it all to their Guardian. Dorothy, one of his consecrated lieutenants, was, like her fellow believers, enabled by his messages to cherish, as Horace Holley expressed it, "completely superhuman sources of confidence and hope."[14] The more the Guardian asked, the more Dorothy did. Neither she nor Frank would have had it any other way.

Their children grew up and established busy lives away from Elm Street, but the center of the household for Frank was Dorothy, and she was often on the road. Frank knew she often drove too fast; she prayed intensely as she drove so that she risked becoming unaware of the road; she picked up hitch-hikers no matter how disreputable they looked; she spoke of racial integration to hostile audiences; she suffered from painful and potentially dangerous attacks of asthma. No one will ever know what Dorothy's travels meant to Frank in terms of loneliness, worry, and sacrifice; but he took his recompense in his great pride in Dorothy.

According to the Guardian's wishes, she concentrated on speaking at universities during the early 1940s, while many of her "Bahá'í children" from Lima went pioneering.

In 1943, she was able to witness and experience some of the hardships and joys of pioneering when she went to visit her daughter, Louise, in Bogota, Colombia. But her mission was larger than that. It was, as always, to teach. The Guardian cabled, "Fervent prayers accompanying you loving appreciation Shoghi."[15] With characteristic thoroughness, she prepared for the trip by learning Spanish from language records, and she set up a weekly class so others could be included in the process. However, when she arrived in Colombia she found that, when people spoke to her, she couldn't understand a word: it was nothing like the slow and steady records. Louise translated for her. But that wasn't good enough for Dorothy. With Louise's help, she memorized some of her favorite stories in the simplest possible Spanish so she could pepper her talks with them, and this greatly endeared her to her listeners.

Dorothy with her daughter, Louise Baker Matthias

After her visit, the first Local Spiritual Assembly of Bogota was formed.

She proceeded to Caracas, and by that time she could communicate fairly well in Spanish. Things went slowly for the first few weeks, but then, with the help of a woman who edited a magazine, "a world of friendships opened up," Dorothy reported. "The meetings grew to about 40 in attendance."[16] She was in Caracas for five weeks, and ten people became Bahá'ís. Four months after that, a new Venezuelan Bahá'í was a special guest at the celebration in the U.S. in May, 1944, marking the conclusion of the Seven Year Plan. She spoke at a youth banquet, and, directing her remarks to Dorothy, said, "I became a Bahá'í because I realized that a religion that can make such wonderful people as you are must be a good religion."[17]

Dorothy had realized that pioneering was "cold rooms, dark *pensiones,* and periods of fruitless waiting; yearning souls, sudden illumination . . . and new conviction of the 'power that is far beyond the ken of men and of angels.'"[18]

****

For the Bahá'ís in the Americas, 1944–1945 was a kind of grace period granted by the Guardian between teaching plans. But the world had no grace period. World War II ended with a bang at Hiroshima, and then the abominable wound opened: the revelation of the horrors of Nazi death camps, the sufferings of prisoners of war, the desolation of the battlefields, the desecration of the cities. Many of the Bahá'ís, like Dorothy, did not interpret grace to mean rest. Dorothy kept traveling throughout North America and also to the Caribbean, Mexico,

Central America, and South America. Her tasks became increasingly significant and delicate, her insight more profound, her prayers more ardent, her yearning towards God—her sincerity—ever greater.

Eloquent as she was, it was Dorothy's sincerity, and not her words, which inspired her hearers. Rita Van Bleyswijk Sombeck entered the Bahá'í Faith and gave up much that she treasured for it because of Dorothy. Rita had been an atheist before she began attending Bahá'í meetings. She had a great prejudice against missionary work. Then, 1945 in New York, she heard Dorothy speak about the Bahá'í Administration. While she listened, she realized it was an unwillingness to sacrifice that held her back from becoming a Bahá'í for, as a Bahá'í, she would feel she must return to the Netherlands as a pioneer. That would mean relinquishing her newly attained and highly valued U.S. citizenship. She said Dorothy's voice faded as her life passed before her in a flash. She was deeply immersed in thought when, suddenly, she looked up. Dorothy's talk was over and Dorothy was standing directly before her. Dorothy told her that she was now a Bahá'í and advised her to pioneer.

By 1946, the Guardian was unfurling the banner of another Seven Year Plan. He said the North American Bahá'ís were the torch-bearers of a new civilization, and their responsibility was two-fold: to strengthen and broaden Bahá'í roots in Latin America, and to initiate teaching in war-ravaged, spiritually starved Europe.

As the Plan progressed, a small flood of pioneers left America for overseas teaching goals, among them over thirty from Lima. They were mobilized by their love of the Guardian and his stirring words, such as these: "Not ours . . . to unriddle the workings of a distant future, or to dwell upon the promised glories of a God-impelled and unimaginably potent Revelation. Ours, rather, the task to cast our eyes upon, and bend our energies to meet, the challenging requirements of the present hour."[19]

That was the trumpet call: the challenging requirements of the present hour. Peace had come, but people did not feel secure. The threat of apocalypse, nuclear war, the final self-immolation of the human race, had arisen. The Bahá'í pioneers, leaving the United States for Europe, arrived in devastated lands among weary and dejected people. They felt they were helping to fulfill the destiny of their country, which was, 'Abdu'l-Bahá had told them, to spiritually lead the world. Shoghi Effendi wrote that, during World War II, the United States had "decisively contributed . . . to the overthrow of the exponents of ideologies fundamentally at variance with the universal tenets of our Faith," and he saw the United States in a process that "must, however long and tortuous the way, lead, through a series of victories and reverses, to the political unification of the Eastern and Western Hemispheres, to the emergence of a world government . . . as foreshadowed by the Prophet Isaiah." However, he also said the U.S. would suffer "tribulations, on a scale unprecedented in its history . . . calculated to purge its institutions, to purify the hearts of its people, to fuse its constituent elements, and to meld it into one entity with its sister nations in both hemispheres. . . ." Yet he was certain that the United States, the "shell which enshrines so precious a member" of the Bahá'í world community, would evolve, "undivided and undefeatable," to complete its contribution to the rise of a new world civilization.[20]

The American Bahá'í pioneers were sustained, then, by an immense sense of mission, but that didn't diminish the pain of being far from home. And many of them, like Rita Van

Bleyswijk Sombeck, felt called upon to pioneer particularly because they'd originally come to the U.S. as immigrants and fluently spoke European languages. Their sacrifice in returning to Europe was tremendous. They were cheered and sustained by visits from Dorothy Baker.

For Anna Kunz, establishing the Bahá'í Faith in Bern, in her native Switzerland, Dorothy's visit in February, 1948, was, "a full but glorious week." She said, 'I feel it will leave signs of its beauty and blessedness for ages to come." She pointed out that tourism was down in Europe, because most people felt another war was imminent, and the Europeans believed in the *Utergang des Abendlandes* (the Decline of the West). She said, "It is for this reason, I feel, that our teaching methods in Europe bring us, almost in the first session with new inquirers, to the point that indeed a great God-sent Messenger, *'ein neuer Offenbarer,'* has come. We used to reveal the full truth only slowly, but it will not work under present conditions. Only a superman can save us from the *'Utergang.'*"[21]

Dorothy Baker arose to meet the needs of the hour, and her talks and classes were crowded. Anna translated for her, but said little in her report of her own tremendous love and admiration for Dorothy. It is meaningful, however, that she, a reticent person of highly disciplined emotions, left just one personal paper in her well-worn prayerbook after she died. It was a quote from Bahá'í Scripture about the power of Divine assistance, copied out in a fine hand on paper that had turned brittle with the years, and under the quote Anna had written in pencil, "Handwriting of Dorothy Baker."[22]

Alice Dudley, who pioneered in Stockholm in 1948, recalled that Dorothy was majestic, authoritative, and very considerate: she invited the pioneers to her hotel to take hot baths, a rare luxury at the time because of fuel shortages.

Dorothy relied on more than her own good instincts to help her as she journeyed. She wrote to friends that she felt her ability to assist in Europe was limited because she was so peripatetic, and that even if she had a million dollars to distribute it wouldn't compare with the gift of daily, ardent prayer. It seemed to her that she was traveling into a fog. She said she knew her friends' love would add potency to their prayers, so she especially wanted them.

With her usual attention to detail and devotion to family, she found time in Portugal to match-make for her daughter, Louise, who was pioneering there. Later, when Louise and her husband, Hubert Matthias, were newlyweds living in a cottage in Birre, Dorothy led study classes for the new Bahá'ís. As she did everywhere she went in the world, she told stories of 'Abdu'l-Bahá; and she was able to recite prayers and quote from Bahá'í writings without books, because she knew so much by heart. When people manifested hostility towards the Bahá'í Faith, her attitude was one of tolerance and compassion, for she felt they were only depriving themselves of the greatest gift.

Dorothy did not neglect Latin America for Europe. She continued to travel there and, somehow, though she never spent long periods of time there, she played a pivotal role in Latin American Bahá'í development. She often said that her heart was in Latin America.

Nor did she neglect her home community. She continued to serve on the National Spiritual Assembly, often as its chairman, and on various committees, and to travel and teach throughout the United States.

* * * * * * * *

Shoghi Effendi was well aware of Dorothy's worth. A brilliant and selfless Bahá'í administrator and teacher, she was already doing the work of a Hand of the Cause of God, for the "obligations of the Hands of the Cause of God," as described by 'Abdu'l-Bahá in His Will and Testament, were "to diffuse the Divine Fragrances, to edify the souls of men, to promote learning, to improve the character of all men and to be, at all times and under all conditions, sanctified and detached from all earthly things. They manifest the fear of God by their conduct, their manners, their deeds and their words."[23] When Shoghi Effendi appointed Hands of the Cause to assist him (hitherto, all Hands of the Cause had been named posthumously), Dorothy was a natural choice. But she didn't see it that way.

On December 24, 1951, Shoghi Effendi sent a long cable to the Bahá'ís of the world. The first part of it had to do with the development of the Bahá'í World Centre on Mount Carmel. Then he announced four conferences embracing eleven National Spiritual Assemblies to mark the "intercontinental stage" of Bahá'í activity and serve as precursors to a great Bahá'í World Congress. With all this, the time had come to appoint the "first contingent" of Hands of the Cause of God—three in Asia, three in America, three in Europe. He saw the newborn institution of the Hands of the Cause "forging fresh links binding" the World Centre to the international Bahá'í community.[24] He then listed his appointees. For America, he named Horace Holley, Leroy Ioas, and Dorothy Baker.

Edna True, at the U.S. Bahá'í National Center, called Dorothy in Lima. Too excited to read the whole cable, she jumped to the part about the Hands of the Cause and named all of them. When Dorothy heard her own name, she thought Edna was kidding, playing some kind of crazy practical joke. Edna kept insisting she was telling the truth. Then Dorothy decided the Guardian must have made a mistake, even though he was the soul of precision. Edna kept talking and Dorothy responded that the whole thing must be some kind of a fluke, and that was the way things stood when they hung up. Soon after the conversation, Dorothy lost her voice for three days.

A few weeks later, she managed to begin putting things into perspective, to see herself, as she always did, as part of a vast plan. She sent a copy of the Guardian's cable to Hubert and Louise in Portugal, saying, "Wanted you to see this first from me, and not from outside sources . . . I am amazed, thrilled, baffled, and uplifted, and only realize vaguely what it all means. Above all, I am humbled to a small spot. . . . It is the International phase opening up, and it is overwhelming."[25]

Outwardly, Dorothy's activities didn't change much because of the appointment, but they increased. She remained in place on the National Assembly and committees, and she kept traveling and teaching.

And Frank Baker's sacrifices grew. When another Hand of the Cause, 'Alí Akbar Furutan, asked Frank about Dorothy, her services, and their life together, Frank answered simply, "First of all, she's not just my wife. She's my queen. I would never consider myself her equal. As far as her services go, my main recollections are of packing and unpacking. I send her off on a teaching trip and when she returns I help her unpack. Those moments when we're home together are the sweetest moments of my life."[26] Frank had witnessed the growth of Dorothy's unmatched faith and conviction. He knew the depth and passion of her prayers, and he had the purity of heart and humility of spirit to place no obstacles in her path—in fact, he cleared her path. He was a very great man.

* * * * * * * * *

In 1953, when the second Seven Year Plan came to a triumphant conclusion, the Guardian announced a Ten Year Plan, also called the global Crusade, which was to begin with four Congresses—in Africa, the U.S., Europe, and India. The American Bahá'ís were no longer the only ones called upon to pioneer; European, African and Asian communities had been rapidly expanding, and they now received their own pioneering mandates. Places like Togoland, Mauritius and Reunion Island suddenly became glamour spots; these remote, seemingly unimportant places were goals named by the Guardian where Bahá'í pioneers were to settle.

Dorothy was to attend and address each of the four Congresses, but first, in February, 1953, she made her long-awaited pilgrimage. She had just a few days in Israel before the conference in Kampala, Uganda, February 12–18. She drank in the Guardian's explanations of subjects dear to her heart and found, as she had anticipated, that "at the Guardian's table . . . new vistas" opened up, and she was able to sense "indescribable joy ahead."[27]

She left Mount Carmel without regret, though her stay had been so brief. Ruḥíyyih Khánum, an old friend, knew how Dorothy had longed for pilgrimage and felt sad that it was so quickly over. She wrote, "I remember going up to her bedroom the night before she was to leave and telling her how distressed I was that . . . she only had seven nights. She gave me an answer which I have very often quoted. . . . She said

that she felt that when people came here they were like a dry
sponge and that when they had the experience of the pilgrimage . . . in an instant they were filled like a sponge being plunged
into water and that very little more could be added, so I should
not feel sad that she had only had seven nights. Her beautiful
eyes were shining when she said this and I was deeply
touched."[28]

After the pilgrimage Dorothy wrote,

> I would not attempt to write the real things, the things
> of the heart, but I can say this that the Glory of the Cause,
> its grandeur, shines like the sun, and, as for our beloved
> Guardian, he is at times a servant and again a king; and he
> is at once the point of all joy and again the nerve center of
> suffering. He is, alas, a ransom, we are his beneficiaries. He
> suffers the grief of the Prophets and yet is the 'true Brother.'
> And as he casts himself into the sea of sacrifice, he is willing
> to cast us, one and all, into that shining sea also. America is
> the lead horse. He drives the chariot that must win over the
> combined forces of the world. He cracks his whip over the
> lead horse, not the others. Do the friends realize this? The
> pilgrimage begins when you take his hand, and ends when
> you last look upon his dear face, and in between you kneel
> at the Shrines and ask for divine direction to serve him.
> And when your prayer is answered there is no doubt about
> it at all; a thousand mercies circle around the answer, and
> the Guardian is in the center of them all."[29]

With the thousand mercies circling around her, Dorothy
boarded the plane for Kampala. She couldn't sleep on board.
She never could sleep on planes. She once told a friend that
her greatest sacrifices were leaving her husband and traveling

by plane. She arrived in Africa spiritually abloom and physically exhausted, a condition to which she was well-accustomed.

The first thing she did in Africa was visit some villages. She also gave public talks in the city. Her effect on the Africans was instant: they felt that quality which the Latin Americans call *simpatía* and always applied to Dorothy; if the Africans had had the same word, they would have used it for her, for it perfectly describes the charm she exerted: it means warm, sincere, compassionate, empathetic. As for Dorothy, her meeting with the Guardian and then with the Africans made her feel more sensitive than ever to the issue of equality.

At the All-America Conference, May 3–6 in Chicago, she spoke of it: "My sights were lifted immeasurably," she said, "and I saw the vistas of these social repercussions (the result of racial oppression) coming because of our spiritual negligence through the years."[30] And she emphasized the need to teach the Native Americans.

In Stockholm, in July, 1953, at the Intercontinental Conference, Dorothy—as she had at the two preceding conferences—stirred and inspired the Bahá'ís to volunteer for pioneering, often to places they'd never heard of before, such as Liechtenstein and San Marino, the Shetland Islands, the Faroe Islands. Meanwhile, she decided the time had come to fulfill a long-deferred dream of hers and Frank's.

Soon afterwards, she wrote to her daughter, "Well, all the world is on the move, pioneering, and I do want you to have the wonderful news. . . . That Dad and I are setting sail in January for the Windward Islands, British West Indies, to settle as resident pioneers. . . . Aunty Lou [Luella, Dorothy's mother] is to go back with us next year, when we have a more definite set-up in Grenada, in fact, she is counting on it." She enthused, "Grenada . . . brings me still closer to the Latins and puts us under the NSA of South America." And she expressed her tremendous admiration and love for Frank Baker, and her own humility: "I think Dad is going to love it; he is genial by nature and a better mixer, and in the first stages at least I am sure he will accomplish more, just by his presence and general personality. But we do not wish to make 'in-a-hurry-Bahá'ís;' first we make friends, and go slowly."[31]

So, Dorothy was one of the five members of the U.S. National Spiritual Assembly who resigned in 1953 to go pioneering. The Guardian kept a photograph of that Assembly in his room at Bahjí.

Dorothy planned to go with Frank to Grenada right after her return to Lima, following the fourth Intercontinental Conference in New Delhi, October 7–15, 1953. But Dorothy was a tremendous success in India; indeed, her work in the villages there opened the way to the mass teaching that began a few years later. She said the best way to teach the Hindus was "to attain the station of a lover to his beloved."[32] And the Guardian asked Dorothy to extend her stay.

* * * * * * * * *

At last, on January 10, 1954, Dorothy, longing for reunion with Frank and the beginning of their pioneering venture, departed India aboard a Comet jet. When the flight stopped in Rome, she mailed reports of her work and observations in India to the Guardian. At 9:31 A.M., she left on the same plane for London. Shortly afterwards, a fisherman on his boat out on the Mediterranean, just south of the island of Elba, heard the whine of a plane high above the clouds. Suddenly, he heard three explosions, one right after the other. There was an ominous silence, then he saw a silver thing flash from the clouds and, trailing smoke, plummet into the sea.

All passengers and crew were lost.

When the Guardian heard the news, he bowed his head and was silent for a very long time.

Some days afterwards, Dorothy's family, with other Bahá'ís and the mourners of Dorothy's fellow travelers, went out to the site of the disaster on an Italian naval corvette. They threw floral wreaths into the sea, while wreaths also dropped from a Naval plane flying overhead, bugles sounded Taps, and flags were lowered to half-mast.

The Bahá'ís read prayers and tossed carnations onto the water. As the flowers drifted away on the blue face of the Mediterranean, the ship returned to Elba. The Bahá'ís learned that a handbag, not Dorothy's, had washed up onto the beach; it contained a Bahá'í pamphlet. So, Dorothy had been teaching up to the moment of her death. They also learned that a copy of May Maxwell's little booklet, *An Early Pilgrimage,* had been found floating on the waves. A journalist took it up, glanced at it, and tossed it back into the sea.

Later, Frank Baker went with Dorothy's mother, at the Guardian's invitation, on pilgrimage, and then they pioneered in Grenada. Frank bought a home, opened it as a Bahá'í Center, and supported pioneering and teaching efforts throughout the West Indies, residing alternately in Grenada and Lima until his death in June, 1963.

Many Bahá'ís were puzzled by Dorothy's death: what did it mean, that one so consecrated, so dedicated, should be subject in her prime to such a violent accident and torn from her loved ones and her duties? They pondered it and came up with various explanations.

But the Guardian offered no explanations. He cabled that Dorothy was an "indefatigable supporter" of the Bahá'í institutions and a "valiant defender" of Bahá'í precepts; he said her "long record" of "outstanding service enriched" the history of her Faith; and he felt sure her "noble spirit" was "reaping (a) bountiful reward."[33]

There was no solution to the mystery; there never is. But Dorothy herself had pointed the path of her soul when, in writing of her beloved grandmother, she quoted the 47th Psalm: "Sing praises to God; sing ye praises with understanding."[34]

Chapter 8

Ella Bailey

Ella Bailey, circa 1882

In April of 1912, Ella Bailey, a forty-eight year old school-teacher born and raised in the American west, journeyed across the continent by rail from San Francisco to Washington D.C. to meet 'Abdu'l-Bahá. As the train sped along, she wondered, she later recalled, "what He looked like, the color of His eyes, of His hair,"[1] and she firmly resolved not to weep in His presence.

Nevertheless, during private moments with Him, she found herself dissolved in tears. During one interview, He looked off into some blue distance all His own, repeating her name many times: "Oh, Ella Bailey, Ella Bailey!"[2] Speaking of it later, Ella said that He seemed to put into her name every possible emotion. But she rarely mentioned his amazing concluding statement: "He who loves Ella Bailey loves Me."[3]

She interpreted the varying emotions in His repetitions of her name to mean that she would suffer much sorrow and pain; her life would be hard; yet she felt He'd granted her a lifetime of faith and strength equal to her trials, and she was convinced of His spiritual power and truth. As for His physical attributes, she said, "After I had once seen Him, I never had words with which to express these things. They seemed so unimportant."[4]

* * * * * * * * *

When Ella Bailey met 'Abdu'l-Bahá, she had already experienced much affliction. She was a child of the western desert and its mining camps, born on December 18, 1864, in Houston, Texas. When she was two, she had polio; one of her legs was paralyzed for life. She was never free of pain.

When she was about three, her family moved to a ranch in San Diego County, in arid southern California near the Mexican border. She grew to love the outdoors and, despite her crippled leg, became a fine horsewoman. As a young woman, she studied at a teachers' college near the family ranch. When she was about twenty, she went to teach in the Banner Mining Camp.

Ella looked winsome and pretty in photographs taken of her when she was in her twenties, but she decided not to marry in order to dedicate her life to the education of children. Teaching in a mining camp—where just about everything was fueled by whiskey and punctuated by gunfire—was no light proposition for an idealistic, attractive young lady. And in the late 1800s, the camps seethed with labor unrest that frequently exploded in pitched battles between strikers and strike-breakers or government troops.

At one time, Ella jotted on a scrap of paper some cryptic notes about her life at Banner: "dance," "shower of confetti," "children," and "funeral." Her notes finish: "After 2 years taught at Los Angeles, there 2 years, then to San Diego, then to . . ."[5] And thus ends our existing record of Ella Bailey's youth. She taught in San Diego around 1888, and at some point after that she went to teach in Berkeley, near San Francisco.

Lua Getsinger came to teach the Bahá'í Faith in San Francisco in 1898, and again in the early 1900s. It was through Lua and one of Lua's first converts, Helen Goodall, that Ella became a Bahá'í. Ramona Allen Brown remembered Ella attending gatherings at Helen Goodall's home, before 'Abdu'l-Bahá came to America.

Helen's daughter, Ella Cooper, initially met 'Abdu'l-Bahá in 1899 as one of the first group of American pilgrims, and then, in 1907, she accompanied her mother to 'Akká. Mother and daughter wrote a booklet called *Daily Lessons Received at*

Acca, and delighted in telling the new Bahá'ís about 'Abdu'l-Bahá. They had learned from observing Him that He lived by His own teaching: whatever is done with love is never trouble, and there is always time. They themselves beautifully manifested this attitude.

Bahá'í literature had not yet been published in book form; 'Abdu'l-Bahá's tablets and prayers, often sent to Helen Goodall, were typed and copied. It took weeks for His messages to reach the U.S. by boat, and the Bahá'ís looked to Ella Cooper and Helen for a living example of His philosophy; fortunately, the two women were worthy of such a trust.

Ramona Allen Brown remembered that, before attending a Unity Feast, each Bahá'í prepared with private prayers centered in the assurance that 'Abdu'l-Bahá promised to be present in spirit whenever His friends gathered together in love. At the Goodall home, Helen and her daughter graciously welcomed the Bahá'ís and ushered them to seats at two long tables in the dining room. There was no chatter or frivolous talk; just a hush.

At each place setting was a slip of paper bearing a verse from *The Hidden Words of Bahá'u'lláh.* After the guests were seated, all silently said the Greatest Name, and a Bahá'í went from person to person, anointing each forehead with attar of roses, while everyone remained quiet and prayerful. Then they read from The Hidden Words, enjoyed refreshments and, when they left, received from their hostesses the flowers that had adorned the tables.

Ramona remembered an evening when Ella Bailey was the one who anointed each brow with perfume. She recalled Ella's charming, sweet smile and said she always felt that Ella, a joyous soul, was an example of courage, for she couldn't walk easily and never felt in good health.

'Abdu'l-Bahá knew Ella's heart, and in 1909 sent her a Tablet counseling,

> Be thou not sad on account of past vicissitudes and troubles, neither be thou discouraged by hardships and difficulties. Be thou hopeful in the bounty of the True One, and be thou happy and rejoiced in the love of God. This world is the arena of tests, trials and calamities. All the existing things are targets for the arrows of mortality; therefore one must not feel sad or disheartened on account of the travails or become hopeless over the intensity of misfortune and distress. Praise be to God that thou hast found the guidance of God, hast entered into the Kingdom of God, hast attained to peace and tranquillity, and hast obtained a share from the Everlasting Bounty and Mercy. Therefore pass the remaining days of thy life with the utmost joy and fragrance, and with joyful heart and tranquil mind, live and act under the protection of His Highness, the Clement.[6]

* * * * * * * *

Because of her afflictions, Ella may have felt that "the remaining days of her life" were destined to be brief. But the best days were yet to come. A few years later, 'Abdu'l-Bahá was in America, and Ella, traveling with Helen Goodall and her daughter, stayed close to Him throughout much of His visit. She later recalled that, in Washington, D.C., where they first met Him, "He greeted me by saying that he was happy to see me with my spiritual mother (Mrs. Goodall), thereby confirming a beautiful spiritual relationship that continued for life between Mrs. Goodall and myself." The greeting also cemented the sisterly bond between the two Ellas. 'Abdu'l-Bahá told the three ladies, "It makes me very happy to see you. When the hearts are pure it makes me very happy. This is what we came for—that the hearts might be made pure. I care not for ease, I care not for comfort, and when I see the pure hearts nothing else matters."[7]

'Abdu'l-Bahá was lionized in Washington. The Secretary of the U.S. Treasury, Lee McClung, came to see Him, and wept and embraced Him. Supreme Court Justices sought Him out, as did doctors, lawyers, diplomats, and the president of the militant new American Federation of Labor, Samuel Gompers. At the Turkish Embassy, a teary-eyed ambassador, knowing far too well all that 'Abdu'l-Bahá had suffered as a prisoner of the Ottoman Empire, acclaimed Him as a peerless Being. 'Abdu'l-Bahá left the Turkish embassy via His preferred mode of transport, the trolley, and returned to Agnes Parsons' house, where He was visited by the former U.S. President, Theodore Roosevelt, who was just beginning his new presidential campaign against William Howard Taft. The Washington press reported how all Bahá'í meetings in that racially segregated city were integrated at the insistence of 'Abdu'l-Bahá. When He spoke to over 1,000 people at Rankin Chapel in Howard University and said that the establishment of racial unity would assure world peace, He received a standing ovation. But it exhilarated Him more to speak in a Bahá'í home where people of all shades of brown and white gathered: He praised the group as a beautiful cluster of jewels.

He afterwards went to the stately home of Alexander Graham Bell, the inventor of the telephone, and was taken there in a car. Perhaps the Bahá'ís thought he would rest during the ride, but His voice could be heard forcefully above the noise of the vehicle: "Oh Bahá'u'lláh! What hast Thou done! O Bahá'u'lláh! May my life be sacrificed for Thee! Oh Bahá'u'lláh! May my soul be offered up for Thy sake! How full were Thy days with trials and tribulation! How severe the ordeals Thou didst endure! How solid the foundations Thou hast finally laid, and how glorious the banner Thou didst hoist.'"[8]

When 'Abdu'l-Bahá proceeded from Washington to Chicago to dedicate the land for the Bahá'í House of Worship, Helen Goodall and the two Ellas followed. They took rooms in the Plaza Hotel, where 'Abdu'l-Bahá was staying. In Chicago, among His many activities, He spoke at Jane Addams' famous settlement center for the indigent, Hull House, and afterwards gave coins to the children and unemployed men who crowded around Him. He addressed an audience of 2,000 at the Fourth Annual Convention of the Bahá'í Temple Unity. The *Chicago Examiner* hallucinogetically reported that there were fifteen million Bahá'ís in the world and 'Abdu'l-Bahá's room "had the appearance of an oriental court" since the women (Ella Bailey, the schoolmarm, among them) were wearing "blue robes and turbans" and all the men were "garbed in flowing robes and fezzes." Not to be outdone, the Chicago newspaper *Inter-Ocean* announced that 'Abdu'l-Bahá was the leader of forty million "Bahaists." Another paper said He was wearing "a gown and turban with red and white stripes." 'Abdu'l-Bahá had infinite patience, but being described as wearing red and white stripes was too much even for Him. He set the reporters straight: "I never wore such colors."[9]

The Bahá'ís trailed after 'Abdu'l-Bahá as He took frequent strolls in Lincoln Park, which stretched greenly from the doors of the Plaza. Sometimes, He would pick up a fallen bough and use it as a walking stick. There was a menagerie in the park, and He liked to stop and watch the polar bear. He also used to pause and contemplate the statue of Abraham Lincoln.

Ella Bailey was present on that cold and wet May 1 when He dedicated the Temple property, and she was also the alternate delegate from San Francisco and Oakland at the Convention. She spoke up during the consultation, and it was mentioned in the convention report. This is one of the only references ever found to Ella Bailey taking a vocal part in a large activity, since her preferred place was behind the scenes.

On May 5, she attended a children's gathering hosted by 'Abdu'l-Bahá, and later described it in an article written with Ella Cooper for the *Star of the West:*

> Although many lived a considerable distance away and found it necessary to arise as early as five o-clock, yet promptly at the appointed hour of eight, about thirty-five children were on hand to greet Him. . . . They were gathered in a circle in the middle of the beautiful parlor of the Plaza, the parents and friends making another circle behind them. When 'Abdu'l-Bahá entered, all arose. While He took the seat prepared for Him, the children sang without accompaniment, 'Softly His Voice is Calling Now.' . . .
>
> Then followed the scene that is indelibly stamped upon the minds and hearts. He called each child to Him in turn, took them in His lap, petting and stroking the hair and hugging and kissing the little ones, pressing the hands and embracing the older ones, all with such infinite love and tenderness shining in His eyes and thrilling in the tones of His voice, that when He whispered in English in their ears to tell Him their names, they answered as joyfully and freely as they would a beloved father. To each child He gave a little different touch, patting some on the breast, some on

the back and some on the head. He blessed them all. There was no suggestion of haste and a hush fell upon the group— a quiet, vibrant, eloquent silence. . . . The children's joy and His own happiness seemed to culminate when one dear little tot ran to Him and fairly threw herself into His arms. When he let her go she stood for a second and then suddenly laughed aloud with perfect joy, which found its instant echo in a ripple around the whole circle.[10]

Ella, with her spiritual mother and sister, returned replete to California. They didn't expect that 'Abdu'l-Bahá would visit there. A few months later, they learned He would arrive in San Francisco on October 3.

Several times, He told the California Bahá'ís, "Your love drew me to you."[11] With His first greetings at the house at 1815 California St., which Helen Goodall and Ella Cooper had chosen for Him, He pointed out how rare His journey was, that it was common to cross a continent for the sake of tourism or trade, but not "simply for the sake of spiritual communion." He said it had occurred "through the bounty of Bahá'u'lláh. We witness how He has brought about the spiritual connection among the hearts."[12]

During His three-week stay in California, the Bahá'ís, among them Ella Bailey, tried to serve Him as much as they could. They went into the kitchen and cooked for Him. He especially liked different kinds of broth. And they brought Him his favorite foods, such as Edam cheese and cucumbers. They spent every moment they could in the house, sitting in the hall or the living room, just to catch a glimpse of Him when He passed and hear His voice. When He went out to speak publically, they followed, and when they saw that He was fatigued or seemed to be ailing, they prayed.

There was were several children's parties with 'Abdu'l-Bahá, reminiscent of the one in Chicago. During a fête at Helen Goodall's house, marshmallows were the treat of the day, and 'Abdu'l-Bahá gave them out, walking among the children and telling each one, "Two hands! Two hands!" because He wanted to make sure every child got as many as possible.[13] Then He addressed the children, saying that they were all good, all illumined. His spontaneity and generosity with youngsters must have meant a great deal to Ella Bailey, since she was such a devoted teacher.

On October 24, as 'Abdu'l-Bahá took His leave of San Francisco, He told the Bahá'ís the tragic story of Bahá'u'lláh's banishment from Iran. Ramona Brown recalled how tears coursed down His cheeks as He spoke, for He seemed to be reliving that heart-breaking journey; and the Bahá'ís also wept. Then 'Abdu'l-Bahá recaptured joy. His voice rang and His eyes sparkled as He authoritatively described the Declaration of Bahá'u'lláh in the Garden of Riḍván, and explained how, in 'Akká, Bahá'u'lláh elucidated His Covenant, which would forever safeguard His Cause. Then He rose from His chair and powerfully proclaimed, "I am the Center of that Covenant!"[14] The Bahá'ís, their faces alight with joy and wonder, also rose. A silence fell, and after a few minutes, 'Abdu'l-Bahá spoke again. Looking into each face, He asked His friends to be faithful, and to teach, not merely by words, but in action. He said, "These wonderful days are passing swiftly, and, once gone, they will never come again."[15] Then the Bahá'ís approached Him to say goodbye. Taking their hands, smiling into their eyes, He repeated, "Allah'u'Abhá!" (God is Most Glorious!)

Throughout Ella Bailey's quiet and humble life, she acted upon 'Abdu'l-Bahá's message and followed His example of selfless love and service. And when she arose to perform her last act of service, her greatest deed, she revealed how deeply and eternally she had given her heart to Him.

* * * * * * * * *

When 'Abdu'l-Bahá died in 1921, Ella was fifty-seven, and she must have felt His loss deeply, especially because Helen Goodall, already aged, felt destitute without Him and died soon after He did. Ella Bailey went on, however, bringing to everything she did a compassion born of her own suffering, and a clear-headed pragmatism that was greatly appreciated by all her associates. She had breadth of vision, and she abhorred niggling, picayune thinking.

Year after year, she taught elementary grades at the McKinley School in Berkeley, and, as former students grew up, they always remembered her. Her health forced her to retire in 1924, at the age of sixty, and the principal of the school wrote to her, thanking her for her services, concluding, "I cannot close this letter without telling you again what a precious thing your friendship has been to me and will continue to be, and how we all have been inspired by your courage and faith."[16]

In 1925, the first Local Spiritual Assembly of the Bahá'ís of Berkeley was elected, and Ella was the first chairman. At that time, a Bahá'í Home was established at 2108 Scott Street in San Francisco, and all the Bahá'í communities in the area worked jointly. Ella wrote proudly, in a report about a children's party at the Bahá'í Home, that the place had been dubbed the House of Light "because it is so filled with sunshine and already emits a Bahá'í spirit." Speaking lovingly of her spiritual sister, she added, "Mrs. Cooper presided (at the party) and if any old care or worry had slipped in, her charming graciousness would soon have routed it."[17]

Ella was reelected annually to the Assembly for over two decades. She never sought the limelight. Her friend, Robert Gulick, said,

> In over twenty years of association with her, the writer does not remember having once seen her on a public platform. Far from seeking publicity, she avoided it. During her long residence at the Berkeley Women's City Club, she used her membership to sponsor many Bahá'í gatherings. Her room became a kind of clinic for the distressed and disconsolate. Hundreds have partaken of her spiritual and material hospitality and generosity.[18]

Recalling 'Abdu'l-Bahá's suggestion that a Bahá'í should teach as if offering a gift to a king, Robert further recalls of Ella,

> Her presentation of the message of Bahá'u'lláh was indeed like that of a royal subject giving his most precious possession to his sovereign. Gentleness and sweetness were her abiding traits. She never tried to force her opinions on anyone but ever beckoned the thirsty to come to the fountain and drink of the water of life that will bring healing to men and nations. Her saintly life proved the best means of promoting the prestige of the Faith she so ardently espoused. Sound in judgment, she never aroused hostility nor did she compromise on principle. Many were her secret sacrifices. She would give sumptuous dinners for friends who were oblivious to the fact that their hostess very often contented herself with tea, toast, and perhaps a little soup. Her whole

day passed in cheering the brokenhearted, in helping the needy, in visiting the sick, and in refreshing the spirits of the unending stream of guests that came to see her.[19]

Robert's wife, Bahia, recalled of Ella, "This club where she lived had a big dining room with expensive, good food, where she would take her guests, but while eating alone in her room she would have very simple, canned food. When we took food which my mother had cooked, Ella would put it in the bathtub in her room. She didn't even have a refrigerator."[20]

By 1937, Ella was physically feeling her age, for she'd had an appendectomy and a series of falls. Her handicap made her increasingly accident-prone as she grew older. Undaunted, she wrote enthusiastically to Martha Root, "Your letter is a wonderful document and reaching me near the time Shoghi Effendi's letter 'The Advent of Divine Justice' was put into my hands I have been having a glorious uplift. What a wonderful time this is in which we are living. What a heart searching time! The very stones must feel the urge to serve! Your work is a marvel! I have, in my mind, pictured your long journeys, your constant and untiring efforts—surely all this will cause the Work to grow in wonderful rapidity and I know His strength is given you to 'carry on' and His protection is constantly with you."[21]

Ella had helped Martha complete a cherished project by planting a rose bush on Howard Carpenter's grave. Martha had worked with him and his wife, Marzieh Gail, in Austria and Bulgaria; at that time, he and Marzieh were en route to Iran at the behest of the Guardian, where Howard's skills as a doctor were sorely needed. Sadly, long months passed in Iran before Howard could get a license to practice medicine, and then he became desperately ill, returned to California for treatment, and died there. In her letter to Martha, Ella continued, "I must tell you about the rose bush you helped put on (the) grave . . . I asked his mother . . . and his sisters what color they would prefer. They decided upon a yellow so when the proper season for planting came Marion Yazdi and I went to the nursery and selected a rose tree, a healthy plant and a yellow color that has pleased them all very much. When you come to Berkeley we will visit that sacred spot again and have prayers. I hope our rose will be blooming."[22]

On the whole, that letter encapsulated Ella: her support of others, her willingness to render loving care, and her secret yen for adventure. As her life stretched into the 1950s, she saw her Faith growing apace all over the world, carried forward by bold pioneers, and she had always been a homebody. Perhaps it had not been very easy for her stay at home. A photograph of her, taken in May, 1950, when she was eighty-six, shows her looking trim, spry and natty in a plaid blouse, a tailored suit with a long skirt, a hat with a snappy brim, and an umbrella and efficient-looking purse hanging from her wrist. She definitely seemed ready to travel.

* * * * * * * *

When Ella was eighty-eight, in 1953, Shoghi Effendi launched the Bahá'ís on the Global Crusade, and Ella responded with gusto. The name Africa was on the lips of many Bahá'ís, for, during the closing years of the second Seven Year Plan, which had begun as a concentrated effort in Europe, pioneers had gone for the first time to Africa, something which hadn't been contemplated when the Plan was initiated—but the Bahá'is were in a state of great enthusiasm. After that Plan, Shoghi Effendi had projected a three-year respite, but the Bahá'ís were so vigorous and motivated that they needed no rest.

When Ella read Shoghi Effendi's stirring messages, and heard that he wanted Robert Gulick and his wife, Bahia, to go to Libya, she secretly yearned to accompany them, but did not tell them. However, they intuited her wishes, and when they told her they would enjoy having her come with them, Robert said she "beamed gratefully." Then her face clouded, and she said, "It would be selfish of me to go to Africa and be a burden." Yet the Gulicks felt her presence would be a blessing. To make sure of doing the right thing, they cabled the Guardian, who responded, "Approve Bailey accompany you." Robert said that cable constituted Ella's "marching orders."[23]

Ella had no living relatives, and was really part of the Gulick family. Bahia Gulick remembers,

> Ella Bailey was my closest friend. I was but a bride— really still a youth—and she was in her eighties . . . I missed my grandmother, whom I had loved very much, and Ella really replaced that grandmother. My mother also missed her mother, and Ella was a mother for her. My best hours were those spent close to Ella listening to all the beautiful Bahá'í stories and her experiences in life. . . .
>
> An outstanding characteristic of Ella Bailey was that she always had a smile on her face. I never heard her complaining. It was very difficult for her at her age to be active, and it took her a long time to dress. I do remember I had to help her put on her shoes; it used to take a long time because she had polio as a child and she had special shoes made for her. She always walked with a cane, which I still have as a remembrance of her. . . .

Ella guided me in everything and taught me particularly how a Bahá'í can sacrifice. . . . In that regard, an incident just happened to remind me of her generosity. . . . I was recently going over the papers which she left to us and I came upon a canceled check. It was Ella's check for $1,000 to the National Fund. Ella was not a wealthy person. . . . Looking at the date, I noticed it was just a few months before she accompanied us to North Africa as pioneers.[24]

Bahia called Ella, in the Persian way, "Ella-Jún" (Ella darling), and cherished her so much that, while preparing to go to Libya, her only worry was about leaving Ella behind. "I thought, 'How can I tell Ella Bailey we are going?'"[25] So of course Bahia was relieved when it was determined that Ella would accompany them and live with them. The Gulicks offered to pay for Ella's ticket but, somehow, she managed it on her own.

Ella then wondered whether it would be wise for her to also go to Chicago to the great Jubilee Celebration: the All-America Intercontinental Teaching Conference combined with the dedication of the finally completed House of Worship. Since she had been present when 'Abdu'l-Bahá dedicated the Temple grounds in 1912, it seemed a shame for her to miss the festivities, and friends encouraged her to go. The Gulicks took her with them.

And so it was that Ella Bailey was one of the people described by William Sears when he wrote about the public dedication ceremony under the lofty, lacy dome of the Temple: "Across the aisle could be seen the glowing and triumphant faces of those apostles of Bahá'u'lláh who had stood upon this same plot of ground with 'Abdu'l-Bahá on that cold, windy May day, forty-one years ago. They had watched their beloved Master dedicate the spot, then an empty, open field, to the welfare of all humanity. The real Temple, He had told them, was the Word of God... Then He looked up, smiled, and assured them that 'in the unseen world, the Temple is already built.'"[26]

Having seen the Temple, a solid reality, in the visible world, Ella also partook of the conference sessions and heard the Guardian's ringing appeal for pioneers. He placed no material expectations on the pioneers; all they needed was purity of heart. He called upon people of all ages, telling the elderly to leave their homes and lay their bones on distant shores, encouraging the young to go forth in the full flood of their ardor. As volunteers for pioneering ascended the stage during the conference, Ella, with her usual avoidance of public platforms, did not join them, but she had already answered the Guardian's appeal; when Robert Gulick announced his intention of going to Libya, he announced Ella Bailey's, too.

* * * * * * * * *

When Ella returned from Wilmette to California, one of her friends noticed that her voice hadn't sounded so light and gay for forty years. But, just a few days later, she became ill with pneumonia. She had to be hospitalized, and then she couldn't go back to the Berkeley Women's Club but had to take a bed at a nursing home. The Gulicks had already left for Tripoli, and Ella was determined to join them.

Robert recalled, "Old friends of older Faiths were horrified at her decision to pull up stakes in California and settle on the old Barbary Coast of North Africa, and they warned her that such a move would shorten her life. She smilingly answered,

'I do not find it such a great sacrifice to give up living in a rest home.'"[27]

On July 14, 1953, she left California, her home for eighty-five years since she moved there with her parents from Texas when she was three. The next day, at the New York apartment of a Bahá'í friend, she was honored with a visit from two Hands of the Cause of God, Dhikru'lláh Khádem and Musá Banání. She had a fall in New York, but an examination revealed no fractures, so she continued on. In Italy, one of the distinguished Italian Bahá'ís, Mario Fiorentini, did all he could for her, and was worried when she fell again, but she was so eager to reach Africa that the fall only inspired her to cut short her stay in Italy. Robert Gulick said, "Equipped with an oxygen mask, Miss Bailey was an excellent traveler. She arrived at Tripoli on July 20."[28]

She wasn't at all well, yet she was conscious of where she was and of the mission she'd undertaken. However, she sustained further falls, and at last became bedridden. Robert Gulick said she "sometimes was not conscious of her condition. " And then again, "she would become painfully aware of her infirmities and would apologize for the work her sickness entailed. She knew that she was in loving hands and, when possessed of her faculties, repeatedly thanked Mrs. Shawkat-Alí Faraju'lláh (Robert's mother-in-law) for nursing her day and night. The presence in the room of two-year old Robert Gulick III always brought a smile to her face."[29]

Ella was not afraid to die. A decade before she went to Africa, she wrote, in a sympathy note to a friend who had lost her husband, "Perhaps my own hampered body has enabled me to look forward to this change as a visit from 'the messenger of joy' and with the assurance that only fuller joy and union with loved ones 'gone before' awaits us . . . in the world of the Kingdom."[30]

Bahá'ís were gathered at Ella's bedside, praying, when she died as twilight neared on August 25, 1953. An Egyptian Bahá'í wept as he kissed her forehead and murmured, "Goodbye, Miss Bailey."[31]

The Guardian cabled that she was a "valiant exemplary pioneer," and her "reward in (the) Kingdom (was) bountiful."[32] At the end of 1953, he sent a telegram to the Intercontinental Conference in New Delhi, saying that the "irresistibly unfolding Crusade" had been "sanctified" by the death of the "heroic . . . Ella Bailey." He said she was "the first American martyr to be laid to rest in African soil," and this had shed "further luster" on the American Bahá'í community, while it consecrated the soil of the "fast awakening African continent."[33]

She had certainly fulfilled the destiny 'Abdu'l-Bahá evoked for her on that April day in 1912 when he repeated her name so magically and then said, "He who loves Ella Bailey loves Me."

But despite her great devotion and her long years as a Bahá'í, Ella had never met the Guardian. She had never even written to him. She knew his workload and was unwilling to burden him; besides, in her humility she followed her simple and singular path and had no pressing inner unrest, no major questions. Yet the Guardian knew her worth. To the Bahá'ís in Libya, he wrote that he personally wished to bear the cost of a marker for her grave.

He often did this for the pioneers. They meant everything to him. Ruḥíyyih Khánum has commented about how touched she was, in Switzerland with the Guardian for one of his rest cures, when he went on a special pilgrimage to pray at the grave of Dagmar Dole, a pioneer who had died there.

The pioneers were the ones who answered the Guardian's summons to carry the Bahá'í Faith forward to every spot on the globe, to make the earth as one country—a country to be ultimately swaddled and lapped in love, in fulfillment of the prophecy of Habbakuk: "The earth shall be filled with the knowledge of the Glory of the Lord as the waters cover the sea."[34] Towards that outcome, the Guardian devised his teaching plans, based on the Divine Plan of 'Abdu'l-Bahá, and he made maps showing the goals of the plans and the victories won. On one of his maps, he put a gold star on the place where Ella Bailey died.

Chapter 9

Marion Jack

Marion Elizabeth Jack, circa 1885

"Come to me." So 'Abdu'l-Bahá instructed Marion Jack when He realized that she had wept alone in His house at 'Akká, where she lived during 1908 and taught English to His family.

A letter from Marion to Ella Cooper tells why she wept while observing 'Abdu'l-Bahá at that time, when He was surrounded by malicious enemies: "Anyone who thinks life for me here is pure joy should try a little of it in my place. . . . Our Dear One saw me one day when I had given way and whether He noticed my red eyes or only felt the depressing atmosphere He asked me how I was and I said quite well. He said *not* quite well and told (His daughter) to tell me I must come to Him when I feel sad. . . ."[1] As the daughter related those words to Marion, 'Abdu'l-Bahá stood by and repeated, "Come to me."

He was under severe surveillance in 1908 because of the rumor-mongering of jealous relatives. While Marion was living in His household, His enemies succeeded in scaring authorities into thinking the square sandstone Shrine of the Báb that He was building on Mount Carmel was a fortress and 'Abdu'l-Bahá intended to usurp Ottoman Rule and establish His own kingdom. A Commission of Inquiry sent by the Sultán dogged 'Abdu'l-Bahá's every move, and He was threatened with exile or death. Visits by western pilgrims stopped, because 'Abdu'l-Bahá deemed them unwise. Things were so bad that He sent His favored grandson, Shoghi Effendi, to live in Haifa, and He instructed the boy not to drink any coffee in other people's homes, because it might contain poison.

The defection of those who should have been staunch grieved and angered 'Abdu'l-Bahá, but He was never distressed by the needs of those who truly loved Him, such as Marion Jack. However, Marion was deeply aware of her own failings and appreciative of His forgiveness, so that she wished the trouble-makers could "feel their own sins" as she felt hers, for then, she said, "they might have more mercy" on 'Abdu'l-Bahá.[2]

Beset as He was by troubles, He yet found His joys, and one of them was Marion herself. She had a hearty good humor and a take-charge spirit. She wrote to Ella that 'Abdu'l-Bahá called her General Jack, and joked that His household was her camp. Contrasted with the flitting and gliding of veiled oriental women and the arch mincing of prim occidental women, Marion's forthright stride amused 'Abdu'l-Bahá. He liked to tease her about getting married, and His daughter said He was only half-joking, for He always wanted those He loved to get married and have families. But Marion had decided long since that she never wanted to be tied down by marriage, so she elected to take it all lightly.

When 'Abdu'l-Bahá gave her a pair of Persian silk socks in rainbow colors, she put them on her hands and said she'd wear them as gloves to her wedding. He laughed and said He'd give her better than that, and anointed her with attar of roses. Marion was pleased that she'd made Him laugh. She wrote to Ella, "I do wish you had seen His amusement that day. I have never seen Him so merry before or since. Often He comes in laughing and making jokes to the family—I think to cheer them up—and sometimes when He looks so tired and ill Himself that one sees it is all pure exertion for His dear family's sake."[3]

It isn't known exactly when Marion left 'Abdu'l-Bahá's household, but it is clear that, all her life, she communicated the *joi de vivre* that He had found so precious. Friends recalled, "Everyone who recounts some acquaintance or association with (Marion) always does so with a smile which seems to spring spontaneously from the mere mention of her name."[4] Marion regarded herself simply as a friend to all people, calling herself "a common or garden woman."[5] Such a reference makes one think of the kinds of flowers that brighten kitchen doorways—hollyhocks, marigolds, mums. Those flowers are not the most delicate and royal, but they are often the most beloved. And this "common or garden woman," known as Jacky to her friends, followed 'Abdu'l-Bahá's example of hardiness: blooming so radiantly that she became, despite disaster, in the words of Shoghi Effendi, an "immortal heroine."[6]

* * * * * * * * *

Marion Elizabeth Jack was born on December 1, 1866, in St. John, New Brunswick, Canada. The child of a happy marriage between Henry and Annie Jack, Marion had five brothers and sisters. Her father, a kind and generous man, served as Vice Consul to Spain and was chief founder of the Reformed Episcopal Church in St. John; both her parents were deeply religious. But her mother's health was delicate. Three of her children died, and then a fire devastated the family home. Broken by these losses, Annie died when Marion was sixteen. Henry Jack couldn't get over his wife's death, and he passed away two years later.

So Marion, the bringer of joy, was no stranger to sorrow. In fact, she wrote, "As I have the capacity of suffering much, so I also enjoy much."[7]

At fourteen, she'd started painting lessons. She also studied music. After considering becoming a musician, she decided instead to be an artist. In 1885, when she was a wistful looking nineteen-year old with a cherubic face, she went to the Lambeth School of Art in London, and soon afterwards she was in Paris. During her twenties and thirties, she traveled and painted landscapes, wintering in Europe and spending summers in North America. On her limited income, she lived with great economy and charming extravagance.

It was in Paris that Marion heard about the Bahá'í Faith. She lived in the Latin Quarter at a pension for ladies kept by a Mademoiselle Philippe who, when the spirit moved her, put on gala costume balls for her boarders and their friends. At one of these parties, Marion, wearing a bright red costume of crinkled tissue paper topped with a huge Merry Widow hat trimmed with big yellow paper flowers, danced and chatted with an architecture student. He looked festive in a light blue silk waistcoat trimmed with white and gold, and he told her about the Bahá'í Faith. Marion immediately began attending meetings, but she said she only understood the Faith some time afterward, when a Persian believer explained it to her.

During 1908, she returned from 'Akká to Canada and helped found an art club in her hometown. In 1910, she went for the first time to Green Acre, the Bahá'í School on the banks of the Piscataqua River in Eliot, Maine, and fell in love with the spot. She bought a cottage in Eliot, just one room up on stilts, reached by a gangplank, with a small, two-story studio behind it. For some years, she spent every summer at Green Acre, painting and teaching.

Green Acre was born of the vision of Sarah Farmer, who, influenced by the Transcendentalist teachings of Ralph Waldo Emerson, first established it as a spiritual retreat dedicated to world peace and the harmony of religions. Then she heard about the Bahá'í Faith, went to see 'Abdu'l-Bahá, became a Bahá'í, and bequeathed her property and her dream to the United States Bahá'í community.

The grand ideal of peace, to which Sarah Farmer dedicated Green Acre, became more potent after 'Abdu'l-Bahá visited the place in 1912, and Marion felt it strongly. A Green Acre landscape that Marion painted many times was the grove called the Lysekloster (Cloisters of Light) Pines. People invested those beautiful old trees with singular personalities because of their age and the mystical events that transpired in their shade. One was called the Persian Pine, another the Swami Pine. In Marion's day, an arched Chinese bridge spanning a small pond led to the Lysekloster Pines, and she painted so many pictures of the scene that Green Acre regulars called the water Marion Jack's Pond.

It is probable, but not certain, that Marion was with 'Abdu'l-Bahá at Green Acre in 1912, but she was definitely with Him in London in 1911 when He made His first visit to the occident. She shared a London flat with a Bahá'í named Elizabeth Herrick at 137 High Street, Kensington, and she and Elizabeth hosted a meeting for 'Abdu'l-Bahá there on a cold, damp September 22. About eighty people attended.

'Abdu'l-Bahá had suffered tuberculosis as a child and doctors advised Him not to go out in raw weather. At Marion's apartment, He told the gathering, "Although the day is cold for me to go out, yet I have come to see you. For the lover there are no difficulties; all is easy. For love I have journeyed to London. . . ." He spoke of the unity of East and West, and told the assemblage, ". . . Ye are all the waves of one sea, the birds of one heaven and mirrors of the same Bounty."[8]

Marion based herself for some years in London; in 1914, when World War I began, she was attending the Bahá'í Temple Unity Convention in Chicago as a delegate from London. Afterwards, she stayed in North America, particularly in Canada.

Much of the time, she was in Montreal with May Maxwell. In 1915, she wrote to Helen Goodall, "I am now . . . in Montreal where the Beloved ('Abdu'l-Bahá) wants me to be."

She added that the Montreal Bahá'í group wasn't large, but "full of spiritual love and unity. . . . And dear May Maxwell is always so lovely and so loving. I am indeed grateful to the Heavenly Beloved for allowing me to be a worker in this assembly in which she is the teacher. I have what May Maxwell calls the social instinct and can gather the people together for her to talk to and teach, so we do beautifully."[9]

Marion was in her mid-forties by that time, and she had developed some eye problems, but she continued producing and exhibiting landscapes and portraits. When she sold a painting of the Lecture Pine at Green Acre, she was thrilled because, she said, "nearly all the Artists are having such poor luck everywhere," and, also, she had "little luck in such sales as a rule."[10] She contributed the money to the Bahá'í Temple Fund.

A charming photograph shows Marion at Green Acre during this period, performing a pageant outdoors with three other women. It was the style at the time, set by Isadora Duncan, to imitate the nymphs painted on the sides of ancient Greek vases and dance in tunics with flower-bedecked hair flowing free. Marion, dimpling wryly at the camera, kicked up her heels and certainly didn't look her years.

In 1916 Marion responded to May Maxwell's encouragement to travel from Canada and teach at Chatauqua, a famous cultural spa in New York State. She went with a feeling of inadequacy offset by a lesson she'd learned from her painting professor: never fear to dare. Although Marion never failed to initiate Bahá'í teaching work, she always hoped that Bahá'ís she considered more capable would step in and take over. But fate called her to pioneer. In answer to 'Abdu'l-Bahá's plea in the "Tablets of the Divine Plan" for Bahá'ís to teach in Alaska, she made an epic journey there with Emogene Hoagg in 1919.

* * * * * * * * *

Alaska was the last frontier of the U.S., pictured by most people as an empty white wilderness. It had been called derogatory names like Icebergia until gold was discovered, whereupon it became an official U.S. territory with its own legislature. When Marion and Emogene visited, it was a rough and tumble hodgepodge of prospectors and missionaries; salmon canneries, general stores and saloons; and Chinese immigrants, Eskimos, Indians, and rustic white Alaskans called "sourdoughs."*

Margaret Duncan Green, a Bahá'í who was a poet, had pioneered from 1915–18 in Alaska, working in the Juneau library; and another Bahá'í named Susan Rice had traveled up the Yukon River in Canada to Dawson, then westward to Fairbanks. Now Marion and Emogene added to those efforts.

Emogene, taught by Lua Getsinger, had become a Bahá'í in California in 1898, and had made a pilgrimage to 'Abdu'l-Bahá in 1900. Widowed in 1918, she was financially independent and gave most of her time to pioneering and travel teaching; Alaska was one of her great adventures.

She and Marion left California in June, 1919, on the Alaskan steamship *Victoria,* and reached Nome in July. They planned to stay in Nome a week, but weather conditions might have stranded them there for a month or more, so they went right on to St. Michael, on the Yukon Delta, across Norton Sound from Nome, and boarded the little steamer *Julia B.* for their trip down the river.

Accomplishing that was not as easy as it sounds. First, they had to cross the water from Nome on a small launch and

---

*A veteran inhabitant and especially an old-time prospector of Alaska or northwestern Canada.

reboard the *Victoria*. The wind was wild, and the waves crashed over their heads, lifting the launch to dizzying heights and then dropping it, soaking the travelers. The *Victoria*'s crew lowered a rope ladder, expecting the drenched passengers to climb up from the launch. That offer was refused, so they improvised a gang plank and, as big waves lifted the launch, passengers were grabbed by a man on the plank from the hands of a man on the launch.

Then the trip to St. Michael took twelve hours, and there was a five-day wait till the wind subsided and they could board the river steamer. When they got to the mouth of the river to continue their trip, there was another wait, eighteen hours, because the flat-bottomed steamer had to come to the mouth when the tide was high, so as not to get caught on sand bars and, because of strong wind and an extra load of freight on their conveyance, the travelers got to the mouth too late for the tide. When it finally came, and the *Julia B.* arrived and made a start, they were again halted by high winds, and they had another eighteen-hour wait.

All this was good practice for the river journey, which was glacially slow. There was plenty of time to get acquainted with fellow travelers, crew members, and riverfront townsfolk. The freighter, carrying 1,400 tons, traveled, at most, at three miles per hour, and there were long stops, sometimes for periods of days, to load and unload.

Marion and Emogene traveled the Tanana River into the Yukon, along a stretch where the Alaska Highway now runs. For eight months and hundreds of miles, they followed the strategy Marion preferred. She went out and sketched portraits, won her subjects over with smiles and little jokes, and led the conversation to the query as to whether her new friends had ever heard of the Bahá'í Faith. Few people had, but, at one point, a Mrs. Hirsch said she had seen 'Abdu'l-Bahá when He was in New York. When Marion found an interested party, she took her to Emogene for further enlightenment. Emogene also wrote newspaper articles and gave public talks.

Marion did a lot of portraits of native people. In this, she veered far from popular sentiment. People wondered why she spent time with the Eskimos. Early in the trip, she and Emogene noticed the prejudice against the Eskimos, and how they and other native people were at the mercy of commercial interests. That wasn't the only kind of prejudice they observed. Emogene reported that, at a small town called Marshall, a woman of color boarded the steamer with a first class ticket, but when she came into the diningroom to eat, the steward told her there was no seat and she left the room, looking, Emogene reported, deeply wounded. Marion and Emogene informed the steward that they would like to be seated with her, and then another woman and a few sourdoughs said they would dine with her, too, so, when the next meal was served, the new passenger had a place.

Emogene found the winding river a wonder, and deemed the rough little towns, with their howling sled dogs, to be picturesque. She and Marion said everyone they met was friendly, and they stopped for three weeks in Fairbanks and then again in Dawson, where Marion gave an exhibit of her paintings as a benefit for war veterans, and amused children who came to the show by making quick, colorful sketches as she told them about 'Abdu'l-Bahá. During the slow river voyages, Marion liked to get on a bare barge and paint, and people would gather around to watch her. Once Emogene and Marion discovered a barge with an organ on it, and, Emogene reported, they gave a concert. Though Marion and Emogene were well received by the relatively cultured establishment in the new little cities, some of the rustic sourdoughs were their most sensitive listeners, and kept up a correspondence with them for years.

At Juneau, Marion stayed in town while Emogene traveled on to Cordova, Valdez, Seward, and Anchorage, accompanied by Georgia Ralston. Though no one that Marion, Emogene, and Georgia spoke to became a Bahá'í, they felt the trip was worthwhile. Marion remarked that it was wonderful how she, a stranger who considered herself neither a teacher nor a speaker, could teach her Faith to well over a hundred people. She and Emogene both lived to see the Bahá'í Faith well established in Alaska, and they were content with their part in pioneering in that rugged frontier.

****

Marion returned to Canada and, in April, 1920, moved to Vancouver on the western shore; she was the first Bahá'í to reside there. She enjoyed it, praising the open and unbiased attitude of the people. She was joined by May Maxwell, and soon Vancouver had a Bahá'í group. With May, Marion was suggested as a delegate to a National Convention. "But I begged off," she wrote to a friend. "I cannot speak publically and . . . I am feeble in business ability . . . and therefore feel it as well to keep in the background. . . . Each one has his own little work to fill in the great scheme of things—mine seems to be to work quietly in new fields or in assisting the real teachers. So I always think it wisest to try and do one's own work and not think of attempting the line of other people."

In the same letter, she mentioned an acquaintance who had "found her affinity" (romantically speaking), and she philosophized about herself, "I . . . have not time to devote to partners or affinities . . . I often raise my heart in thankfulness for the freedom that is mine so that I may roam into places where those who are tied down cannot venture. And, after all, no matter how beautiful married life is, the life of the spirit is even more beautiful—blessed be liberty I say."[11]

Despite Marion's self-depreciation, she and May Maxwell, by popular demand, both represented Canada at the 13th Annual Convention and on the newly formed Teaching Committee for North America.

When Marion attended events in Chicago or passed through the city during her travels, she often stayed with Emma Lundberg and her daughter, Elfie, in their big old Victorian dwelling. Some six decades after the fact, Elfie's face would light with amusement as she remembered how Marion used to descend upon them, stringing clotheslines from room to room so she could dry her wet canvases and her clothes, and scattering paints and brushes, in various states of use and disuse, all over the house.

A cryptic telegram from Marion in Winnipeg, Manitoba, dated March, 1922, cited Mrs. Emma Lundberg as her picture agent in Chicago; to this, Marion added that she'd forgotten all about those pictures. Clearly, if Marion did not consider herself a real teacher she was drastically under-estimating her capacity, but, when it came to business, she knew her limits. However, that didn't stop her from being a constantly productive artist, and friends loved to visit her at her studio in Green Acre, to listen to her stories and see the landscapes and portraits she'd made as she traveled.

In 1921, Marion received a tablet from 'Abdu'l-Bahá, written during the last week of His life. "Wherever thou art take into thy hand the cup of the wine of the love of God, give it unto the friends and make them intoxicated. . . . Engage thou in teaching. . . ." He assured her, "I never forget thee, and think always of thee."[12]

Then, another tablet to her was found, unsigned, among His papers. It instructed her to teach in Toronto and St. John, and contained His prayer for her success so that she would be continually blessed.

In 1922, Marion had a one-woman exhibit in Moncton, New Brunswick, which received critical acclaim. Then she went to Winnipeg. From there, she wrote Ella Cooper, "I have come here . . . alone to struggle with the Message. . . . I am not at all satisfied with my work—nor with myself. Oh to be one of those who are so shining that their very presence speaks."[13]

She didn't realize that she was precisely what she longed to be, and that her star, although she was fifty-six years old, had really only just begun to rise.

* * * * * * * *

In one of His tablets to her, 'Abdu'l-Bahá had promised Marion that she would again visit Mount Carmel. This promise was fulfilled in 1931, when Shoghi Effendi invited her to make another pilgrimage. She was lodged in Bahjí, where she made some paintings for the Guardian. She wrote to another Bahá'í artist, Victoria Bedekian, known to all as Auntie Victoria, of Shoghi Effendi's joy that Bahjí, which had declined during the years that 'Abdu'l-Bahá was oppressed, had been restored and was all illuminated by electric lights. She said she was painting two canvases, one of which was about twelve feet long, a panorama of 'Akká and the Sacred Shrines. The Guardian framed that one and displayed it in Bahjí, and it is still there.

Marion recorded that when Shoghi Effendi took her to the Shrine at Bahjí, he himself chanted, and then he ushered Marion, with Emma and Louise Thompson, from the courtyard into the inmost Shrine, where, at his request, Emma recited the Tablet of Aḥmad. He told the three that this was a very great privilege.

During her pilgrimage, the Guardian asked Marion to visit Louise Gregory, wife of Louis Gregory and the Bahá'í pioneer in Sofia, Bulgaria. So, Marion went from Haifa to Bulgaria for a few months. But Louise Gregory was not well, and it was she who went home after a few months. Marion, sixty-five years old and with a heart ailment, stayed—and stayed, and stayed. In 1933, in his letter which has been titled "America and the Most Great Peace," the Guardian wrote, "In the northernmost capitals of Europe, in most of its central states, throughout the Balkan Peninsula, along the shores of the African, the Asiatic and South American continents are found this day a small band of women pioneers who, single-handed and with scanty resources, are toiling for the advent of the Day 'Abdu'l-Bahá has foretold."[14] Marion was one of this small band, and she had all the qualities the Guardian cited for pioneering success: "renunciation, tenacity, dauntless and passionate fervour."[15]

* * * * * * * *

Bulgaria was not, in the eyes of the world, a desirable place to settle or even to tour. The travel writer Patrick Leigh Fermor, who hiked through middle Europe and the Balkans to Istanbul in 1934, said that he met no one who had been to Bulgaria, for eastern Europe looked westward, towards Vienna, Berlin, London and Paris. The great Bulgar Empire had fallen to the Turks during the Fourteenth Century, and Bulgaria's glories had never risen again; people residing north of the Danube deemed the country charmlessly backwards. However, upon visiting Bulgaria, Fermor found this estimation to be unjust. Bulgaria, with its long, deep history, had its own allure of the orient and of Byzantium.

Marion, to whom allure was a matter of doing the Guardian's wish, went to Sofia in the fabled Valley of Roses and took a hotel room, found a vegetarian restaurant where she habitually dined, and looked into the eyes of everyone she met, giving her Message, searching for receptive hearts. She knew it would be difficult; it had always been difficult. A few years before, while teaching in the southern United States, in Louisiana, she had written to Auntie Victoria, "This 'path-finder' knows too well that patience is the 'password' at every milestone, but I try to persevere."[16]

Louise Gregory had established a Bahá'í group in Varna; and Martha Root had visited Bulgaria, and would visit again during Marion's first years there. In 1931, George Adam Benke, born in Russia, resident in Germany and one of the early German Bahá'ís, came to Sofia for three months to help Marion. He was a linguist, and he quickly began learning Bulgarian; he could already speak other languages current in the country. Marion only spoke some French, and she never did learn Bulgarian.

George attended an Esperanto Congress at Stara Zagora, and served as honorary vice-president of the gathering. He returned to Sofia in 1932, to again serve as vice-president at an Esperanto Congress, and he visited Varna and Stara Zagora.

He was constantly busy talking with people in his wonderful pot pourri of languages until, one night, he died of a sudden and unexpected heart attack. He is buried in Sofia, and it is said that Shoghi Effendi called him the first European Bahá'í martyr.

After that, Marion was mostly alone as a pioneer in Sofia. Because of political and religious conditions, she had to be circumspect in her teaching. The Greek Orthodox church was the only religious institution recognized by the State. Every government employee had to belong to the church, and the country was liberally sprinkled with cathedrals and monasteries. Marion spoke to people individually and invited them to her room for small meetings.

One of her friends described that room as "a museum full of her pictures, books and papers all over. We sat wherever there was some place—on 'the' chair, the bed, on the floor, and she always had some refreshments. . . . The discussions of the Faith were handicapped by the complicated language question. Marion had nothing in the Bulgarian language, few people understood English and her favoured book, 'Abdu'l-Bahá's *Paris Talks,* had to be translated by one person from French into German or English, and by someone else into Bulgarian."[17]

At times, Marion had a few pamphlets in Bulgarian. Martha Root, while visiting in 1932, got out the first Bulgarian edition of *Bahá'u'lláh and the New Era* with Konstantin Dinkloff, and, in 1937, *The Hidden Words of Bahá'u'lláh* was printed in Bulgarian. But those books weren't always available and, most of the time, Marion's supply of literature was scanty.

The Guardian always kept her in mind and showered her with love, praise and encouragement through his letters. In November, 1931, when she'd formed a Bahá'í group in Sofia, he lauded her, "Your splendid services, rendered with such faith, such humility, such perseverance and devotion, have at last been crowned with success. You have achieved a task that will ever live in, nay adorn and enrich, the annals of God's immortal Faith. What is now necessary is to consolidate the work already achieved."[18]

At the same time, in a letter written by his secretary on his behalf, he commented that, for the past one hundred years, the Balkans had been torn by strife and hatred, with wars spreading misery on all sides, so that the region stood in sore need of the message of peace.

In July, 1932, he advised Marion not to measure the value of her teaching by the number of people who became Bahá'ís, for conversion was a long process; Marion only had to teach the Faith as thoroughly as possible, and let time do the rest.

In 1933, Bulgarian authorities restricted Bahá'í activities. Marion wrote to Emogene Hoagg, "Things have been topsy turvey here for months. . . . The Holy Synod is against us." She added that the Bahá'ís in Bulgaria were not, as yet, a very "robust group" of believers; she said, "We are only kids."[19]

During that period, she enjoyed the visit of Marzieh Gail and Howard Carpenter. They were a humorous pair, fun to have around. Marzieh's letters home from Bulgaria give some idea of Marion's environment. She described the market: "Lots of third-rate industrial products such as lilac cotton bloomers, a good deal of metalware leftover from the Turks: bracelets and bangles, incense burners, a case with a little crank that had contained the Book of Esther . . . some peasant dresses and weaves, very uninteresting pottery . . . halva, hens, lambs, and so on."

She recorded a sight of the sort that Marion saw frequently: "The enormous pink theater here is hung with crepe—famous actor dead. We saw his funeral the other day, from Miss Jack's window. First a silver coffin tilted in an open carriage (and held up by an uncomfortable-looking man seated under it), then the corpse himself, right out in the open, up to his neck in flowers and carried by a crowd of friends, then a battalion of priests in black and silver robes, then the empty hearse rattling along as an anti-climax—thousands of people, and chanting, and red student-caps."

She reported that it was a small world in Sofia: "The whole town knows who we are, where we're going, and in fact our every secret thought." And she said, "As for Bahá'í news, there's plenty of it. . . . The main thing is we have a meeting every night in Miss Jack's rooms at the hotel; people come and we talk. . . . They come of their own accord and stay for hours. The situation is complicated by language difficulties. . . . Never talked so much in our lives. Miss Jack is dear to us— some of our friends want to know if we can't settle in Sofia!"

She philosophized, "I know if the Cause didn't spread itself because it has a power in it, no one could spread it; when you consider that it has been done here without material means, and often makes the person who hears it sacrifice some of his most cherished beliefs."

Another passage from Marzieh's correspondence gives a glimpse of one of the diverse people Marion befriended: "We've met a fascinating Armenian lady. She lives in an enormous Turkish room at Miss Jack's hotel. She has silver hair to her shoulders, endless eyebrows, and huge red-brown eyes. She wears black velvet, a gray fox scarf and diamonds that make you dizzy. Her heels are incredible, she speaks seven languages, she's trying to reduce on lamb, fried potatoes and Turkish Delight. . . . She comes to our talks and asks many questions about the Cause."[20]

During the summer of 1933, Marion was in Budapest at the Guardian's suggestion, helping Martha Root. She stayed for a month, and then, in autumn, 1933, she and Martha took the Orient Express to Edirne to find the places where Bahá'u'lláh lived during his five-year exile there.

During the time when Bahá'u'lláh lived in Edirne, that part of Turkey was called Rumelia, and the southern part of Bulgaria was Eastern Rumelia. Adrianople (Edirne), near the borders of Greece and Bulgaria, separated from the Turkish mainland by the Bosphorus, was called by Bahá'u'lláh the Land of Mystery, and Shoghi Effendi felt that Bahá'u'lláh's years there had closely associated His presence with Europe, especially with the Balkans, and particularly with Bulgaria. One of his letters to Marion refers to Bulgaria as the portion of the Balkans chosen by God to receive the blessing of Bahá'u'lláh's presence.

During her visit to Edirne, Marion was ill, but she kept going. Following her usual pattern, she rendered her services as an artist, sketching and painting the sites that she and Martha discovered. Martha wrote, "People were intensely interested in the paintings of Miss Jack; each time she went out to sketch they gathered about her, and I know the artist was pleased when the Turkish women would give her shoulder a loving little pat and exclaim, 'Aferin! Aferin!' (Bravo! Bravo!) Children flocked about her to see the picture grow, and in the eyes of many men and women was the question: 'Why are these sites so dear to you?'"[21]

With the dearness of what they'd found treasured in their hearts, recorded in Marion's sketches and reported to the Guardian, Marion and Martha returned to Sofia. In December, 1933, Martha wrote that she believed "General Jack" was a great power in the Balkans. She was also a kind friend.

Martha reported that Marion had made her soup at midnight, following a meeting; and she generally made the tea and served cakes for gatherings, since she wanted Martha to concentrate on speaking. The two ladies boarded in the same house, and every evening Martha carried her chairs, table and two cups to Marion's room. She said that, after so many years of working alone, she enjoyed the privilege of being with Marion, a sincere, great Bahá'í who had known 'Abdu'l-Bahá.

By 1934, there were over thirty Bahá'ís in Sofia, and the first Local Spiritual Assembly was elected. Shoghi Effendi wrote to Marion, "Your patient and strenuous labours in the service of so great a Cause and in circumstances that are truly difficult and trying have endeared you to us all and deserve to rank as high as the great achievements that have signalized the establishment of the Administrative Order of the Faith of Bahá'u'lláh. You should be intensely happy, and profoundly grateful for having rendered such distinguished and never-to-be-forgotten services to the Sacred Threshold." He added, "Your great and historic work is by no means ended. Greater triumphs still await you." He did not necessarily mean that she must dedicate the rest of her life to Bulgaria. In a letter written shortly afterwards, he said, "I leave it entirely to your discretion as to whether you should extend your stay in Bulgaria or initiate a new chapter of your historic work in some other country in Europe. I feel truly proud of the constancy and courage that distinguish your pioneer services."[22]

Although religious prohibitions persisted in Bulgaria, and political parties were outlawed in 1934, Marion elected to stay. The Local Spiritual Assembly of Sofia was the first one in the Balkans, and she was determined to maintain it. In March, 1935, the *Bahá'í News* reported, "Miss Jack writes that the card list of interested people has almost 150 names. 'It is thrilling to meet so many interested people as we have here in Bulgaria. How we could do with half a dozen teachers!'"[23] But she had to continue alone.

Shoghi Effendi, always concerned about her loneliness, sent May Maxwell's niece, Jeanne Bolles, with her mother, to visit Marion in 1936. That same year, Marion made a trip to Germany to attend the Bahá'í Summer school in Esslingen. There, she was reunited with May Maxwell and with May's daughter; they were making the whirlwind teaching tour of Europe that culminated in their pilgrimage to Haifa, during which Shoghi Effendi took Mary Maxwell as his bride. Anna Kunz, one of the founders of the Bahá'í community of Switzerland, who would later be a member of the first Italo-Swiss National Spiritual Assembly, was also at that historic Summer School, held when Germany was on the brink of disaster.

In 1936, Nazism, so inimical to everything the Bahá'í Faith stands for, gripped Germany in its hideous fist, and by the next year the Faith and its institutions had been banned by special order of the Reichsfuhrer Himmler. Bahá'í books were confiscated, including those in personal libraries, and some meetings were proscribed. The Gestapo made so-called domiciliary visits to Bahá'í homes, questioning Bahá'ís for hours, menacing them with pistols. A Dresden Bahá'í spent six months in prison because a Bahá'í prayer was found in his possession. Bulgaria allied itself with the Nazis and was a center of German espionage. Nevertheless, at the Guardian's suggestion, Marion visited the German Bahá'ís in 1937. It was the last time she ever left Bulgaria.

* * * * * * * *

Oppression, along with natural attrition, thinned the ranks of new Bahá'ís in Nazi Bulgaria, leaving only those who truly believed. Marion saw a mercy in that: a few of her worst problems were solved. She wrote to her niece,

> Some of the least desirable have been weeded out. I have ceased to be a fighter. I believe in leaving it in prayer and of course in higher hands. You would be amused at those who have been removed. At one time there were those who were inclined to be snarly dogs. One left for America, one for the Provinces. There was a spiritualist. . . . who believed that God was directing him to lead the Cause through Spiritism. He got huffed over nothing and withdrew. Another was an unrepentant magdalene. She has gone to Paris. Another, a good looking rather charming kleptomaniac, has gone for two years to do military service.[24]

By 1939, World War II was inevitable, and the Guardian advised Marion to leave Bulgaria. Marion had a British passport, and she was residing in a country that would fight with the Axis powers against the British-led Allies. She was definitely persona non grata in Bulgaria. But, there were over one hundred Bahá'ís and many Bahá'í sympathizers in Sofia. Marion couldn't conceive of leaving this promising, but immature, community.

She wrote to her niece,

> He (Shoghi Effendi) first advised Canada, but... I suggested Geneva thinking I had found a man who could re-

place me... Shoghi Effendi wired 'approve Switzerland,' but... I was now disillusioned... with those who should have replaced me, so a few days ago he advised 'remain Sofia.' There is one fine man who could do much better than I, but there is a law forbidding any government official to take part in anything other than the Orthodox Church... So this gentleman cannot be (a leader), though he has the courage to attend... And the young have no place (of their own to live), or are unable to come forward, so, though I could easily be replaced in one way, there is no one in a position to hold the fort."[25]

In March, 1941, Nazi troops snuck into Bulgaria determined to undermine Soviet Russian influence and force Greece and Yugoslavia to cut ties with England and join the Axis powers. In November of that year, Bulgaria declared war on England and the U.S.

Marion, General Jack, at the age of seventy-five, was an illegal alien in Bulgaria. Aid from her friends outside the battle zone could not reach her, and her life was endangered by her heart condition, the constant threat of imprisonment, and poverty. She now attained her most sublime heights of heroism. Ruḥíyyih Khánum recorded in her diary a remark of Shoghi Effendi's, "You cannot be a hero without action. This is the touchstone. Not movement, coming and going, but in the evidences of your character. Jacky . . . is a heroine because of her conduct, the heroic spirit reveals itself in her."[26]

The ordinary observer, looking at Marion, the unwanted British subject in Nazi Bulgaria, would not have seen a heroine, but merely a gentle, humble old lady in a patched coat. Gustav Lowe might have been, at first, just such an ordinary observer, but then he became a devoted friend of Marion's, and a Bahá'í. When he first met Marion in the restaurant where she always dined, in 1938, he was an immigrant from Austria after Hitler's take-over, and Marion impressed him with her friendly smile. One day he interpreted for her when her regular waiter had his day off and there was no one else who spoke English. From then on, he lunched with her daily, and was soon attending Bahá'í meetings in her hotel room.

She had to discontinue the meetings when war broke out. Gustav, as a German citizen opposed to the Reich, couldn't be seen with her, and kept in touch with her through friends. In October, 1940, when he got a visa to emigrate to the U.S., he dared to phone her, and even to visit her. "She had moved to a cheaper hotel," he said. "Her room was probably too small for two people and we met in the lobby. I told her of my plan to go to the United States by the complicated way, crossing the Black Sea to Odessa, through Russia on the Trans-Siberian Railroad and across the Pacific from Japan . . . I invited her to come along and promised that I would take care of her. But she declined. . . . We exchanged letters until Bulgaria became part of the Iron Curtain and she indicated that it was too dangerous to receive my letters and to write to me."[27]

By 1941, messages from outside Bulgaria got through to Marion only sporadically. When the Allies bombed Sofia on January 10, 1944, the place where she lived was destroyed. The house where all the Bulgarian editions of *Bahá'u'lláh and the New Era* were kept was also devastated, and the Bahá'í who lived there was killed. Marion, along with thousands of others, was homeless and had to be evacuated. She managed to find ironic amusement in the fact that, when she and a friend were trying to leave Sofia, they thought they'd have to "board an open cattle car," but, as they approached the miserable conveyance, their way was barred by an officious young man, who intoned, "You can't come in here if you are English or American." Marion said that, although it was "zero weather," they had to laugh at the pompous defender of the cattle car, and they told him, "O.K. We'll get into the next." But they didn't have to. The man who was watching their baggage found what seemed like luxury accommodations in a second class passenger car. Shortly after that, all Marion's luggage was stolen. She merely commented, "It seems wonderful, what one can do without."[28] She lived in a village outside of Sofia for about a year.

Following the bombing, Bulgaria started peace talks with the Allies. But, before any results were reached, the Soviet Union declared war on Bulgaria. In September, 1944, the Soviets occupied the country and the Bulgarian Communists, who had been awaiting their chance, took power.

* * * * * * * * *

In November, 1945, the *Bahá'í News* published a report that "Miss Jack, the well-known pioneer in Bulgaria, who is eighty years old, has returned to Sofia... She and all the Sofia believers, with the exception of one, have survived and are now trying to resume their teaching activities."[29]

Also in November, 1945, Ella Robarts received a letter from Marion. Ella wrote a note on the letter saying it had taken about seventy-eight days for it to reach the U.S. Shortly afterwards, she received a second letter, written by Marion in January, 1946, that took forty-one days to arrive. Marion said she was writing from a coffee shop and apologized for using pencil, but said it couldn't be helped because the ink in her portable ink pot had dried up. Her handwriting, which had always been artistic, almost calligraphic, was as beautiful as ever. She said of her setting, "I like this place as I have had the chance of speaking to a couple of fine men here, so lately I try to frequent it in the hopes of catching a listening ear, and an ear which may not only listen but pass on the Glad Tidings by way of another member of the head. . . ." She told Ella that she liked to affectionately recall "our dear little Alma Knobloch," who, pioneering to Germany during the lifetime of 'Abdu'l-Bahá, used to "haunt" restaurants. She said, "God grant that there may be as much success in this corner of the world as she had in hers."[30]

Marion, at her great age, was starting over. And it didn't shake her faith in the least that Alma Knobloch's efforts had been in Germany—and look what happened in Germany. It didn't phase Marion that, after the Bahá'í Message had been given around the world, in some places even by 'Abdu'l-Bahá Himself, two calamitous global wars had ensued within less than fifty years, and a third and more calamitous one loomed. As far as she was concerned, the old armies fought their wars to destroy the old world order. She fought in a new army, to build a new world order, and no setbacks could stop her, for she was certain of victory. Bulgaria was under Communist rule, yet she said, "All in God's good time I feel there will be active doings in the Balkans of a spiritual nature as well as elsewhere in Europe."[31]

Back in 1908, when 'Abdu'l-Bahá had nicknamed her General Jack, she thought it was because of her forthright, athletic stride. Doubtless, in her humility, in 1946, as she dauntlessly raised the banner of her convictions in a shell-shocked and oppressed little country, she still thought that. How wrong she was.

Despite her invincible faith, she didn't witness Bulgaria's torment with an untroubled heart. The remnant of the Bahá'í community was more a fragile flock than an army, and she gathered it around her and wrote, "We are looking forward to the ringing of the Liberty Bell in this country. It takes untold patience to bide the time, but maybe we are accomplishing as much in seed sowing as when we had certain group meetings. That is not for me to judge. I only know from a fine Persian Bahá'í brother passing through here that they added many more to their members (in Iran), when they were deprived of meetings. . . . So, here's hoping."[32]

She had not been exempt from political pressure. She said, "The people here have not the perfect freedom of America— and especially in the German domination were very closely watched. I was called to the police and asked to disgorge names (of Bulgarian Bahá'ís). But I politely refused. They had a few (names), but received no satisfaction from yours truly. Since then I have been caution personified."[33]

When she wrote to Ella, she was living in a tiny room half-filled with wood for the stove, and she spent about one third of whatever money she had on wood. She had beans, peas, lentils, and cabbage, but they upset her stomach, so she made do mostly with bread, usually eaten without butter.

She felt people were interested in her Message, and told Ella she couldn't credit herself for that: "In fact I can claim nothing for myself. The beloved Guardian told me to arise and he knew of course from whence would come the real help if I obeyed." With a rare admission of loneliness, she added, "I am pining for news. Don't think I am forgetting any of you precious friends for that is farthest from my thoughts." Remembering her halcyon days at Green Acre, she said, "In the summer you all seem nearer even than at other times."[34]

Winters were harsh and Marion suffered as money and cloth-ing sent by friends and family failed to arrive. She wrote to her niece, "My old rabbit skin has sadly lost its feathers and really looks forlorn in big spots, nevertheless it keeps one warm and that is the chief thing. I could not get it restored for lack of funds, and my cloth coat is that of a real hobo—mended until it fairly groans in self-defense. The two pockets are sending up their dying gasps. As I usually carry two bags, I hustle and cover the worst spots on the pelt if anyone is coming who seems to matter."[35]

Marion found it impossible to reorganize the Bahá'í group under prevailing political conditions, but she held three gath-erings a week in her tiny, comfortless room, one in English, one in French, and one in Bulgarian. In 1948, she was eager to attend a European conference for new Bahá'ís and pio-neers, in May, in Geneva. She yearned to be reunited with old friends, and the Bahá'ís longed to honor her, for Shoghi Ef-fendi had recently cabled that she was an heroic soul who merited being regarded as a shining example to all pioneers in the Americas and Europe. She wrote to Edna True, "Well now here goes! All aboard! Am I the glad one?"[36]

But it was not to be. Marion couldn't get a visa to leave Bulgaria. War and oppression had not vanquished her, but this disappointment was almost too much for her. She wrote to Edna,

> I should have written . . . but the fact is that I was so blue for a few days and could write nothing . . . I am longing for news of the joyous event . . . I have started five times to write the beloved Guardian, but found myself telling too much and made a blot on the last effort when nearly fin-ished. I wish I could give you details of the two rather hid-

eous months of the catastrophes in my efforts (to leave Bulgaria), for we British are quite *demodé* here, and how finally a good hearted but naive professor . . . put me in the hands of a Travelers' Agent—a deep dyed chimpanzee and a well-known _____. Well, I had perhaps better not say what so many others say about him. . . . In any case I met my Waterloo from beginning to end. . . . My only consolation is that I mean to make a greater effort in the work here. I am sorry I cannot say just how through the post. It may be true as the English papers state that there is freedom in religious matters here but alas! I am the doubting Thomas and remain cautious, as I do not want the dear ones to get into trouble, and hope to stay with the darlings yet a little while. And some of the newest believers are among the best.[37]

Marion asked if she could keep the $200 Edna had sent for traveling and use at least part of it "for having things typed in Bulgarian. No chance for any printing now."[38] Edna replied that she should use the money to travel to Switzerland for a rest and a change of scene, and Marion answered,

Don't speak of my trotting off to travel in Switzerland or anywhere else, *cherie*. I need neither 'change' nor 'rest.' The greatest rest and change to me is to see things stirring heavenward in the souls of the dear ones here. . . . This little country is my job dear Edna, and the effort to get about in a new one is not in the least attractive to me. I love beauty, but the greatest beauty to me is to see the light of attraction to the sacred teachings in the faces of the beloved of God. . . ." She had to meet individually or in very small groups with her "dear ones," because the regime had forbidden Bahá'í meetings. She said hopefully, "Should we again have permission to meet things will open up. God is caring for us all. That is not only sure it is 'sartin.'"[39]

Nothing could induce her to try to leave Bulgaria again. She mentioned some friends, two teachers and a missionary, who had left Bulgaria and longed to return, but were refused visas. "Once out of this country one may have to stay out," she said.[40]

Obviously, she'd found her consolation for missing the conference. She added that, instead of using part of the $200 to go to Switzerland, she'd use it for the luxury of taxis, "for my silly old back needs help in getting about," she said. "Honestly, girlie, 81 years old is quite an age. None of my forebears achieved it."[41]

The Guardian's secretary wrote to North America on his behalf: "He feels that the spirit of Marion Jack, her evident desire to stay with the community she loves so dearly and has fostered through thick and thin, reflects glory not only on the North American Bahá'í community but on the entire Faith. She should be left free to remain in Bulgaria, and your Assembly should see to it that she receives a sufficient income to end her life in peace and with no more hardships to be endured."[42]

Despite Shoghi Effendi's clearly stated admiration and gratitude to her, in a later letter to Ella Robarts, Marion referred to Louise Gregory as the "Mother of Bulgaria. She and sweet Martha—twin mothers—a new species." She never stopped missing these and other friends, and she said, "We will all be together one of these days. Think of the Glory of it! It seems too good to be true!..." She was sure that "so many beloved ones" awaited her, and that she would again meet and talk with 'Abdu'l-Bahá.[43]

On March 17, 1954, her moment came. At the age of eighty-eight, she passed away after being bedridden and in pain for some months. She was buried among the soldiers in the British Military Cemetery in Sofia.

The Guardian cabled that she was "surpassed in (her) constancy, dedication, self-abnegation and fearlessness by none except (the) incomparable Martha Root." And he echoed and fulfilled her hope of reunion when he said her "triumphant soul" had now joined her "distinguished band (of) co-workers in (the) Abhá Kingdom: Martha Root, Lua Getsinger, May Maxwell, Hyde Dunn, Susan Moody, Keith Ransom-Kehler, Ella Bailey and Dorothy Baker whose remains lying in such widely scattered areas (of the) globe as Honolulu, Cairo, Buenos Aires, Sydney, Teheran, Isfahan, Tripoli and (the) depths (of the) Mediterranean Sea attest (the) magnificence (of the) pioneer services rendered by (the) North American Bahá'í community." He wrote that Marion's grave was destined to confer an "eternal benediction" upon Bulgaria, the "country already honored" by its link with Edirne, that "sacred city" associated with the Proclamation of the Faith of Bahá'u'lláh.[44]

And yet, Marion, the "immortal heroine," thought of herself only as a "common or garden woman." In that light, remember her with this verse from a lyric, "The Hardy Garden," by Edna St. Vincent Millay:

Now let forever the phlox and the rose be tended
Here where the rain has darkened and the sun has dried
So many times the terrace, yet is love unended,
Love has not died.[45]

* * * * * * * * *

And the time has come to end this book. Except, for lives lived in the spirit of a love which does not wait but which goes forth, selflessly giving, there really is no ending; "love has not died." It's like the flame of the candle 'Abdu'l-Bahá described to May Maxwell which weeps away its life drop by drop so that it can radiate light. The candle is eternal. No matter the gales of war and calamity, the flame endures.

* * * * * * * *

Notes

Notes

Beginnings

1. *Bahá'í World Faith,* p. 162.
2. *An Early Pilgrimage,* p. 42.

Chapter 1: Lua Getsinger

1–6. Lua Getsinger, Letter to Spiritual Assembly of Chicago, December, 1898.
7. *God Passes By,* p. 253.
8–16. Lua Getsinger, Letter to Spiritual Assembly of Chicago, December, 1898.
17. *Memories of 'Abdu'l-Bahá,* pp. 16–17.
18. *The Flame,* p. 17.
19. Ibid.
20–22. Ibid., pp. 19–20.
23–26. Ibid., pp. 25–26.
27. *Bahá'í Prayers,* p. 135.
28. *The Flame,* p. 128.
29–31. *Some Bahá'ís to Remember,* p. 120.
32. *The Diary of Juliet Thompson,* p. 281.
33–34. *God Passes By,* p. 276.
35. *Star of the West,* Vol. 1, No. 17, pp. 2–3.
36. *239 Days,* p. 47.
37. *The Diary of Juliet Thompson,* pp. 313–314.
38–39. Ibid., pp. 324–325.
40. *Star of the West,* Vol. IV, No. 12, p. 1.
41. *Star of the West,* Vol. VII, No. 4, p. 2.

42. *Star of the West,* Vol. VI, No. 12, p. 1.
43. Sears and Quigley, *The Flame,* p. 129.
44. Ibid., p. 134.
45. Ibid., p. 139.

Chapter 2: May Maxwell

1. *An Early Pilgrimage,* p. 11.
2–3. Ibid., p. 13.
4–5. "The Life of May Maxwell," cassette tapes.
6. *An Early Pilgrimage,* p. 10.
7–8. Ibid., pp. 10–11.
9–11. Ibid., pp. 11–13.
12–14. Ibid., pp. 14–16.
15–17. Ibid., pp. 25–26.
18. Ibid., p. 17.
19. Ibid., p. 32.
20–22. Ibid., p. 34–37.
23–24. Ibid., pp. 39–40.
25. Ibid., pp. 41–42.
26–27. Ibid., pp. 42–43.
28–29. Rúḥíyyih Khánum, Letter to Janet Ruhe, August 13, 1995.
30. *A Compendium of Volumes of the Bahá'í World,* p. 516.
31–32. Ibid.
33. "The Life of May Maxwell."
34. *Compendium,* p. 521.
35. Ibid., p. 523.
36. Rúḥíyyih Khánum, letter to Janet Ruhe, June 19, 1988.
37. *Compendium,* p. 519.
38. *The Bahá'í World, Vol. XIII,* p. 818.
39. *Bahá'í News,* Feb. 1965, p. 10.

40. *Bahá'í News,* Oct. 1983, p. 8.

41–42. "The Life of May Maxwell."

43–48. *Star of the West,* Vol. V, No. 19, pp. 6–7.

49. *Compendium,* p. 521.

50. Ibid.

51–52. "The Life of May Maxwell."

53. *Compendium,* p. 521.

54. *Compendium,* p. 641.

55. "The Life of May Maxwell."

56. Ibid.

57. *Compendium,* p. 641.

58. "The Life of May Maxwell."

59. *Compendium,* p. 522.

60. *Tablets of the Divine Plan,* p. 51.

61. *Compendium,* p. 523.

62. *God Passes By,* p. 304.

63. *Star of the West,* Vol. 12, No. 15, p. 1.

64. *Bahá'í World Faith,* p. 449.

65. "The Life of May Maxwell."

66. *Compendium,* p. 525.

67–69. "The Life of May Maxwell."

70. *Compendium,* p. 524.

71. Ibid., p. 525.

72. *The Priceless Pearl,* pp. 153–154.

73–74. *Compendium,* p. 526.

75. Leonora Holsapple Armstrong, "Personal Recollections 1919–1923," (unpublished), U.S. Bahá'í Archives, p. 1.

76. *The Priceless Pearl,* p. 154.

77. *Compendium,* p. 526.

78. Ibid., p. 527.

79. "The Life of May Maxwell."

80. *Compendium,* p. 527.
81. *The Priceless Pearl,* p. 154.
82. *Compendium,* p. 524.

Chapter 3: Martha Root

1. *God Passes By,* pp. 386–387.
2. *Compendium,* p. 530.
3. *Bahá'í News,* July, 1948, p. 6.
4–5. *Martha Root: Herald of the Kingdom,* pp. 9–10.
6. Ibid., p. 42.
7. Ibid., p. 40.
8. Ibid., p. 42.
9–11. Ibid., p. 46.
12. Ibid., p. 49.
13. *Ṭáhirih the Pure,* p. 4.
14. *Herald,* p. 67.
15. Ibid., p. 68.
16. Ibid., p. 74.
17. Ibid., p. 73.
18. Martha Root, Letter to Agnes Parsons, 24 Oct. 1921, Agnes Parsons Papers, U.S. Bahá'í Archives.
19. Martha Root, Letter to A. Parsons, 25 Sept. 1932, Parsons Papers, U.S. Archives.
20. *Martha Root: Lioness at the Threshold,* p. 167.
21. *Bahá'í News,* Nov. 1947, p. 6.
22. *Lioness,* p. 172.
23. Martha Root, Letter to "Angela," undated, Martha Root Papers, Literary Notes, U.S. Bahá'í Archives.
24. *Compendium,* p. 515.
25. *Lioness,* p. 183.
26. Martha Root, Pilgrim Notes, 1925, Martha Root Papers, U.S. Bahá'í Archives.

27. *Lioness,* p. 217.
28. *Herald,* p. 106.
29. Ibid., p. 112.
30. *The Priceless Pearl,* p. 109.
31–32. *Lidia,* p. 70.
33. *Lioness,* p. 320.
34–36. Ibid., p. 331.
37. Shoghi Effendi, Correspondence, Martha Root Papers, U.S. Bahá'í Archives.
38. *Lioness,* p. 343.
39. Ibid., p. 350.
40. *Bahá'í News,* Nov. 1930, p. 10.
41. *Bahá'í News,* Oct. 1930, p. 7.
42. *Bahá'í News,* Nov. 1930, p. 11.
43. "Memories of Martha Root," cassette tape.
44. *Lioness,* p. 387.
45. *Compendium,* p. 531.
46. *God Passes By,* p. 386.

Chapter 4: Hyde Dunn

1–3. *Some Bahá'ís to Remember,* p. 153.
4–5. *Star of the West,* Vol. VII, No. 4, p. 10.
6–10. *The Bahá'í World: Vol. XIII,* p. 859.
11. *Bahá'ís to Remember,* p. 156.
12–14. *Compendium,* pp. 553–54.
15. *Some Bahá'ís to Remember,* p. 197.
16–18. *Herald of the South,* Vol. 5, July 1985, p. 23.
19. *Compendium,* p. 554.
20. *God Passes By,* p. 308.
21. *Herald of the South,* Vol. 5, July 1985, p. 23.
22–23. Ibid., p. 24.
24–25. *Compendium,* p. 559.

26. *Star of the West,* Vol. XIV, No. 1, p. 25.

27. *Star of the West,* Vol. XIV, No. 11, p. 345.

28. *Herald of the South,* Vol. 5, July 1985, p. 42.

29. *Some Bahá'ís to Remember,* p. 161.

30–32. Martha Root, "Notes from Martha Root," 1924, Martha Root Papers.

33. *Some Bahá'ís to Remember,* p. 161.

34. Ibid., p. 162.

35. Hyde Dunn, letter to Clara Dunn, Feb. 21, 1926.

36. Hyde Dunn, letter to Ernest Brewer, Mar. 17, 1926.

37–39. Ibid., Apr. 2, 1926.

40. Dunn, letter to C. Dunn, Apr. 11 1926.

41. Dunn, letter to Brewer, Aug. 29, 1926.

42. Dunn, letter to Keith Ransom-Kehler, Aug. 3, 1931, "Scrapbooks," Keith Ransom-Kehler Papers.

43. Keith Ransom-Kehler, "Australia Diary," Sept. 8, 1931, Keith Ransom-Kehler Papers.

44. Ibid., Oct. 5, 1931.

45. Ibid., Oct. 18, 1931.

46. *The Bahá'í World: Vol. V,* p. 520.

47. *Herald of the South,* Vol. 5, July 1985, p. 46.

48. *The Bahá'í World: Vol. XVII,* p. 515.

49. *Herald of the South,* Vol. 5, July 1985, p. 48.

50. Martha Root, "Letter from Sydney," 1939, Martha Root Papers.

51. *Some Bahá'ís to Remember,* pp. 166–167.

52. Ibid., p. 167

Chapter 5: *Keith Ransom-Kehler*

1. Keith Ransom-Kehler, "Chinese Diary and Voyage to Australia," Sept. 13, 1931, Ransom-Kehler Papers.

2. *Compendium,* p. 523.

3. *The Bahá'í World: Vol. II,* p. 130.

4. *Other People, Other Places,* p. 179.

5. *The Bahá'í World: Vol. II,* p. 132.

6–7. *Bahá'í News Letter,* No. 13, p. 3.

8. *The Bahá'í World: Vol. II,* p. 133.

9. Ibid., p. 136.

10. Keith Ransom-Kehler, Letter to Fanny Knobloch, Ransom-Kehler Correspondence, Hannen Family Papers.

11. Keith Ransom-Kehler, "Japanese Diary," June 27, 1931, Ransom-Kehler Papers.

12. Ibid., June 28, 1931.

13. Ibid., July 7, 1931.

14. Ibid., July 12, 1931.

15. Ibid., July 15, 1931.

16. Ibid., Aug. 9, 1931.

17. Ibid., Aug. 15, 1931.

18. Keith Ransom-Kehler, "Chinese Diary, Voyage to Australia," Aug. 19, 1931, Ransom-Kehler Papers.

19. Ibid., Aug. 16, 1931.

20. Ibid., Aug. 18, 1931.

21. Ibid., Aug. 20, 1931.

22. Ibid., Aug. 19, 1931.

23. Ibid., Aug. 20, 1931.

24. Ibid., Aug. 21, 1931.

25–26. Ibid., Aug. 27, 1931.

27. Ibid., Sept. 5, 1931.

28. Keith Ransom-Kehler, "Australian Diary," Sept. 23, 1931, Ransom-Kehler Papers.

29. Ibid., Oct. 16, 1931.

30. Ibid., Oct., 1931.

31. Ibid., Oct. 9, 1931.

32–33. Ibid., Oct. 29, 1931.

34. Ibid., Nov. 9, 1931.

35. Ibid., Nov. 15, 1931.

36–38. Keith Ransom-Kehler, "New Zealand and Australia Diary," Nov. 23, 1931, Ransom-Kehler Papers.

39–42. Ibid., Nov. 30, 1931.

43. *The Bahá'í World: Vol. V,* p. 664.

44. "New Zealand & Australia Diary," Dec. 6, 1931.

45. Ibid., Dec. 11, 1931.

46–47. Ibid., Jan. 21, 1932.

48. Ibid., Jan. 26, 1932.

49. Keith Ransom-Kehler, "Javanese, Singapore, Burmese Diary," Feb. 14, 1932, Ransom-Kehler Papers.

50. Ibid., Feb. 18, 1932.

51–54. Keith Ransom-Kehler, "Indian Diary," Mar. 25, 1932, Ransom-Kehler Papers.

55. Ibid., May 1, 1932.

56. Ibid., Mar. 11, 1932.

57–58. Ibid., Apr. 9, 1932.

59. Ibid., May 6, 1932.

60. *Other People, Other Places,* p. 177.

61–62. *Bahá'í World: Vol. V,* p. 187.

63. *The Bahá'í Magazine,* Vol. 24, No. 1, p. 13.

64. *Bahá'í Prayers,* p. 129.

65–66. *Bahá'í Magazine,* Vol. 24, No. 3, p. 81.

67. *Other People, Other Places,* p. 179.

68. *The Bahá'í World: Vol. V,* p. 402.

69. Ibid., p. 395.

70. Ibid., p. 26.

71. Ibid., 398.

72. Ibid., p. 409.

Chapter 6: Susan Moody

1–2. *The Bahá'í Magazine,* Vol. 25, No. 12, p. 376.

3–13. Susan Moody, Letter to Eva Russell, Oct. 24, 1909, Thornton Chase Papers, Susan Moody–Eva Russell Correspondence.

14. *'Abdu'l-Bahá,* p. 96.

15–28 Moody to Russell, Nov. 27, 1909.

29. Ibid., Dec. 27, 1909.

30. Ibid., Jan. 24, 1910.

31. Ibid., Jan. 2, 1910.

32. Ibid., Jan. 11, 1910.

33–34. Ibid., Jan. 24, 1910.

35. Ibid., Feb. 13, 1910; and *Bahá'í News,* Vol. 1, No. 6, p. 6.

36. *Bahá'í News,* Vol. 1, No. 15, p. 9.

37. 'Abdu'l-Bahá, Tablet, translated Oct, 1912, Tablets of 'Abdu'l-Bahá to Susan Moody.

38. 'Abdu'l-Bahá, Tablet, undated, translated in Chicago.

39–40. *Star of the West,* Vol. II, No. 18, p. 13.

41–42. Moody to Russell, Jan. 29, 1910.

43. Susan Moody, Letter to Agnes Parsons, Nov. 24, 1912, Mary M. Rabb Papers, Susan Moody Correspondence.

44. Moody to Russell, Jan. 19, 1910.

45. 'Abdu'l-Bahá, Tablet, undated, trans. in Chicago.

46. Susan Moody, Letter to Joseph Hannen, July 15, 1917, Joseph Hannen-Susan Moody Correspondence, Hannen-Knobloch Family Papers.

47. Moody to J. Hannen, Oct. 25, 1917.

48. *Star of the West,* Vol. VI, No. 7.

49. Joseph Hannen, "Persian-American Educational Society." *Star of the West,* Vol. VI, No. 7.

50. Susan Moody, letter fragment, Hannen-Knobloch Family Papers, Joseph Hannen-Susan Moody Correspondence.

51. Elizabeth Stewart, "News from Persia," portion of her letter dated 25 Nov. 1918 to Isabella Brittingham, *Star of the West,* Vol. X, No. 3.

52. Moody, Letter to Pauline Hannen, May 20, 1920, Hannen-Knobloch Family Papers, Pauline Hannen-Susan Moody Correspondence.

53–54. Moody, "Obituary, Lilian Frances Kappes," *Star of the West,* Vol. XI, No. 19.

55. 'Abdu'l-Bahá, "Requiem Tablet Revealed for Lilian Kappes." *Star of the West,* Vol. XII, No. 19.

56. *Arches of the Years,* pg. 240.

57–58. Moody, Letter extracts, July 15 & July 21, 1924, Mary M. Rabb Papers.

59. Ibid., Aug. 214, 1924.

60. *Bahá'í News,* No. 1, p. 1.

61. *Compendium,* p. 488.

62. *Bahá'í News,* No. 15, p. 3.

63. *Compendium,* p. 488.

64. Moody, Letter to Shahnaz Waite, Feb. 16, 1932, Mary M. Rabb Papers.

65. *The Bahá'í World: Vol. V,* p. 524.

66–67. *Compendium,* pg. 489.

Chapter 7: Dorothy Baker

1. *From Copper to Gold,* p. 10.

2. *Compendium,* p. 654.

3. *Copper to Gold,* p. 89.

4–5. Margaret Ruhe, "Notes on Dorothy Baker," 1976.

6. *Copper to Gold,* p. 119.

7. Ibid., p. 126.

8. Ibid., p. 135.

9. Ruhe, "Notes."

10. *From Copper to Gold*, p. 139.

11. *Compendium*, p. 388.

12. *The Bahá'í World: Vol. VII*, p. 19.

13. *From Copper to Gold*, p. 144.

14. *The Bahá'í World: Vol. VII*, p. 15.

15. *From Copper to Gold*, p. 226.

16. Ibid., p. 227.

17. *Bahá'í News*, No. 170, p. 17.

18. *Bahá'í News*, May 1948, p. 9.

19. *The Challenging Requirements of the Present Hour*, p. 5.

20. Ibid., pp. 33–35.

21. *World Order*, Vol. XIV, pp. 406–411.

22. From a paper that is the property of Janet Ruhe.

23. *Compendium*, p. 320.

24. Ibid., pp. 320–321.

25. *From Copper to Gold*, p. 256.

26. Ibid., p. 274.

27. Ibid., p. 262.

28. Ibid., p. 264.

29. *Bahá'í News*, No. 280, p. 17.

30. *From Copper to Gold*, p. 270.

31. Ibid., p. 274.

32. Ibid., p. 286.

33. *Compendium*, p. 653.

34. *The Bahá'í Magazine*, Vol. 24, pg. 283.

Chapter 8: Ella Bailey

1. *Compendium*, p. 668.

2–3. *Memories of 'Abdu'l-Bahá*, p. 30.

4. *Compendium*, p. 668.
5. Ella Bailey, "Notes," Ella G. Cooper Papers.
6. *Memories of 'Abdu'l-Bahá*, p. 29.
7. *Compendium*, p. 668.
8. *'Abdu'l-Bahá*, p. 183.
9. *239 Days*, pp. 37–40.
10. *Star of the West*, Vol. III, No. 7, p. 6.
11. *Memories of 'Abdu'l-Bahá*, p. 33.
12. Ibid., p. 35.
13. Ibid., p. 78.
14–15. Ibid., pp. 84–85.
16. *Compendium*, p. 668.
17. Ella Bailey, Letter, Jan. 3, 1925, Ella Robarts Papers.
18–19. *Compendium*, pp. 668–669.
20. Bahia Gulick, Letter to Janet Ruhe, Aug. 21, 1995.
21–22. Ella Bailey, Letter, undated, Martha Root Papers.
23. *Compendium*, p. 669.
24–25. B. Gulick, Letter.
26. *Compendium*, p. 116.
27–29. *Compendium*, p. 669.
30. Ella Bailey, Letter, 1943, George Latimer Papers.
31. *Compendium*, p. 670.
32. Ibid., p. 668.
33. Ibid., p. 671.
34. *The Holy Scriptures*, p. 751.

Chapter 9: Marion Jack

1–3. Marion Jack, Letter, "Acca—Date Unknown," Ella G. Cooper Papers.
4. European Teaching Committee Records, "Marion Jack Memorial," p. 2.
5. Jack, Letter, "Acca."

6. *Compendium,* p. 657.

7. Jack, Letter, "Acca.".

8. *Star of the West,* Vol. II, No. 12, p. 5.

9–10. Marion Jack, Letter, Dec. 11, 1915, Helen Goodall Papers.

11. Marion Jack, Letter fragment, Vancouver, Ella Robarts Papers.

12. 'Abdu'l-Bahá, Tablet to Marion Jack, Nov. 1, 1921, Ella Robarts Papers.

13. Jack, Letter, Apr. 2, 1922, Ella G. Cooper Papers.

14. *The World Order of Bahá'u'lláh,* p. 93.

15. *The Priceless Pearl,* p. 415.

16. Marion Jack, postcard, Louisiana, Victoria Bedikian Papers.

17. *Compendium,* p. 659.

18. *Marion Jack: Immortal Heroine,* p. 6.

19. Ibid., p. 7.

20. *Other People, Other Places,* pp. 22–24.

21. *The Bahá'í World: Vol. V,* p. 593.

22. *Immortal Heroine,* pp. 8–9.

23. *Bahá'í News,* No. 90, p. 10.

24–25. *Immortal Heroine,* p. 9.

26. *The Priceless Pearl,* p. 161.

27. *Compendium,* p. 659.

28. *Immortal Heroine,* p. 10.

29. *Bahá'í News,* No. 177, p. 18.

30–31. Jack, Letter, Nov. 26, 1945, Ella Robarts Papers.

32–34. Ibid., Jan.2, 1946.

35. *Immortal Heroine,* p. 11.

36. Marion Jack, Letter, Mar. 12, 1948, European Teaching Committee Records.

37–38. Ibid., June 7, 1948.

39–41. Ibid., July 8, 1948.
42. *Immortal Heroine,* p. 11.
43. Jack, Letter, May 31, 1949, Ella Robarts Papers.
44. *Compendium,* p. 657.
45. Millay, *Collected Lyrics,* p. 161.

Bibliography

Bibliography

'Abdu'l-Bahá. *Tablets of the Divine Plan.* 1ˢᵗ ps. ed. Wilmette, Ill.: Bahá'í Publishing Trust, 1993.

The Bahá'í World: A Biennial International Record, Volume II, 1926–1928. Compiled by the National Spiritual Assembly of the Bahá'ís of the United States and Canada. New York: Bahá'í Publishing Committee, 1928.

The Bahá'í World: A Biennial International Record, Volume IV, 1930–1932. Compiled by the National Spiritual Assembly of the Bahá'ís of the United States and Canada. New York: Bahá'í Publishing Committee, 1933.

The Bahá'í World: A Biennial International Record, Volume V, 1932–1934. Compiled by the National Spiritual Assembly of the Bahá'ís of the United States and Canada. New York: Bahá'í Publishing Committee, 1936.

The Bahá'í World: A Biennial International Record, Volume VII, 1936–1938. Compiled by the National Spiritual Assembly of the Bahá'ís of the United States and Canada. New York: Bahá'í Publishing Committee, 1939.

The Bahá'í World: An International Record, Volume XIII, 1954–1963. Compiled by the Universal House of Justice. Haifa: The Universal House of Justice, 1970.

The Bahá'í World: An International Record, Volume XIV, 1963–1968. Compiled by the Universal House of Justice. Haifa: The Universal House of Justice, 1974.

The Bahá'í World: An International Record, Volume XV, 1968–1973. Compiled by the Universal House of Justice. Haifa: Bahá'í World Centre, 1975.

The Bahá'í World: An International Record, Volume XVII, 1976–1979. Compiled by the Universal House of Justice. Haifa: Bahá'í World Centre, 1981.

The Bahá'í World: An International Record, Volume XVIII, 1979–1984. Haifa: Bahá'í World Centre, 1986.

Bahá'u'lláh and 'Abdu'l-Bahá. *Bahá'í World Faith*. Wilmette, Ill.: Bahá'í Publishing Trust, 1956.

Bahá'u'lláh, the Báb, and 'Abdu'l-Bahá. *Bahá'í Prayers: A Selection of Prayers Revealed by Bahá'u'lláh, the Báb, and 'Abdu'l-Bahá*. New ed. Wilmette, Ill.: Bahá'í Publishing Trust, 1993.

Balyuzi, H.M. *'Abdu'l-Bahá: The Centre of the Covenant of Bahá'u'lláh*. London: George Ronald, 1971.

Brown, Ramona Allen. *Memories of 'Abdu'l-Bahá: Recollections of the Early Days of the Bahá'í Faith in California*. Wilmette, Ill.: Bahá'í Publishing Trust, 1980.

Freeman, Dorothy. *From Copper to Gold: The Life of Dorothy Baker*. Oxford: George Ronald, 1984.

Gail, Marzieh. *Arches of the Years*. Oxford: George Ronald, 1991.

Gail, Marzieh. *Other People, Other Places*. Oxford: George Ronald, 1982.

Gail, Marzieh. *Summon up Remembrance*. Oxford: George Ronald, 1987.

Garis, M.R. *Martha Root: Lioness at the Threshold*. Wilmette, Ill.: Bahá'í Publishing Trust, 1983.

Heller, Wendy. *Lidia: The Life of Lidia Zamenhof, Daughter of Esperanto*. Oxford: George Ronald, 1985.

Jewish Publication Society. *The Holy Scriptures*. Philadelphia: Jewish Publication Society, 1917.

Marie, Queen of Rumania. *My Life*. London: Cassell & Co. Ltd., 1934.

Martin, Douglas. *The Persecution of the Bahá'ís of Iran 1844–1984*. Ottawa: The Association for Bahá'í Studies, 1984.

Maxwell, May. *An Early Pilgrimage*. Oxford: George Ronald, 1969.

Millay, Edna St. Vincent. *Collected Lyrics*. New York: Perenniel Library, Harper and Row, 1981.

Morrison, Gayle, *To Move the World: Louis G. Gregory and the Advancement of Racial Unity in America*. Foreword by Glenford E. Mitchell. Wilmette, Ill.: Bahá'í Publishing Trust, 1982.

National Spiritual Assembly of the Bahá'ís of Canada. *Marion Jack: Immortal Heroine.* Thornhill, Ont.: Bahá'í Canada Publications, 1985.

Rabbani, Rúḥíyyih. *The Priceless Pearl.* London: Bahá'í Publishing Trust, 1969.

Root, Martha. *Ṭáhirih the Pure.* Introduction by Marzieh Gail. Rev. ed. Los Angeles: Kalimát Press, 1981.

Sears, William and Robert Quigley. *The Flame.* Oxford: George Ronald, 1972.

Shoghi Effendi, *The Challenging Requirements of the Present Hour,* Wilmette, Ill.: National Spiritual Assembly of the Bahá'ís of the U.S. and Canada, 1947.

Shoghi Effendi. *God Passes By.* Rev. ed. Wilmette, Ill.: Bahá'í Publishing Trust, 1974.

Shoghi Effendi. *The World Order of Bahá'u'lláh: Selected Letters.* New ed. Wilmette, Ill.: Bahá'í Publishing Trust, 1991.

Thompson, Juliet. *The Diary of Juliet Thompson.* Los Angeles: Kalimát Press, 1983.

Ward, Allen L., *239 Days: 'Abdu'l-Bahá's Journey in America.* Wilmette, Ill.: Bahá'í Publishing Trust, 1979.

White, Roger, Ed. *A Compendium of Volumes of the Bahá'í World I–XII, 1925–1954.* Oxford: George Ronald, 1981.

Whitehead, O.Z. *Some Bahá'ís to Remember.* Oxford: George Ronald, 1983.

Whitehead, O.Z. *Some Early Bahá'ís of the West.* Oxford: George Ronald, 1976.

Zinky, Kay. *Martha Root: Herald of the Kingdom.* New Dehli: Bahá'í Publishing Trust, 1983.

Other Sources

Other Sources:
articles, letters, papers

Chapter 1, Lua Getsinger

'Abdu'l-Bahá. "Tablet of 'Abdu'l-Bahá on His coming to America." *Star of the West,* vol. 1, no. 17 (Jan. 19, 1911).

Alexander, Janet. "Memories of Dr. Edward C. Getsinger." Santiago, 1991 (unpublished).

Bahá'í News, no. 190 (Dec. 1946); no. 196 (Jan. 1947).

"California News." *Star of the West,* vol. 2, no. 14 (Nov. 23, 1911).

Cooper, Ella Goodall. "Preparing the Way in California." *Star of the West,* vol. 2, no. 16 (Dec. 31, 1911).

Faizi, A.Q. "Toward the Unity of East and West." *Bahá'í News,* no. 514 (Jan. 1954).

Getsinger, Edward. Letters to Albert Windust, 1911, 1912, 1914. Windust Papers, U.S. National Bahá'í Archives.

Getsinger, Lua. Letter to Chicago Assembly, Dec. 1898. Parsons Papers, U.S. National Bahá'í Archives.

Goodall, Helen S. "The Work in California." *Star of the West,* vol. 2, no. 13 (Nov. 4, 1911).

"In Memoriam: Mrs. Lua Moore Getsinger." *Star of the West,* vol. 4, no. 4 (May 17, 1916) and vol. 7, no. 19 (Mar. 2, 1917).

Root, Martha. "Memorial Service for Mrs. Lua Getsinger." *Star of the West,* vol. 8, no. 9 (Aug. 20, 1917).

Stockman, Robert H. "The Bahá'í Faith, Beginnings in North America." *World Order,* vol. 18, no. 4 (Summer 1984).

"The Work in India." *Star of the West,* vol. 5, no. 2 (Apr. 9, 1914).

Whitmore, Bruce W. "The Temple is Already Built." *Bahá'í News* (Apr. 1987).

Windust, Albert R. "The Bahá'í Faith in America to 1912." *World Order,* vol. 11, no. 8 (Nov. 1945).

Chapter 2, May Maxwell

Allen, Berthalin. "The Luminous Hour." *Bahá'í News,* Feb. 1965.

Armstrong, Leonora Holsapple. "Personal Recollections 1919–1923." U.S. National Bahá'í Archives.

Hofman, Marion (née Marion Holley). Letter to Janet Ruhe. Oxford, Oct. 2, 1991.

Maxwell, May. "Letter from Mrs. May Maxwell to Mr. Charles Mason Remey." *Star of the West,* vol. 5, no. 19 (Mar. 2, 1915).

Maxwell, May. "The Seed Sowing of the Ages." *Star of the West,* vol. 11 (July 13, 1919).

"The Night has Come." *Star of the West,* vol. 12, no. 15 (Dec. 12, 1921).

Rúḥíyyih Khánum. "The Life of May Maxwell." Cassette tapes, Buenos Aires, Feb. 26–Mar. 1, 1990.

Rúḥíyyih Khánum. Letter to Janet Ruhe, Haifa (June 19, 1988).

Shoghi Effendi [Rabbani]. "Cablegram to American Bahá'ís." *Star of the West,* vol. 12, no. 18.

Sprague, Philip G. "Buenos Aires." *World Order,* vol. 8, no. 6 (Sept. 1942).

Troxel, Duane. "Agnes Alexander: 70 Years of Service." *Bahá'í News* (Oct. and Dec. 1983).

Chapter 3, Martha Root

"Bahá'í Notes." *Star of the West,* vol. 13, no. 7 (Oct. 1922).

Ford, Mr. and Mrs. Harry E. "Pioneer." *Bahá'í News,* no. 200 (Oct.–Nov., 1947).

Gail, Marzieh. "'Abdu'l-Bahá in America—The 25th Anniversary Observance." *Bahá'í News* (April 1987).

"Miss Martha Root in India." *Bahá'í News,* no. 45 (Oct. 1930); no. 46 (Nov. 1930).

National Spiritual Assembly of the Bahá'ís of India, Pakistan and Burma, *In Memory of Miss Martha Root,* 1939.

"News Notes." *Star of the West,* vol. 13, no. 5 (Aug. 1922).

Root, Martha. General Letters to Bahá'is; Literary Notes; Pilgrim Notes, Martha Root Papers, U.S. National Bahá'í Archives.

Root, Martha. "Letter from Miss Martha Root." *Bahá'í News Letter*, no. 35 (Nov. 1929).

Root, Martha. Letters to Agnes Parsons, Parsons Papers, Martha Root Correspondence, U.S. National Bahá'í Archives.

Shoghi Effendi. "Letter from Shoghi Effendi." *Bahá'í News Letter*, no. 14 (Nov. 1926).

Shoghi Effendi. Letter from Shoghi Effendi to the Bahá'ís of Iran, 1929, Martha Root Papers, Correspondence, Shoghi Effendi, U.S. National Bahá'í Archives.

Troxel, Duane. "Agnes Alexander: 70 Years of Service." *Bahá'í News* (Dec. 1983).

Witzel, Mignon. "Memories of Martha Root." Cassette tape recorded for Janet Ruhe, Maracaibo, Venezuela, March 1992.

Chapter 4, Hyde Dunn

Bahá'í Assembly of San Francisco. "Mrs. Fanny Dunn." *Star of the West*, vol. 7, no. 4 (May 17, 1917).

"Bahá'í World News." *Star of the West*, vol. 14, no. 11 (Feb. 1924).

Cooper, Ella. "The New Work Now Before Us." *Star of the West*, vol. 7, no. 11 (Sept. 27, 1916).

Dunn, Hyde and Clara. Letters, Feb., Mar., Apr., July, and Aug. 1926, courtesy of Graham Hassall, Australia.

Dunn, Hyde. Letter to Keith Ransom-Kehler, Aug. 2, 1931, Scrapbook, Keith Ransom-Kehler Papers, U.S. National Bahá'í Archives.

Hassall, Graham. "First and Finest." *Herald of the South*, vol. 4 (July 1985).

Hassall, Graham. "Outpost of a World Religion, The Bahá'í Faith in Australia 1920–47." *The Journal of Religious History*, vol. 16, no. 3, Melbourne (June 1991).

"'Mother' and 'Father' of a Continent." *Herald of the South*, July–Sept. 1992.

Ransom-Kehler, Keith. "Australia Diary" and "Scrapbook." Keith Ransom-Kehler Papers, U.S. National Bahá'í Archives.

Root, Martha. Letters to Bahá'ís, General Correspondence, Martha Root Papers, U.S. National Bahá'í Archives.

Root, Martha. "Notes from Martha Root." General Correspondence, Martha Root Papers, U.S. National Bahá'í Archives.

"The First Bahá'í Feast in New Zealand." *Star of the West,* vol. 12, no. 1 (Apr. 1923).

Chapter 5, *Keith Ransom-Kehler*

Bahá'í News Letter, no. 6 (July–Aug. 1925); no. 7 (Sept. 1925); no. 12 (June–July 1926); and no. 15 (Jan. 1927).

Faizi, A.Q. "Tributes to Heroic Sacrifice." *Bahá'í News,* no. 518 (May 1954).

Giammarrese, Nicholas. "Personal Recollections: 'A Few Words of Grateful Appreciation.'" U.S. National Bahá'í Archives.

Handy, Carol. Article on the 40th anniversary of Keith's death, *Herald-Palladium,* Benton Harbor, Michigan, Oct. 1973; and letter to Janet Ruhe with clippings, documents, papers on Keith, Ludington, Michigan, 1992.

Haney, Mariam. "Keith Ransom-Kehler, A Brief Sketch of a Dynamic Personality." *The Bahá'í Magazine,* vol. 24, no. 9.

Hofman, Marion. Conversation with Janet Ruhe, Haifa, Apr. 1986; letters, to Janet Ruhe, Oxford, Oct. 1991; to Moojan Momen, Oxford, Nov. 1992.

"Keith Ransom-Kehler, First American Bahá'í Martyr." *Bahá'í News,* no. 79 (Nov. 1933).

"Mrs. Keith Ransom-Kehler in Barbadoes." *Bahá'í News Letter,* no. 35 (Nov. 1926).

"Mrs. Ransom-Kehler's Activities on the Pacific Coast." *Bahá'í News,* no. 48 (Feb. 1931).

Notes on Keith Ransom-Kehler by Jeffrey Norman, Vassar College Files, Class of 1898, Poughkeepsie, 1993.

Ransom-Kehler, Keith, Keith Ransom-Kehler Correspondence 1928–1929, Hannen Family Papers, U.S. National Bahá'í Archives.

Ransom-Kehler, Keith. "Letter from Mrs. Keith Ransom-Kehler to the Convention." *Bahá'í News Letter,* no. 13 (Sept. 1926).

Ransom-Kehler, Keith. "Letters Home." *The Bahá'í Magazine,* vol. 24, nos. 1–10 (Apr. 1933–Jan. 1934).

Ransom-Kehler, Keith. Notebooks "Japanese Diary," "Chinese Diary and Voyage to Australia," "Australian Diary," "New Zealand and Australia Diary," "Javanese, Burmese, Singapore Diary," "Indian Diary," and "Scrapbooks," U.S. National Bahá'í Archives.

"San Francisco." *Bahá'í News,* no. 54 (May 1931).

"The Bahá'í Congress for Teaching and the 14th annual Convention." *Star of the West,* vol. 13, no. 4 (May 17, 1922).

Chapter 6, Susan Moody

'Abdu'l-Bahá. "Requiem Tablet Revealed for Lilian Kappes." *Star of the West,* vol. 12, no. 19 (Mar. 2, 1922).

'Abdu'l-Bahá, Tablets of 'Abdu'l-Bahá to Susan Moody, Susan I. Moody Papers, U.S. National Bahá'í Archives.

Bahá'í News, no. 1 (Dec. 1924); no. 6 (July–Aug. 1925); no. 15 (Nov. 1926); no. 25 (July 1928); and no. 81 (Feb. 1934).

Haney, Mariam. "The Passing of Dr. Susan I. Moody." *The Bahá'í Magazine,* vol. 25, no. 12.

Hannen-Knobloch Family Papers, Joseph Hannen-Susan Moody Correspondence, and Pauline Hannen-Susan Moody Correspondence, U.S. National Bahá'í Archives.

Kappes, Lilian. "Miss Lilian Kappes Arrives in Persia." *Star of the West,* vol. 2, no. 18 (Feb. 7, 1912).

"Kappes Memorial Fund" and "Dr. Sarah Clock." *Star of the West,* vol. 12, no. 19 (Mar. 1922).

Moody, Susan. "Bahá'í Martyrdoms in Persia." *Star of the West,* vol. 6, no. 7 (July 13, 1915).

Moody, Susan. "Lilian Frances Kappes." *Star of the West,* vol. 11, no. 19 (Mar. 2, 1921).

Moody, Susan. Susan Moody Correspondence, Mary M. Rabb Papers, U.S. National Bahá'í Archives.

Moody, Susan. Susan Moody-Eva Russell Correspondence, Thornton Chase Papers, U.S. National Bahá'í Archives.

"News from Persia." *Star of the West,* vol. 10, no. 1 (Mar. 1920).

Root, Martha. Letters to Susan Moody, Martha Root Correspondence, Susan I. Moody Papers, U.S. National Bahá'í Archives.

"Societe Nonahalan or Children's Savings Institution." *Star of the West*, vol. 11, no. 19 (Mar. 2, 1921).

Star of the West, vol. 1, nos. 1, 2, 5, 7, 11, and 15; vol. 2, no. 3; vol. 4, no. 7, 19; vol. 5, no. 5; vol. 10, no. 3; and vol. 15, no. 10.

Stewart, Elizabeth. "Letter from Elizabeth H. Stewart." *Star of the West*, vol. 11, no. 1 (Mar. 21, 1921).

"The Unity Band," "Persia," and "The Persian American Education Society." *Star of the West*, vol. 1, no. 1 (Mar. 21, 1910).

Chapter 7, Dorothy Baker

Bahá'í News, no. 170 (June 1944).

Baker, Dorothy. "A View of Pioneering." *Bahá'í News*, May 1948.

Baker, Dorothy, "Letter read at 46th Annual U.S. National Bahá'í Convention," *Bahá'í News*, no. 280 (June 1954).

Baker, Dorothy. "The Evolution of a Bahá'í." *The Bahá'í Magazine*, 1933–1934.

D'Araujo, Victor, letter to Janet Ruhe, Den Haag, Jan. 1992.

Dudley, Alice P., letter to Janet Ruhe, Lucerne, Cal., Dec. 1991.

Kunz, Anna. "A Bahá'í in Switzerland." *World Order*, vol. 14, no. 12 (Mar. 1949).

National Spiritual Assembly of the Bahá'ís of the United States and Canada. "The Guardian's Seven Year Plan." Wilmette, Ill.: Bahá'í Publishing Trust, 1946.

Ruhe, Margaret. "Notes on Dorothy Baker." Haifa, 1976 (unpublished).

Chapter 8, Ella Bailey

Bailey, Ella. Ella Bailey Correspondence, George Latimer Papers, U.S. National Bahá'í Archives.

Bailey, Ella. Ella Bailey Correspondence, Ella Robarts Papers, U.S. National Bahá'í Archives.

Bailey, Ella. Ella Bailey Correspondence, H. Emogene Hoagg Papers, U.S. National Bahá'í Archives.

Bailey, Ella. Ella Bailey Correspondence, Martha Root Papers, U.S. National Bahá'í Archives.

Bailey, Ella. Ella Bailey Notes, Ella G. Cooper Papers, U.S. National Bahá'í Archives.

Cooper, Ella Goodall and Bailey, Ella M. "'Abdu'l-Bahá with the children of the Friends in Chicago." *Star of the West,* vol. 3, no. 7 (July 13, 1912).

Gulick, Bahia. Letter to Janet Ruhe, Sun City, Arizona (Aug. 21, 1995).

Sears, William. "The Commemoration of Historic Anniversaries, The Public Dedication of the Bahá'í House of Worship." *A Compendium of Volumes of the Bahá'í World.*

Star of the West, vol. 3, nos. 4, 5.

Chapter 9, Marion Jack

'Abdu'l-Bahá. Tablets from 'Abdu'l-Bahá to Marion Jack. Ella Robarts Papers, U.S. National Bahá'í Archives.

"Alaska, Planting the Seeds of Victory." *Bahá'í News,* Aug. 1981.

Bahá'í News, no. 90 (Mar. 1935); no. 143 (May 1941); no. 177 (Nov. 1945); no. 182 (Apr. 1946); no. 193 (Mar. 1947); no. 195 (May 1947); no. 199 (Sept. 1947); no. 206 (Apr. 1948); and no. 216 (Feb. 1949).

Behrendt, Judith. Letter to Janet Ruhe. Punta Gorda, Belize, May 20, 1992.

Cuthbert, Arthur. "London, England, News Notes." *Star of the West,* vol. 2, no. 2 (Apr. 9, 1911).

Cuthbert, Arthur. Untitled report on 'Abdu'l-Bahá in London. *Star of the West,* vol. 2, no. 12 (Oct. 16, 1911).

European Teaching Committee. "Report: Marion Jack Memorial." European Teaching Committee Records, U.S. National Bahá'í Archives.

Gash, Andrew. "Fear and Faith in Nazi Germany." *Herald of the South,* vol. 14 (January 1988).

Jack, Marion. Marion Jack Correspondence, Bahá'í Temple Unity, Alfred Lunt Papers, U.S. National Bahá'í Archives.

Index

Index

A

'Abdu'l-Bahá, 3, 4, 6, 8–10,
15–29, 31, 32, 35–42, 44, 46–49,
51–58, 60, 67, 68, 70, 71, 73–81,
85, 87, 88, 96, 99–101, 103, 104,
106–108, 112, 114, 116, 123, 127,
136, 150, 162, 169–174, 177–180,
184–187, 189–192, 201–203, 205,
209–211, 224, 235–243, 245, 249,
250, 252, 253, 257–263, 265, 268,
281, 285, 287
 arrival in
  Canada, 53, 277
  United States, 25
 daughters of, 5
 death of, 56
 departure from
  Canada, 54
  United States, 29
 description of, 5
 funeral of, 56
 grandchildren of, 20
 grandson of. *See* Shoghi Effendi.
 home of, 6
 mandate of, 62
 release from imprisonment, 24
 sister of. *See* Bahíyyih Khánum.
 wife of, 6, 132
 Will and Testament of, 57, 225
Abu'l–Faḍl, Mírzá, 17, 18
 description of, 17
Aconcagua, 77
Addams, Jane, 240
Adelaide, 113, 122, 144, 145

Administrative Order, 58, 119, 121,
275
Adrianople. *See* Edirne.
Advent, 13
Advent of Divine Justice, 216
Africa, 229, 247, 248, 251
 North, 213
 South, 3, 134, 163
African American Bahá'ís, 14, 16, 23
Agra, 152, 153
Akhund, Hájí, 177, 186
'Akká, 3, 5, 10, 15, 21, 30, 35, 39,
41, 46, 54, 55, 100, 169, 236, 260
Aladauleh Street, 179
'Alá'í
 Najmíyyih, 157, 163, 164
 Raḥmatu'lláh, 157–159, 163
Alaska, 262, 263
 Highway, 264
Albah, 74, 75
Albania, 87
 King Zog of, 87
Albion College, 128, 129
alcohol, 15
Alexander, Agnes, 46, 72, 81, 82, 91,
137–139
Aligargh, 152
Alláh'u'Abhá, 164, 176
All-America Intercontinental
 Teaching Conference, 249
Allen, Berthalin, 45
Almond
 Maysie, 113